MORAL ISSUES IN INTERNATIONAL AFFAIRS

Moral Issues in International Affairs

Problems of European Integration

Edited by

Bill McSweeney
Head of the Centre for Peace Studies
Irish School of Ecumenics

First published in Great Britain 1998 by
MACMILLAN PRESS LTD
Houndmills, Basingstoke, Hampshire RG21 6XS and London
Companies and representatives throughout the world

A catalogue record for this book is available from the British Library.

ISBN 0–333–69848–7

First published in the United States of America 1998 by
ST. MARTIN'S PRESS, INC.,
Scholarly and Reference Division,
175 Fifth Avenue, New York, N.Y. 10010

ISBN 0–312–21128–7

Library of Congress Cataloging-in-Publication Data
Moral issues in international affairs : problems of European
integration / edited by Bill McSweeney.
p. cm.
Includes bibliographical references and index.
ISBN 0–312–21128–7 (cloth)
1. International relations—Moral and ethical aspects. 2. Europe–
–Economic integration—Moral and ethical aspects. I. McSweeney,
William.
JZ1306.M67 1998
172'.4'094—dc21   97–40513
                                                                  CIP

This book is printed on paper suitable for recycling and made from fully managed and
sustained forest sources.

10   9   8   7   6   5   4   3   2   1
07   06   05   04   03   02   01   00   99   98

Printed and bound in Great Britain by
Antony Rowe Ltd, Chippenham, Wiltshire

Contents

Notes on the Contributors   *vii*

Introduction: Comments on Morality and Peace Research
Bill McSweeney   1

PART I   MORALITY AND SECURITY: THEORETICAL
ISSUES

1   Morality in International Affairs: a Case for Robust
    Universalism
    Fred Halliday   15

2   Morality and Global Security: the Normative Horizons of
    War
    Richard Falk   31

PART II   NORMATIVE QUESTIONS IN EUROPEAN
INTEGRATION

3   Ideals and Idolatry in the European Construct
    Joseph Weiler   55

4   Moral Choice and European Integration
    Bill McSweeney   89

PART III   MORAL CHALLENGES IN NEGOTIATING AN
EVER CLOSER UNION

5   The Compatibility of EU Membership with Neutrality
    Walter Carlsnaes   117

6   The Indivisible Continent: Russia, NATO and European
    Security
    Michael MccGwire   139

7   European Integration and the Arms Trade: Creating a New
    Moral Imperative?
    Ian Davis   187

8   Leading by Virtuous Example: European Policy for Overseas
    Development
    David Coombes   221

Appendix: Address by Václav Havel to the European
Parliament, Strasbourg, 8 March 1994   246

Index   253

Notes on the Contributors

Walter Carlsnaes is Professor of Government at Uppsala University and the founding editor of the *European Journal of International Affairs*. His publications include *Energy Vulnerability and Swedish National Security* (Frances Pinter, 1988); *The EC and Changing Foreign Policy* (ed. with Steve Smith) (Sage, 1993).

David Coombes is Professor of European Integration Studies at the University of Limerick. His publications include *European Integration, Regional Devolution and National Parliaments* (Policy Studies Institute, 1979); *Politics and Bureaucracy in the European Community* (Allen & Unwin, 1970).

Ian Davis is pursuing doctoral research on the arms trade at the Department of Peace Studies at the University of Bradford and is the author of several reports on UK defence policy.

Richard Falk is Professor of International Law and International Relations at Princeton University. He is the author of *On Humane Governance: Toward a New Global Politics* (PSU Press, 1995).

Fred Halliday is Professor of International Relations at the London School of Economics. His most recent publications include *Rethinking International Relations* (Macmillan, 1994); *Islam and the Myth of Confrontation* (I.B. Tauris, 1996).

Michael MccGwire is former Fellow at the Brookings Institute, Emeritus Fellow at the University of Cambridge, and Honorary Professor of International Politics at University College of Wales at Aberystwyth. His recent publications include *Perestroika and Soviet National Security* (Brookings Institute, 1991).

Bill McSweeney is Senior Lecturer in International Politics and Head of the Centre for Peace Studies at the Irish School of Ecumenics. Publications include *Roman Catholicism: the Search for Relevance* (Blackwell, 1980); *Ireland and the Threat of Nuclear War* (ed.) (Dominican Publications, 1985); *Security and Identity in International Relations Theory* (forthcoming).

Joseph Weiler is Manley Hudson Professor of Law at Harvard University, and Co-Director of the Academy of European Law, European University Institute, Florence. His publications include *Human Rights and the European Community* (Nomos Verlag, 1991); *An Ever-Closer Union: Critical Analysis of the Draft Treaty* (European Policy Institute, 1985).

Introduction: Comments on Morality and Peace Research
Bill McSweeney

It should come as no surprise that an institute founded to advance pluralism and tolerance through its postgraduate programmes of 'ecumenical studies' displays a bias towards issues of morality and ethics. The religious origins of the Irish School of Ecumenics, which was the principal sponsor of this collection of papers, make it predictable and appropriate that it should focus on such questions.

Neither should it puzzle the reader to find that a Centre for Peace Studies – a department of the Irish School of Ecumenics, engaged in teaching and research on a range of Peace Research topics – shows a similar disposition to raise the ethical question in the analysis of security, conflict and its resolution. One should expect this explicit orientation, given the contrast between the ideal and the existing order, the gap between human possibilities for amelioration and nature in the raw, which is filled by the term 'peace' in every language. The option for 'peace' rather than 'international' studies conveys the conviction that any established order is a consequence of choice and is therefore susceptible to change in favour of alternatives.

But it is clear that many Peace Research (PR) institutes in the past, like ours, have been inhibited from displaying the moral concern announced in their name and in the statement which it conveys to students and potential funders in contrast to the discipline of International Relations (IR). We have long co-existed in the academic community in ambiguous relation to our more prestigious IR colleagues. While addressing much the same area of human relationships, we claim to be different from them; while insisting that we apply the same rigorous standards of scholarship, we do so on a different (higher?) moral plane. But the difference has not been apparent to generations of students, trained in an approach to the study of international affairs which is reactive to the judgments and conclusions of the older discipline and uncritical of the theoretical framework that generates them. Above all, we have too easily deferred to the reigning principle of political science which makes the ethical the enemy of truth and the facts sacred and unproblematic.

1

This situation is changing rapidly since the beginning of this decade. Paradoxically, the transformation required to provide a more adequate theoretical foundation for a 'peace' orientation to international affairs is occurring, not in the PR institutes, but in those of International Relations.

Since their inception in the 1960s, institutes of Peace Research have always competed for the rewards of academe at some disadvantage in relation to the discipline of IR. It has never been easy to define their area of interest and competence in contradistinction to that of the IR community. During the Cold War, when the major question demanding attention revolved around the nature, number and deployment of weapons constituting mutual deterrence, PR institutes enjoyed an easy demarcation for students and practitioners, by virtue of their role as critics of the mainstream. For four decades following the end of World War II, the discipline of IR provided a relatively unitary and simple target for the PR community, permitting the latter to rest comfortably with its definition in opposition to the former. In the elaboration of a complex defence of nuclear deterrence on the part of IR scholars, peace researchers found a target adequate to the demands of their constituency of students and peace activists.

The relationship between the two communities of scholars, however, was skewed in favour of IR; the competition for funds, prestige and political support, particularly in the universities, was never equitable. Like women in relation to male centres of power, peace researchers in the universities found they had to work harder to establish their credentials as scholars. In an academic community where the canons of natural science established the measure of scholarly worth, where the whiff of moralizing was deemed in bad taste, and where the scientific standard for the study of international security was set by the realist school of International Relations, Peace Research made a dubious bedfellow. In its defence, peace researchers adopted the analogy of medicine to illustrate the compatibility of ethical commitment with dispassionate objectivity. Like medical scientists in respect of disease and physical suffering, peace researchers saw violence and war as an evil to be controlled or eliminated, and made an ethical commitment to that end; this did not impugn their capacity to employ the same rigorous scientific method to their study of international relations as their colleagues in the other social sciences.

It was an attractive riposte in its day. Who could deny that ethics entered into the choice of the research topic without thereby distorting the objectivity of the research process? If medical research and nuclear physics were not compromised as scientific disciplines by the moral choice which directed their studies, why should Peace Research have any case to answer? Thus fortified against the misplaced criticism of the IR community, peace researchers consolidated their position as the loyal opposition, working to the same principles, following the same rules, as the dominant school of realism.

Having adopted a common focus of study in the military aspects of the Cold War – albeit in opposition – peace researchers (with notable individual exceptions) found themselves drawn into a common methodology also. Whereas the founding sociologist, Galtung, had altered course to a multidisciplinary tack, asking the larger questions about legitimacy and structure, the community of peace researchers competing for recognition and funds in the universities found themselves drawn into the narrow channels of piecemeal, quantitative studies set by orthodox IR. Positivism made political scientists of them all, a principal difference between peace researchers and IR scholars being that the former became parasitic on the standards of truth and analytical rigour set by the latter.

Despite occasional efforts to construct a theory of Peace Research, the only coherent option opened to scholars during its 30 years of existence was a perspective derived from neo-Marxist structuralism. Structuralism invited the sociologically minded and globally oriented peace researcher to develop a research agenda clearly different from that of the IR realist. But it could not compete on the terrain of empirical problem-solving set by the Cold War. It was different – so different in its initial assumptions and method of inquiry that there could be no debate between it and its principal rival in international affairs. They constructed different worlds and there was no common ground on which to contest the question of validity.

Moreover, this PR perspective was no different on the crucial question of moral choice and the agency of change. The moral tone which accompanied its investigations of structures of violence and exploitation served to highlight the greed and rapaciousness of states. But the avarice of states was not a surprise for the world of political science; its discovery by peace researchers did little to challenge the realist view that the laws of nature in the raw determine the behaviour of states. And it did not offer a challenge because Peace Research shared the same epistemological bias towards positivism, the same fundamental philosophical understanding of a deterministic social order, as the dominant school.

Thus, where peace researchers addressed a different world from a different world-view to that of their IR colleagues there was no common ground where commensurable criteria of evidence and inference could be contested. Where the Cold War provided a common field of inquiry, peace researchers found a target to shoot at, a body of data and prescriptions supportive of Western strategic policies to undermine, but at the cost of showing how a different world, a credible alternative, was possible. What military strategists and security specialists wrote today, peace researchers attacked tomorrow. Where the hawks had their facts compiled in *The Military Balance*, the doves corrected them in their *SIPRI Yearbook* (compiled annually by the Stockholm International Peace Research Institute).

By limiting the scope of inquiry to quantifiable data and testable propositions, the subscription to positivism helped to marginalize the kind of theoretical and philosophical inquiry which did not lend itself to the requirements of a cumulative science. Significantly for peace researchers, the list of do's and don'ts for the respectable scholar proscribed the consideration of morality as an inadmissible approach to the building of a science of the international.

Had Peace Research cultivated its intellectual roots in sociology, rather than political science, its deviation into positivism might have been arrested, and its recovery of the normative dimension of international politics facilitated. The pretensions to constructing a science of the social were dominant in sociology also until the 1960s (and continue to lure large tracts of the research community, despite the failed record). But the crisis in the discipline at the end of that decade generated a radical reassessment of its foundations.

Already in the late 1960s, sociology had begun to turn away from the value-free illusions cultivated in its American homeland for decades previously, and to begin the task of constructing an alternative body of theory capable of incorporating human agency and moral choice in the analysis and characterization of the social order. Ironically, it was not the Peace Research community that recognized that positivism had run its course and that the work of Habermas, Foucault, Giddens, and the cognitive turn generally in sociology offered a richer theoretical foundation for the study of security and the international order, but their colleagues in the privileged classrooms of IR.

From the mid-1980s, the post-positivist movement has begun to transform the intellectual ethos of IR – in the United Kingdom, at least, much less so in the United States – from a relative homogeneity of approach to one of expanding pluralism. The influence of this movement is felt, not so much in the number of scholars involved, as in the weight it carries in the IR literature, where a sensitivity to the cognitive construction of once-unproblematic concepts like 'state', 'security', 'sovereignty', is almost *de rigueur*. In its train, this development has elevated the concern with morality from the margins of inquiry to the centre, to the point where the idea of a 'normative perspective' is becoming something of an anachronism. All social theory is normative, in the sense that there is no objective social world out there to be measured and manipulated by the observer, independent of the standards and values of human individuals who constitute it.

A proliferation of labels to characterize particular emphases in the new approach to international relations – 'critical international theory', 'constitutivism', 'constructivism' and more – suggests a pluralism of factions and disguises the common elements in the new approaches. They are united in a basic sociological assumption that the facts and institutions of the social order are socially constructed, cognitive artefacts, which must therefore be unpacked, deconstructed, in terms of the interests, values and ideas which constitute them.

Absent from the *mélange* of labels in the new pluralism is 'peace research'. Either it is not perceived as making a distinctive theoretical contribution to the understanding of international relations, or its theoretical foundations are deemed inadequate to the task of challenging the hold of realism. Either way – and there is probably a measure of both in the perception of the discipline – it is odd that the new shift in IR appears to ignore Peace Research in its quest for cognate disciplinary support.

Though long established as a major site of opposition to the *findings* of realism on questions of security and peace, there is little indication, as yet, that peace research institutes have extended their opposition to the positivism which underpins realism, and recognized the potential for a theoretical and philosophical basis of peace studies in the anti-positivist debate in IR. It is surely of the essence of peace studies that it provide an adequate philosophical basis for the claim that the international order is a product of human choice, not a necessity of history, and that the 'real' world is a consequence of moral decision about a world as it ought to be. Unless human agency is defensible as an elementary component of the very stuff which comprises the social order – social action – the question of alternatives to the established institutions of politics and to the security arrangements which are presented as their necessary outcome, will too easily be consigned to the realm of the 'ideal' and the 'utopian'.

In the lack of an adequate theoretical basis of moral choice and contingency in international affairs, Peace Research implicitly relegates morality to the margins of analysis – to the consequentialist discussion of policy on realist terms, or to the intrusion of moral judgment on the process of objective inquiry. Consequentialist reasoning has its place in moral theory, but it is always hostage to the impossible task of predicting future facts from current alternative options. (The Brandt and Palme Reports of the 1980s furnish an example of limiting moral reasoning to utilitarian or consequentialist premises.) The intrusion of moral judgment on the research process can help to focus attention on distorting factors in the selection of the topic or methods of analysis, but their control or exclusion at this level does not expose the ethical factor which lies at the core of social action and of the process of analyzing it. (A concern with the ethics of war or particular instruments of war in no way exhausts the ethical and the place of values in war and war-making.)

The medical analogy is a dangerous one for Peace Research. By impli-cation, it equates the object of social scientific inquiry with the natural order, and of Peace Research with the physical world of medicine. It rele-gates morality to the margins of research – the initial commitment – where, it is implied, the concern with ethics begins and ends. It tends to confine peace researchers to the arena of 'problem-solving', in the sense popular-ized by Robert Cox, rather than the critical theory which would open up the possibility of alternative structures premised upon the contingency of the established order.

The sudden end of the Cold War has left the formal organization of Peace Research bereft of a clear focus. Scholars in the older discipline of International Relations, on the other hand, for much longer in thrall to the apparent certitudes of realism, have been emancipated by it. The collapse of the bipolar world, and the failure of IR theory to predict it, even to accommodate it within the realm of the realistic, helped to liberate these scholars from a perspective which effectively denied the possibilities now unfolding before their eyes. For centuries, it appeared, the world had pro-vided the empirical evidence which supported the theories of Carr, Morgenthau, Waltz and the school of political science that views the egoistic behaviour of states as the determined outcome of human nature and structural laws. The end of the Cold War was an anomaly which did not fit, and which brought in its wake an outbreak of domestically gen-erated struggles for emancipation which only the dogmatist could explain in terms of the traditional theoretical approach. Others read the omens for positivism and found common cause with anti-positivistic schools of philosophy and sociology, to rebuild the foundations of international theory and, in the process, to rediscover the central place of moral choice and human agency. Paradoxically, this emancipatory movement within mainstream international relations is thus building the theoretical and philosophical foundations of the project of Peace Studies which, above all, rests on the claim that there are alternatives to any existing social order and that human agency and moral choice are fundamental, not marginal, to their realization.

*****

For this book, a number of internationally known scholars were invited to prepare papers on the general theme of morality in international affairs, with a particular relevance to the current debate on further integration and expansion of the European Union. Within this wide remit, three areas were separated for discussion: morality in international affairs in broad theoretical terms, the relevance of ethics and ideals to European integration in general, and the moral import of specific problem areas arising from the current debate on European integration.

Other than selecting a group of scholars known to share the School's concern to focus discussion within the boundaries of these three areas, no attempt was made to define more detailed terms of reference for contributors. In some respects, this results in a less coherent collection than might otherwise be the case. It is a grouping of papers around a theme, rather than a focusing of views on a single topic. But coherence is a hazard of all collections, and I hope this one proves to be no less interesting and useful to students for that.

The range of problem areas from which to choose the topics of Part III is so great that inevitably the choice is something of a lottery. Few will disagree that the issues chosen are among those which pose the significant ethical questions for policymakers and publics over the final years of the millennium.

The foregoing introductory comments on morality and Peace Research are intended to complement the discussion in the opening paper by Fred Halliday, by focusing attention on the normative dimension of research within the PR community, from which International Peace Studies in the Irish School of Ecumenics draws much of its inspiration and resources.

In his paper, Halliday captures the impulse behind the collection as a whole in his opening paragraph. International relations, as a practice and as a topic of analysis, raises moral issues which entail choice; the moral dimension is not an angle, an optional perspective for academics or politicians, still less a distortion of the data and process of understanding.

He illustrates the growing engagement with ethical issues in several areas of international concern – most obviously, and pertinently, the recourse to interstate war. In the field of human rights, an explosion of interest in individual rights since the UN Declaration in 1948 has highlighted the conflict between the collective and the individual subject of rights. In the economic arena, moral considerations focus on the distribution of wealth and on the expanding horizons of a cosmopolitan ethic. The question of migration, which Halliday sees as 'the hottest political potato in the world', presses for academic analysis in respect of the tension between globalizing forces liberating capital, technology and information, and our attitude to nationalism and the state, closing the doors to the suppliers of labour.

The case for a moral cosmopolitanism, Halliday acknowledges, is challenged by various forms of relativism – from the philosophical communitarianism of MacIntyre, Walzer and others, through what he calls the 'fallacy of origin', to the more extreme fallacies of postmodernism.

Richard Falk continues the background-setting of Part I with his discussion of security and morality. With respect to security and war, there is no question but that the moral dimension is central to its conduct and analysis. The problem is, rather, *which* morality should inform debate and policies on global security.

Three types of moral relevance are distinguished and traced historically to illustrate their impact on academic debate and policies. The first is the reliance on morality to constrain recourse to force as an instrument of security; secondly, a realist focus on a morality of means in order to realize most effectively the security goals of the state; a third type is a morality of ends, by which one exerts control over the role of force in world politics through the instruments of disarmament, demilitarization and non-violence.

Since the failure of Wilsonian morality of the first type, the prevailing consideration in international politics has been a morality of means, seeking to place limits to conflict and ensure the preservation of order. Security needs to be redefined on a human and global scale, created from below by transnational agents, rather than imposed from above.

Part II moves the discussion to the consideration of European integration and the relevance of normative analysis to our understanding of its origin and its contemporary significance. Joseph Weiler views the public hostility to the Maastricht Treaty as marking a crisis of values in the history of European integration, which raises the question of ideals over means. 'Ideals', he argues, 'are a principal vehicle through which individuals and groups interpret reality, give meaning to their life, and define their identity – positively and negatively.' His aim is to try to define European integration in terms of its ideals, and not only its structural and material components.

Weiler identifies the ideals which animated the European Community in its foundational period as those of peace, prosperity and supranationalism, and links them with what he terms the 'core values of Christian grace, social responsibility ... and the enlightenment'.

A major theme of Halliday and Falk is that of human agency and choice in the construction of the international order, while Weiler relates moral ideals, and the choice implicit in them, to the definition of collective identities, inclusive or exclusive of others. McSweeney develops this relationship between ideals and identities in Chapter 4. The objective is to argue the case – against the so-called 'intergovernmentalist' school – for conceiving of European integration as a security policy embodied in an integrated security community. This is accomplished, it is argued, through the reconstruction of identities and interests, and is consequent upon a moral choice, not an external determination, of the actors involved.

A third contribution on the theme of Part II is added as an appendix to the collection. Often cited in support of the critique of post-Maastricht integration, the address of the President of the Czech Republic, Václav Havel, to the European Parliament is here reproduced in full. Havel weaves an account of European history with a dream of European Union in order to explain why his country seeks membership and why it should be extended to all who fall within the boundaries of the continent. In one of his finest speeches since the liberation of his country from communism, he postulates a natural interconnectedness of the continent, to which the EU has begun to respond, in building a zone of cooperation with the potential and aim of expanding to embrace the whole area divided by the Cold War.

Havel's metaphors take on a sombre colour as he addresses the EU's task for the future and focuses on the EU of the Maastricht Treaty. His respect for the EU's efficiency and bureaucratic complexity is tainted by his perception of it as the well-oiled machine, the soulless mountain of administration. Echoing Weiler's analysis, he sketches the decline marked by Maastricht from a 'European Union ... based on a large set of values, with roots in antiquity and in Christianity, which over 2000 years evolved into what we recognize today as the foundations of modern democracy, the rule of law and civil society'. For Havel, there is need to establish a charter for the European Union which would clearly define its foundational ideas and the values it intends to embody.

Part III of the book addresses specific problems of integration which pose particular ethical questions for the Community and member states. Reflecting a traditional foreign policy concern of the country where this collection of papers was initiated – though diplomatically steering clear of the Irish case – Walter Carlsnaes discusses the compatibility of neutrality with EU integration.

He distinguishes three ways in which neutrality has been conducted. Exemplified by Switzerland, *defensive* neutrality is a policy aimed at reducing a state's participation in international relations to the minimum, both with respect to the system and to specific actors in it. A *parametric* policy of neutrality, by contrast, seeks to influence the external conditions of the neutral state in a direction favourable to the reduction of international tension. Here, the policies pursued by Austria and Finland during the bipolar conditions of the Cold War provide the model. The *strategic* approach to international relations is represented in Swedish policy, seeking to influence each of the superpowers directly in what he terms 'a reciprocal, asymmetrical relationship'.

Of the three types, Carlsnaes argues that only a parametric policy of neutrality is capable of adaptation to the demands of EU membership. The Swiss model is incompatible with the very nature of the Community as a political system, while the Swedish stands in contradiction to the specific demands of the Maastricht provisions on foreign policy. The defensive neutrality of Austria and Finland, however, may have its place in the post-Cold War period.

On the normative question of the place of neutrality in an expanded Community, he argues that there is 'more reason today than five years ago for not writing off neutrality as a policy with a viable role in contemporary Europe'. Against the backdrop of deep-rooted conflicts on the borders of the Community, there is need for bridge-builders and providers of good offices, both within Europe and further afield.

Whether or not neutrals have a compatible and ethically defensible role in an integrated Europe depends practically, and more immediately, on the fate of the EU's Common Foreign and Security Policy (CFSP). The evolution of this sector of integration, and of the Community's external policies in general, raises a multitude of pressing ethical problems, only some of which are analyzed in the three chapters that follow.

Michael MccGwire's paper looks at the prior condition for a CFSP: the proposed enlargement of NATO and its potential to embrace the continent in a common security system or to redraw the military boundaries in a divided Europe. If the ideal of peace and the construction of a security community remain central to the integration process in the EU, how is this affected by the restructuring of Europe-wide security policies and organizations following the Cold War? A Common Foreign and Security Policy for the Community cannot be realized independently of decisions to reorient the direct relationship between the two antagonists of the Cold War. NATO's response to the decline of its enemy and Russia's response to NATO will inevitably set the scene for any possibilities of security cooperation envisaged by the EU.

MccGwire locates the root pressure for extending NATO eastwards in the sphere of domestic politics in the United States. A historical cleavage concerning the scope of American involvement in world affairs has re-emerged with the collapse of communism. A long tradition of isolationism and distrust of foreign alliances has resurfaced in Congress to challenge the internationalism of NATO enthusiasts in the State Department. The proposal for NATO enlargement, for MccGwire, has little to do with a realistic assessment of Europe's security needs; it is the outcome of compromise reached thousands of miles away between the factions struggling for supremacy in Washington. In his detailed critique of three strategic grounds offered in support of NATO enlargement, MccGwire argues that enlargement is counter-productive for the satisfactory resolution of each: Russia's historic political aspirations; the control of nuclear weapons; and the breakdown of political and civil order following East European democratization.

He concludes in the note of pessimism which characterizes his overall analysis: 'The adverse effect on Russia's legitimate interests of enlarging NATO and our implicit designation of Russia as a potential enemy are a certain recipe for acrimony and dissent, rather than the cooperative engagement on which security in Europe must perforce depend.'

Ian Davis sets out, in Chapter 7, to challenge the conventional acceptability in principle of arms trading, and to demonstrate that the arms trade is *prima facie* morally unacceptable, even if sometimes, in practice, a tolerable case can be made for it. A realist rationale informed the arms trade during the Cold War and continues to do so today, with states appealing to national interest to defend the subsidies which support the continued growth in arms production, research and trade.

There are compelling reasons why the arms trade should be repudiated now, Davis argues. Apart from the insecurity that it engenders, the arms trade does not bring the much-vaunted economic or foreign policy benefits to the participating states, and cannot be morally justified in that it sustains repressive regimes in their domestic reproduction of insecurity. Davis looks to the development of a strong regulatory framework on the part of the European Union and to the influence of the new neutral member states to counter, and ultimately to delegitimize, the arms trade.

Addressing the question of overseas development in relation to European integration, David Coombes begins by questioning the concept of 'overseas' in regard to the 'development' relationship with the European Union. The overdevelopment of Europe as a whole may be the problem and, indeed, the starting point of its resolution.

The Community is committed, not just to internal, but also to external economic development. It has treaty obligations, in particular, to the 'economic and social development' of its members' former colonies, through the association formalized in the so-called Lomé Conventions. Since Maastricht, this commitment has been formally extended to include 'the sustainable economic and social development of the developing countries'. If the European continent must still be seen as a priority for the peace and development of other societies outside it, perhaps its integration in some form can point to a solution.

*****

Finally, a word of thanks to those who contributed to making this modest contribution to the international debate on the part of the Irish School of Ecumenics possible. Firstly, to the eminent contributors themselves – all of them modest enough, in a more personal sense, to give their time and expertise to the project. John Gibson, a Quaker and managing executive of Friends Provident Assurance Company in Dublin, felt strongly enough about the project to commit his organization to supporting it financially and then to become a full-time student on our Masters programme in Peace Studies. Gillian Wylie, while completing her doctoral studies in International Relations for the University of Aberdeen, was happy to join the project as editorial assistant, and merits particular thanks for her intellectual perceptiveness, efficiency and good humour. Dr Jim O'Brien and Dermot Scott were generous, as ever, in making the facilities of the European Parliament Office in Dublin available to the enterprise. The exceptional courtesy and editorial efficiency of freelance editor Sheila Chatten was greatly appreciated.

Lastly, my thanks to my colleagues in the School and its director Geraldine Smyth – with a special mention of Dorothy Maguire – for encouraging the project and putting up with the inevitable disruptions it entailed.

Part 1
Morality and Security:
Theoretical Issues

1 Morality in International Affairs: a Case for Robust Universalism

Fred Halliday

There is no subject more important for the discussion of international relations than that of morality. By morality I mean not only the approach to be taken to a set of unavoidable moral issues that arise in international relations, but also the means to arrive at areas of agreement and standards, and the means to implement and enforce such approaches. The reasons for this importance are several, but there can be little debate as to the starting point: international relations – whether seen as relations between states, or seen as a broader set of relations across frontiers, bypassing in whole or in part the strictly interstate – raises moral issues on which choice, by commission or omission, is essential.

These choices confront all those directly involved in international relations – be they states, interstate organizations, non-governmental organizations, transnational bodies, religious groups – but they also, directly or indirectly, confront every one of us as individuals. We are all presented with choices as to international affairs, choices that we make directly as individuals, or through the political and other organizations we belong to and where we articulate our views. Such choices involve conceptions of obligation and the common good, but they go beyond the two other areas where obligation or conceptions of the good may be found – namely international law and non-legal international convention, the assumptions, regimes, or what some call 'institutions', of relations between states.[1] As in domestic politics law and morality may overlap, but they cover distinct areas. Equally, convention and norms may involve a large measure of moral concern, not least underlying assumptions about the importance of maintaining cooperation and of contributing to a predictable, ordered, set of international relations: but these norms too – such as the rules of diplomacy, or understandings about trade – are not in themselves constitutive of morality.

The unavoidability of morality, and the need for choices, can be illustrated by reference to five major areas of international activity. The first, the classic area for the elaboration of moral codes about relations between communities and states, is war.[2] Modern international society, and every other international system I am aware of, has underlying assumptions about the conduct of war, broadly identifiable in terms of the two classic categories of the right to go to war, or use force, in the first place, *jus ad bellum*, and the proper use of force in war, *jus in bello*. These conceptions are present in classical Greece, as they are in the Islamic tradition. Much of our modern perception of them can be derived from the very clear discussion of Aquinas. No one today looking at the debates on, say, the Gulf War of 1990–1, or the conflict between Serbia, Croatia and Bosnia in the Balkans, can fail to see allusion, conscious or not, to the distinctions and criteria of the Thomist tradition: on the one hand the need for just authority and just cause to go to war, on the other the respect for proportion and discrimination in the conduct of that war. Looking back over international debates of the past half century, we encounter a multitude of debates on war phrased in moral terms: on the legitimacy or not of using nuclear weapons, on the legitimacy of threatening to use nuclear weapons when having no intention of using them, on the 'justness' or not of authorities inviting others in to defend their sovereignty (as in Saigon, Prague, Kabul), on the rights of unofficial combatants – national liberation fighters, guerrilla strugglers, terrorists – claiming to speak in the name of oppressed peoples, classes or nations. Fourteen years ago the British entered the Falklands War: sovereignty was certainly threatened but there were those who debated the legitimacy or otherwise of acting in such a way that 1000 young men died in the south Atlantic protecting not the lives, which were never threatened, but the 'way of life' of roughly 2000 inhabitants of the islands. The latter were invaded by a country where an estimated 100 000 people of the same culture and ethnic stock live quite happily with their Anglican churches, horse-races and Harrods. We can easily recall retrospective and bitter debates about particular acts in wars that are, in broader terms, considered just, such as the bombing of Dresden and the nuclear annihilation of Hiroshima and Nagasaki. We may say that war is an amoral activity, *inter arma silent leges*, as the saying goes: the fact is that in the debates – political, moral, religious – over war and the use of force in the past half-century morality has been as present as ever.

This presence of morality is evident in a second broad area of international affairs, namely that of economics and wealth. It was, of course, long thus: in past centuries it was accepted that, for some states at least, it was legitimate to use force up to and including the seizure of territory and the enslavement or at least severe subjugation of peoples, to promote one's own economic interests, often identified with progress in general. In the seventeenth century Grotius, the father of much contemporary international relations theory, spent his time working on a law of booty. He certainly felt that it was just to wage war to protect one's economic interests. Until at least World War I, the European powers felt it legitimate to seize the territory of weaker states, and to use force to collect their debts. Saddam Hussein's argument, that he had a right to invade Kuwait because that state had damaged Iraq's economic interests, was not accepted in 1990 because it came from him, but it was only a few decades out as far as the general acceptability of the criterion was concerned. While invasion as a form of debt collection is not acceptable today, it is still regarded as legitimate to use other forms of pressure – up to and including forms of economic and diplomatic sanction – to oppose nationalization or expropriation: Ireland had experience of this in the 1930s, and Fidel Castro, were he present here, would no doubt have something, probably a lot, to say about *el bloqueo*.

The issue of wealth has, however, come over recent decades to have a rather different character, based on a broad aspiration towards an equalization of the world's wealth, or, at least, towards the promotion of growth and development in poor countries. At one level this can be seen as an extension to the international level of the assumptions about welfare and equity that have been held, for rather more decades, by developed countries. We can think of the Marshall Plan, of the promotion of Third World growth through foreign aid, of plans to restructure the world economy through a New International Economic Order, launched in 1973, and of many subsequent debates on debt, technological transfer and trade policy. Some of the arguments for global redistribution derive their legitimacy from an argument about history – that the wealth of the rich 10 per cent of the world is based, in whole or in part, on a history of imperial plunder and subjugation. Alternatively, the same argument is applied to the contemporary world – prosperity in the north requires poverty in the south, our OECD wealth is in some sense necessarily oligarchic. This, broadly speaking, is the argument of dependency theory. Others take a more pragmatic approach: whatever the causes, the world is one and an impoverished and embittered south will, sooner or later, threaten the security and prosperity of the north. A programme of global Keynesianism is needed to offset that danger: made with some force when it was first promoted by the Brandt Report in 1980 it has, of course, acquired greater urgency with the onset of the global ecological crisis which will engulf us all, in its environmental or demographic forms, or both, unless enlightened, far-sighted and global policies, of which there is scant evidence to date, are applied. Alternatively, the argument for global redistribution can rest almost entirely on the plea for a common humanity, a strictly moral and cosmopolitan appeal, that, for example, denies specific, exclusive, national claims to raw materials that might happen to lie under their territory and which assumes not the possibility of some conditional redistribution, but an obligation to share the world's wealth equally.[3]

Such redistributive concerns have, it must be noted, had rather small impact. While overall levels of output increase, the inequality of wealth in the world today is growing. Over a fifth of humanity live below a minimum level of basic need satisfaction. Many forms of wealth – technology, finance, control of key industries and markets – are becoming more and more oligarchic. Yet the arguments used to defend this are themselves based on combinations of policy and moral assumptions: that the best way to promote wealth is not to promote state intervention or distribution; that the poverty of many societies is above all due to their internal weaknesses – that is, it is 'their fault'; that the precondition for the maintenance of any international system is the continued strength and prosperity of the rich minority; *in extremis* that the inequality in the world is inevitable, the result of nature, or 'God's way'. Such views, rarely articulated directly in the editorial columns of our serious papers, are rather more widely held than late millennial politesse would have us believe.

This brings me to a third area of moral discourse, and choice, in the international system, that of human rights.[4] We live in a world where some allusion to human rights is almost obligatory, a necessary part of international respectability. Again, the tradition is in some ways a long one. Concern for individual rights was, of course, a major preoccupation of earlier empires and missionary religions, at least as far as their own people were concerned. Bulgarian atrocities or the fate of Christians in China required a response. Concern for group rights, or for those of collectivities we now call nations, developed over the past century and a half, finding its expression in above all the assumption, which developed over the nineteenth century, that nations had the right to self-determination, that is, to the option of independence or, if they forwent it, to equal and just treatment within broader multi-ethnic states. Today conceptions of group rights are still very much with us and are causing many a headache – in Bosnia and Rwanda, but also in supposedly nicer places like Quebec, Northern Ireland or 'Padania'. But what has become most important in the international discussion of human rights over the past half-century has been the explosion of interest in individual human rights, beginning with the Universal Declaration of Human Rights (UDHR) proclaimed by the

UN in 1948. Many other codes have followed, concerning gender, race, torture and the rights of children.

What this commitment to human rights involves is not only the promotion of a particular area of moral concern across frontiers, but also a huge effort to develop and implement such commitments, and standards. At the same time the commitment to this area of morality differs in an important way from the two other areas I have mentioned, war and wealth: for if, in the former case, the subjects of moral action have, with some qualifications, been states, the doctrine of human rights, although wielded by states, has been seen, and rightly so, as in contradiction with the assumption that states are the sole or primary actors. Indeed by introducing the UDHR in 1948 and all that has subsequently been derived from it, the international community has highlighted a fundamental conflict, an incompatibility, between two moral approaches to international relations. This was noted exactly 200 years ago by one of the most perceptive, and short-winded, of writers on international affairs, Immanuel Kant, in his 13-page essay *On Perpetual Peace*, published in 1795; Kant envisaged the spread of a cosmopolitan law and morality that would transcend states and gradually, through the workings of history and nature, and perhaps a bit of conscious human agency, promote a cosmopolitan world.[5] Today this conflict is evident in the rhetoric of those who resist criticism on the basis of human rights, as much as on the part of those who espouse it, or use it for instrumental purposes: the arguments against are rarely about standards themselves, but more often phrased in terms of alternative, but equally universalistic, principles – non-interference, sovereignty, the need for a single standard, the questioning of the motives of those making the criticism. In other words, states resist human rights criticism by defending the rights of states. Equally, many of those who start from a liberal, individualistic, position resist any cogent application of this to international affairs.[6]

This brings me to the fourth, and last, area in which morality is inherent in our discussion and conduct of international relations, namely our attitude to the state itself. We live in a world of sovereign states, a collection of centres of power and authority, arrived at through a pretty arbitrary historical process that corresponds hardly at all to considerations of representativity or logic: in Europe it corresponds to where armies got tired of fighting, in the rest of the world it more or less corresponds to lines drawn by the – equally European – colonial powers. But it is there, we have strong reasons for seeking in most cases to preserve it, and we have come over the centuries to invest it with a moral authority – in earlier times the divine right of kings, since the early nineteenth century increasingly the ethical system associated with nationalism. According to this system, a rather recent package of values which everyone now seems quite happy to regard as natural and inevitable, all of us are in some way 'born' into a national group, to which we owe obedience, and which gives us in return a bundle of desirable things: identity, community, history, language and, not least, territory. If the first four components of the national package may seem straightforward and rationally defensible, the last is a rather curious assumption: the idea that physical terrain – rocks, rivers, mountains, fields, stones – can in any meaningful sense 'have' a nationality is an arbitrary one, a very modern conceit, but one that people are happy to fight and die for. The argument is, of course, that morality, legal and ethical claim, is given by history, by prime occupation, but there are problems with that, and it would create quite a lot of trouble to enforce it and quite a bit of ethnic cleansing to set the clock back to ... when is not quite clear. As a descendant of earlier inhabitants of the British Isles, I could become quite exercised about the Anglo-Saxons, all of whom were illegal immigrants once.

Nationalism has created an ethical system and it is the one that the world holds to, but it has at the same time created many problems.[7] One concerns territory, a problem just alluded to. A second concerns those who are not part of the 'national' group: they should be excluded, or suppressed, or in extreme cases, as in Nazi Germany, killed, finally solved. A third concerns those who like myself have two nationalities: we may regard ourselves as privileged, but others will be quick to say that those who have two nationalities belong to neither. A fourth issue concerns those who while clearly not part of the nation would like to come and live within its boundaries, that is, to migrate. They can promise to assimilate, or come and set up their own well-behaved but distinct communities, or promise to come as second-class citizens. But while the world has become more international and the other factors of production – capital, technology, information – fly round the world, the most traditional factor of production, labour, is becoming less and less mobile. The world was a much freer place to move around in a hundred years ago.

While we hear much about globalization and transnationalism, and the global village, today the doors are closing. The question which this poses, beyond issues of social policy or citizenship law, is what would a morality of migration be? Do states have an absolute right to stop it? Do individuals have an absolute right to migrate? What of the intermediate obligation of which Kant speaks, *Hospitalität*, not full acceptance, but an obligation to treat well those who are already within one's frontiers? What of refugees? Migration is perhaps the hottest political potato in the contemporary world, yet it is the one that politicians and moralists are most uneasy about. The stranger is knocking at the door, and in most cases does not want to become simply one of us, at least in the next generation. It is noticeable in the rush of literature on the fiftieth anniversary of the UN and in such documents as the Report of the Commission on Global Governance, and amidst detailed proposals on all sorts of other things, that this was the issue most dodged, beyond some anodyne injunctions to treat migrants decently.[8] The issue of the claims of nations involves many other problems – of who speaks for the nation, or what happens to those whose interpretation of the nation and its tradition is different, a point made by, among others, feminist critics, of what the relation between national and international values and commitments may be.

The one thing that we can agree on, however, is that throughout this discussion morality is present. In essence, we have three possible positions as to the point of prime moral reference: the state, defined conditionally or unconditionally as the existing government; some broader constituency, be it a religious community, a political grouping, such as the working class, or the intelligentsia, or some more restricted sub-state entity, a locality, a kinship structure, such as a tribe, or an economic entity, be it a firm, a mafia, a bank. Those who are sceptical about the definitions, and hence claims, of nationalism often opt for one of the two other frameworks – be it in the world revolution, or some more intimate group. We may recall, in this context, the scornful discussion of nations in *Ulysses*. For his part Graham Greene once said 'I would rather betray my country than my friends'. For most of humanity, on the other hand, the claim of country is at least formally supreme. We shall know this is not so when the word traitor is no longer a term of abuse.

So far, it would appear, so good. There are lots of moral issues in international relations, and no doubt more that I have not mentioned. If we look at the world of political discourse the presence of moral issues, and an awareness of them, seems not to be in doubt. The whole language of discussion of foreign policy within countries is suffused with moral terminology – claims on loyalty and higher principle clashing with denunciation of betrayal, moral cowardice, sell-outs, self-seeking, inconsistency, cravenness and the rest. Perhaps no area of public discourse is so infused with allegations of immorality, and not least with various forms of excoriation, as is that of international affairs. This tone applies, *inter alia*, to the issue of neutrality. Yet neutrality is not a moral but a legal concept: one would be hard pressed to find a moral obligation to it, in so far as the right to morality can be derived from sovereignty. And yet, for all this, the role of morality in international affairs, indeed the very relevance of morality to international affairs, is often questioned, in public policy as much as in the academic literature. Practitioners are quite quick to invoke national interest, and deploy phrases like 'We cannot afford the luxury of …'. The academic literature, especially that of the 'realism' that has since World War II been the dominant idiom in the Anglo-Saxon world, itself the dominant trend within the field on a global level, has sought to reduce the claims of morality on international relations, and to warn of the dangers of moral discourse. Many of the textbooks of international relations, I would wager the vast majority, have no discussion of it at all. We could revise the old saying about the irrelevance of law to war. *Inter nationes silent mores.* I apologise for the fact that the word 'nationes' in this political sense, although spuriously Latinate, is in fact a more recent invention, coined by Bentham in 1780.

Why is there this silence? At least five broad reasons suggest themselves. The first reason one might consider is the one most present in political discourse today, and especially in the literature on global governance and other attempts to reform the international system today. It is that, while we are broadly in agreement on what should be done, we lack the instruments, the institutions, the funds, the political commitment, to carry out what we would like to do. Some blame this on the weakness of the international institutions themselves, some on the lack of finance, some on the corruption of international bureaucracies and civil servants, some on the timidity of particular leaders – a feeble UN secretary-general here, a weak-willed British foreign secretary there. Alternatively, the blame can be put on the underlying political sources of this international system, namely the national states and, behind them, the public opinion of the countries themselves, and in particular of the major industrialized and democratic countries. Thus the failure to increase foreign aid can be attributed to the selfishness and/or short-sightedness of the rich world, as can the, probably catastrophic, failure to move decisively and quickly to curb CO_2 emissions. Behind all the accusations about what 'went wrong' in Bosnia, the fact is that in no major state, European or North American, let alone Japanese, was there a public willingness to incur the casualties and financial costs of a major intervention, prior to the defeat of the Serbian armies in the summer of 1995. The phrase much beloved of British politicians when accused of chickening out over Bosnia is expressive: 'We cannot wipe the tear from every eye'. The same would apply to the failure to enforce human rights obligations: the costs in terms of lost trade and influence of a harder line towards China or Saudi Arabia are not ones the respective publics, and their flimsily legitimated politicians, are prepared to pay. One could go on. The point is, however, that if this is the problem, a lack of will and of properly financed and supported institutions, then the solution is somehow to do more – to lobby, to educate, to polemicize, to organize so that a broader international coalition of the good can be brought into being to feed, protect and care for those in need across the world.

This argument is in itself a contingent argument, suggesting that more could be done if only we tried harder. But there is a second, more intractable, argument that makes such appeals appear trivial or ineffective, if not downright misleading and dangerous. This is, in essence, the argument that morality cannot play a significant role, or indeed any role, in international affairs, because relations between states are based on power, and above all military power, and when not armed power then economic interest.[9] This has been the claim of the realist school of international relations, and it derives its authority from the critique of an earlier moral and legal approach, the mistakenly named 'utopian' approach, of the 1920s and 1930s. In one of the classic statements of this approach, E.H. Carr's *The Twenty Years' Crisis*, first published in 1939, and still the book with which our postgraduate students start their compulsory course in international theory, Carr argues that the failure of the League of Nations was above all a result of a failure to look at international relations as they are. It rested on a confusion of wish with reality, and a mistaken, in the end disastrous, reliance on law, trust and consensus when states were pursuing their selfish national interests through the maximization of power. Carr invokes Machiavelli, not to legitimate deceit or cunning, but to warn against the replacement of realism by wishful thinking.[10] Others – Hans Morgenthau, Reinhold Niebuhr, Henry Kissinger, my former colleague Fred Northedge, Martin Wight – have written in similar vein.

While domestic politics involves consent, law, and some play for morality, international relations is the domain of power politics. Morality, as Michael Howard wrote, is of 'quite Merovingian ineffectiveness' in the field of international affairs. Others, somewhat less bleak in their approach, such as Hedley Bull in his *The Anarchical Society*, have argued that morality may have a role but only when it is within the constraints of power. Law, morality, and appeals to interests other than the state can only succeed if backed by power, and in particular by the actions of the great powers. Thus an international security system based as was the League on unanimity, or founded on some broader consensus of the UN General Assembly, would be doomed to ineffectiveness. The best you could hope for would be today's UN Security Council, based as it is on a small group of great powers – all the more so since the formal reality of a US control, backed up by compliant Britain and France, is even more centralized than the illusion of a five-power coalition would suggest. Had Hedley Bull lived he could, with much justification, have claimed endorsement for his insistence on the need for great powers from the outcome of two recent world crises: in Kuwait in 1990–1, and in former Yugoslavia after 1991, nothing got done till the single really great power remaining in the world decided to do something. If the US had not acted, Saddam would be in Kuwait, and Karadzic might be in, or still on the hills surrounding, Sarajevo. It may not be how we would like to see the world, and it is certainly not the best of all possible worlds. But who can easily say that this is not the case?

The realist critique of morality in international affairs involves, however, another element, a third argument to the effect that morality and international relations cannot be combined. This is the argument, derived in part from the sociology of knowledge, that proclamations of morality are duplicitous, that they conceal hidden interests, that, in effect, those who claim to be acting, or appeal to others to act, in the name of some common good are using such language to conceal their own concerns. This was the gist of Carr's critique of liberal internationalism between the wars. As Adam Roberts, Professor of international relations at Oxford, and not someone shy of pushing moral claims, once put it: 'The problem with internationalism is that it is really just a way of saying why can't the rest of the world be like us.' In an area of great international activity, albeit one little studied by academic specialists, sport, this self-interest disguised as universalism is evident: there is nothing so parochial as the World Series. This is the basis of contemporary opposition, by say China or Iran, to human rights criticisms from the UN or the USA. Much of the debate on reforming the international economic system revolves around competing charges of concealed special pleading – the richer countries, who would benefit from it, proclaiming free trade, the poorer countries, who would not, calling for various forms of protectionism and interstate intervention to alter the workings of the market. The object of international contention most of all, the environment, gives us plenty of examples of this, the Third World seeing the north's proposals as reflecting their already established benefits and, simultaneously, their refusal to give up their wasteful, automobilized, life-style, and the concerned enlightened ecologists of the north seeing southern states as selfishly putting the exploitation and running down of their forests or whatever before the broader interests of mankind. *Ceteris paribus*, we can see the same issues in the debate on migration, on intellectual copyright, and of course on that much-protected vested interest nearer home, a common agricultural policy. More general public discourse on the proposals of other states reflects this – one need only look at reactions to proposals to broaden the permanent membership of the Security Council, or at debates on deepening and/or widening the European Union, or at the debate on removing subsidies to the French film industry, to see that the suspicion of special interest masked as international policy remains.

This has, of course, long been the resort of those who have criticized the neutrality option of European states: behind the pretence of high-mindedness on the part of small nations has lain, it is argued, the selfishness of those who do not want to share the burdens of promoting a better world. One can think of those who have used their neutrality to sell arms, others who used it to launder money, others who abuse their vote to disrupt international conferences, others to protect anomalous and, by international standards, autistic moral choices, others to elect war criminals as presidents. Moreover, most neutral and non-aligned states were, in the broader scheme of things, free-riders: had the third world war become imminent they would have jumped one way or the other, mainly one way I suspect, and they were throughout this period sheltering behind the security of the big military alliances.

These three arguments constitute what may be termed the classical critique of the role of morality in international affairs. They recur again and again in the literature and in debates on what could or should be done about particular international issues. I doubt if recent disputes about, say, Bosnia or Rwanda or the imprisonment of dissidents in China, have thrown up many new questions: they have, however, underlined the continued relevance of these issues and the lack of clear thinking, or progress, on them. There are, however, two other lines of argument concerning the role of morality in international relations which merit attention, one of them of comparatively recent formulation, if not origin, the other enduringly present but all too little articulated by those concerned with this issue. Both are, at least initially, philosophic in form.

The first of these philosophic arguments questions not the relevance of morality to international affairs but rather our ability to formulate, and hence even try to implement, any general moral principles at all.[11] Hitherto most discussion about morality and international relations has assumed that, whether implementable or not, certain principles exist to which we may refer: these may be derived from religion, or natural law, or positive international law, or reason, but at least they are there. You can look them up in a book, get worked up about them, and then argue about how or if they can be applied. This can, however, no longer be said. We live in an era when the authority of such moral codes or grand narratives or enlightenment projects or international standards, or whatever you want to call them, is being questioned. The questioning comes from three broad directions. One line of argument is that of the moral philosophers – writers such as Alasdair MacIntyre, Stuart Hampshire and Raymond Plant – who question whether any moral principles, derived from reason, can be arrived at.[12] Their position, broadly categorizable as 'communitarian', is both anti-individualistic and anti-universalistic: no Kant for them. Our morality, they say, is only capable of definition between communities, groups into which we are born or where we find ourselves, and the moralities of different groups are not only different, but incommensurable. No universal codes are possible and indeed, linking up with the critique of internationalism, they suspect that attempts to do so are a form of rationalist or enlightenment arrogance. The best we can do is promote some tolerance, and procedures for adjudicating between traditions. They are, of course, deeply moral and concerned men, but, regretfully, tell us that we must ditch any aspirations to make our morality universal. Morality between nations or states would therefore be an exiguous, limited one, or, in Michael Walzer's terminology, a 'thin' morality in contrast to the 'thick' morality found in societies.[13]

To this, moral philosophic critique, is added a second one, ever present but today very much part of current concerns, of a relativist *Zeitgeist*, which challenges the authority of values, or any codes, because of their association with a particular European or more broadly hegemonic origin. This is broadly speaking the argument that the values articulated by the west, and diffused throughout the world, are invalid because they are 'ethno-' or 'Euro-centric', and not just those of one particular region but of a region that has, over the past five centuries, imposed itself by force on the rest of the world. Drawing on critiques of cultural imperialism, and augmented by more recent thinking on multiculturalism and the importance of difference, this form of relativism proceeds from an historical identification of origin to an invalidation of the universal applicability of moral principles arrived at in this way. In one sense this is a contemporary, anti-hegemonic or anti-imperialist, version of Carr's suspicion of the universality of moral codes. But it contains within it another premise, one rarely articulated, and too easily accepted, namely what I would call the fallacy of origin, whereby a set of ideas or moral principles are deemed invalid just because they have a specific origin. This invalidity does not follow for ideas of engineering or medicine or music, nor is the critique of ethnocentrism much in evidence when we come to such Eurocentric ideas as national self-determination or the sovereignty of states, or commercial profit. Moreover, this critique, for all its invocation of history, rests upon a quite ahistorical and simplistic view of the 'west', one that omits the degree to which the moral principles of today's 'west' – for example, human rights, rule of law, democracy – were ones formulated not by an undifferentiated, dominant, west, but by social and political movements themselves opposed to the dominant order in the west and taken up by others, outside the 'west', who shared a similar, oppositional, perspective.

To these two critiques is now added a third, the dominant spirit of much social science in the west today, what is in broad terms called 'post-modernism'. According to this approach, we must reject the pretensions of the enlightenment, towards any rational or universalizable codes or grand narrative, and accept an inevitable profusion of values, meanings, codes, a discursive plurality that is both inevitable and desirable. We must, to use one of their favourite words, be intellectual nomads. We can no longer talk of truth, or of shared human aspirations, but must rejoice in the diversity of images that go to make up our contemporary post-enlightenment, post-rational, postmodernist condition. Those who want to promulgate general codes and implement them are stuck in some now overtaken time-warp, the enlightenment condition that has given us two centuries of brutalism and hegemony in the name of progress towards the modern. There is much that could be said about postmodernism, and the conceits of its proponents. One can, however, content oneself with saying very little. It is a monstrous conceit, banal when it is not second-rate, and of arguable relevance to either international relations or morality. If one is languishing in jail or suffering racial or gender or other oppression in some country the last thing one wants to be told is that one is still a victim of the enlightenment project. It has an important place in art and literature. It is, in this context, a silly approach and one that as much as any other reflects the irresponsibility of much of the intelligentsia in the developed world.

CONCLUSION

I have tried in what has gone before to sketch out both the positive and negative sides of the attempt to apply morality to international relations, and to show that, for all the enthusiasm and commitment we may feel for particular values, there are substantial obstacles, some long established, some comparatively recent, to arguing the case. It would seem to be the first precondition for any serious discussion of the role of morality in international relations that these difficulties be recognized. Far too often discussion of morality in international affairs, in part provoked by the predominant amoralism of policy and academic study alike, resorts to an impatient, angry and utopian assertion of alternatives. Indeed one of the difficulties of arguing *for* a moral position in international affairs is that so much of what is proposed is of a wishful, sincere but impractical kind, and one that too easily falls into the traps identified by Machiavelli and his successors. In this case the old Gramscian injunction, 'pessimism of the intellect, optimism of the will', seems especially relevant. This goes for the rules of war, for reforming global governance, for human rights, for the international economy. We can come up with grand ideas, and envisage radically different worlds. This is what people did when, for example, they opposed slavery or colonialism, or proposed the setting up of the UN – all grand, apparently unattainable goals. But we should take on board the more subtle version of the realist case and always be able to show how we get there from here, what the practical steps would be, what the stages would be, how support, and money, for such an advance could be mobilized and maintained. A kind of robust universalism, or, if you like, a Scandinavian consensus with teeth, is needed to push forward these issues.

Once we start to do this we shall encounter another difficulty, one too easily forgotten, but one which also highlights the possibility as well as the difficulty of practical action. This is that we face not one but many choices; that is, the choice is not just whether to apply morality to international affairs but rather to recognize the range of choices which are offered and on which sincere, morally concerned, people may disagree. If the realists and pragmatists sin by denying the importance of moral claims, the moralists fail too often by simplifying the issue, by denying the need for argument and choice, as between moral actions. There is no necessary compatibility, no harmony of values, to fall back on once morality is invoked: choices still have to be made. This is, in effect, the greatest weakness of the moral denunciation of states, the implication being that if only states or electorates were moral then they would know exactly what to do.

This is rarely the case. Whether on the issue of sovereignty versus human rights, or economic reform versus market forces, or waging war versus conciliation, difficult, but not irresolvable, moral choices arise. In the case of the wars of former Yugoslavia, for example, there were clear differences of policy depending on whether primacy was given to humanitarian aid, or to protecting human rights, or to seeking peace through diplomatic conciliation, or to defending the sovereignty and integrity of states. If you made humanitarian aid the priority, you had to deal with, and pay off, criminals and murderers. If you defended the sovereignty of states you prolonged war. At the same time, the no doubt justified refusal to talk to some mass murderers in Serbian Bosnia contrasts with a continued eagerness to engage in diplomatic dialogue with others whose record of killing is at least as great: Boris Yeltsin in Chechnya and Hafiz al-Asad in his suppression of his Islamist opponents have at least as much blood on their hands as Radovan Karadzic and Radko Mladic. Equally, in former Yugoslavia as elsewhere, support for the principle of self-determination, for any people who looked reasonably like a candidate to be a people and clearly wanted separation, had to be balanced against other factors: the international community, for all its support for self-determination, has always been selective in recognizing its relevance. In the situation we now find ourselves in, when the collapse of communism has added 22 new states to the international system, no government in the world wants to see many more sovereign entities emerging. The parking lot is full, with perhaps a space or two still be filled by, say, Palestine or Quebec. This reflects not justice towards peoples, but rather calculations of international order. We can go through the whole gamut of policies and moral choices in the international system and make similar discrimina-tions. There is no harm in that, of course: in international affairs, as in domestic politics, or one's private life, there are too rarely clear moral choices. Maturity lies not in denying this but in thinking the choices through and making as informed and discriminating a decision as one can.

The greatest of all realist putdowns is the claim that there is no progress in international relations and that those who think there is, or could be, such progress are the most dangerous of all people. To quote Graham Greene again: 'An innocent person is like a leper walking the world without his bell.' Such indeed would be the realist view of moralists. But the realists are wrong now, indeed they have always been wrong, and there is, in a cautious, positivistic, sense a considerable accumulation of under-standings, laws and codes which have helped to make the world a some-what more moral place: states, and others, violate these morals, but that is the case everywhere. The end of the Cold War and the emergence of a somewhat greater international consensus also provides an opportunity to promote these values, even as we argue over the content of relevant codes, and come face to face with the choices involved. I would, therefore, end by putting my own voice behind those who, with all the pessimism of the intellect and of experience, continue to try to push forward the codification and implementation of moral concerns, and to educate public opinion, above all that in democracies, about the possibility and need for morality in international affairs. We need, if anything, to be somewhat more forceful, even benignly impatient, in our approach to these matters.

Notes

1. Hedley Bull, *The Anarchical Society* (Macmillan, 1977).
2. Michael Walzer, *Just and Unjust Wars* (New York, Basic Books, 2nd edition, 1992).
3. Charles Beitz, *Political Theory and International Relations* (Princeton: Princeton University Press, 1979).
4. R.J. Vincent, *Human Rights and International Relations* (London: Cambridge University Press, 1986); Jack Donnelly, *International Human Rights* (Oxford: Westview Press, 1993).
5. Thomas Donaldson, 'Kant's Global Rationalism' in Terry Nardin and David Mapel (eds), *Traditions in International Ethics* (Cambridge: Cambridge University Press, 1993).
6. John Rawls, 'The Law of Peoples' in Stephen Shure and Susan Hurley (eds), *On Human Rights* (New York: Basic Books, 1993).
7. David Miller, *On Nationality* (Oxford: Clarendon Press, 1995) offers an ethical defence of nations.
8. *Our Global Neighbourhood* (Oxford: OUP, 1995).
9. For example, Michael Howard 'Ethics and Power in International Policy' in *The Causes of War* (London: Temple Smith, 1983).
10. E.H. Carr, *The Twenty Years' Crisis* (London: Macmillan, 1983).
11. Chris Brown, *International Relations Theory: New Normative Approaches* (Hemel Hempstead: Harvester Wheatsheaf, 1992).
12. Alasdair MacIntyre, *After Virtue* (London: Duckworth, 1981); Stuart Hampshire, *Innocence and Experience* (London: Penguin, 1989); Raymond Plant, *Modern Political Thought* (Oxford: Blackwell, 1991).
13. Michael Walzer, *Thick and Thin: Moral Argument at Home and Abroad* (London: Notre Dame Press, 1994).

2 Morality and Global Security: the Normative Horizons of War
Richard Falk

I. PRELIMINARIES

The topic of morality in the global sphere of politics is complex, confusing, controversial and, in the end, unavoidable. It is finally unavoidable because the undertaking of war is inconceivable in the modern world without accompanying justifying and discrediting arguments; even non-democratic governments do not in modern times generally embark upon war without elaborate public efforts to legitimate their actions. But whether explicitly moral/legal claims and counter-claims are more than displays of adherence to rhetorical styles of diplomacy evolved over the course of several centuries remains inherently controversial, being subject to contradictory conceptual and historical modes of interpretation.

Recently the relevance of morality to international or global security has been further problematized by suggesting a wide range of reference points for security other than the independence and territorial integrity of the sovereign state and its population. These have included various elements of human well-being such as freedom from fear and satisfaction of basic survival needs, the conditions of domestic political order that shape attitudes toward war in foreign policy, the role of international institutions in specifying limits on the permissible, and most recently, the demographic, environmental and resource dimensions of sustainable development. International security becomes, then, a synonym for whatever is valued in international life.[1]

There are two forms of this broader conception of security: the broadest of all is to regard security as the condition of individual and collective existence that aspires to eliminate insecurity in all its forms; the more restricted expansion of international security is to connect it only with the conditions associated with the minimization of threats arising from adversary recourse to the use of force across international boundaries. The narrow conception of international security is concerned only with the military means, including closely related financial capabilities, relied upon by states and their representatives to uphold the relative position of their country in the world, but most significantly to sustain sovereignty in relation to people, resources and territory subject to their lawful authority. An important reformulation of the narrow conception would include military initiatives mandated or undertaken by the United Nations or regional actors, such as NATO in relation to Bosnia. The importance of these developments, generally expressive of globalization tendencies, explains the choice here of 'global security' rather than 'international security' to identify the topic.

Of course, the complexity doesn't end here. There is, above all, a fundamental distinction between the security of the state or unit and the security of the system as a whole. For instance, the elected leaders of France are presumably sincerely persuaded that France will be more secure with respect to potential threats directed at its vital interests as a result of its controversial series of nuclear tests in the Pacific during 1995–6, but the system may be less secure, either because other states will feel encouraged to test by the French precedent or because of harm done to health and environmental conditions in the affected region. Global security encompasses both discourses, that on behalf of particular states and that on behalf of the past, present and future of global society conceived as a whole.

There is also the closely related issue of the locus of relevant authority: major states have long regarded it to be an element of their sovereignty to determine their national security policy with virtually no duty of external accountability. Thus, France, as represented by its political leaders, expresses the last word with regard to French security even if, arguably, it reaches decisions that are felt by other major governments, as well as in regional and global arenas, to be 'wrong' for France, much less for the wider community. Minor or outlaw states have more restricted discretion to define their own security, being subject to such geopolitical constraints as those associated with nuclear non-proliferation norms; in particular, countries such as North Korea, Iran and Iraq are perceived as threats to the established regional orders and are subjected to various constraints on the exercise of sovereign rights with respect to security. These constraints are set and enforced by hegemonic actors and their allies.

One source of widespread confusion is the indeterminate relationship between law and morality as it bears upon our thinking about global security. Generally, it is quite possible for these two sources of normative authority, which are commonly treated as mutually reinforcing, actually to point in divergent, even contradictory, directions. For instance, a lawful peace treaty can validate an immoral outcome in warfare, quite clearly the impact of the *de facto* state-splitting character of the 1995 Dayton Peace Agreement on the 'ethnically cleansed' peoples of former Yugoslavia; international law for decades lent an aura of legality to colonial relationships and exploitative foreign investment arrangements, but questions of morality were never put to rest by such a legalistic facelift.

At the same time, there is a continuous moral pressure to make law into a vehicle for the realization of moral goals, including the informing moral idea in international life that there are strict limits on the discretion to use force that apply to states and other political actors, and that these have a *moral* duty to uphold international law, and that the law, in effect, embodies agreed, generally applicable and authoritative standards of morality that confine discretion to use force to 'defensive' modes. But even if the authority of law is affirmed in such telling circumstances, the nature of the guidance provided is often vague and unsatisfactory, allowing multiple self-serving interpretations, especially of the doctrine of 'self-defence'. For decades prominent diplomats laboured to agree upon a definition of 'aggression', which when finally achieved, turned out to be useless, given its abstractness and vulnerability to loopholes. Law on such fundamental matters as the right of states to use force is open-textured both as to the authority to interpret its meaning and with respect to the proper delimitation of the right of 'self-defence'.[2]

There is the related daunting problem of interpretation in a political order in which authority is dispersed and decentralized. Generally, a sovereign state continues to insist on its capacity to interpret applicable moral and legal obligations with only a highly circumscribed willingness to refer interstate disputes to a third party process. Even on the rare occasions when a global arena for decision is available in disputes relating to security policy, as was the case in relation to the Nicaraguan government's complaints about US government efforts during the 1980s to intervene militarily by way of the Contras to destablilize the Sandinista government, the US government did its utmost to prevent the World Court from reaching a decision, and then when its policies were held in violation of international law, defied the decision and avoided any bad effects, even censure.[3] After the decision, US officials attacked the integrity of the World Court as 'Marxist' and 'third-world oriented', and argued that, in any event, a country was not obliged to sign a suicide pact with international law. Deference to geopolitics by international institutions should not have been surprising, but what may have been less expected was the degree to which distinguished international law specialists of realist persuasion came rushing to the defence of that part of the US position that denied the relevance of international law to claims involving recourse to force even as they urged the US government for pragmatic reasons to restore its adherence to the compulsory jurisdiction of the World Court.[4]

The proper application of morality to political behaviour of an international character is also far from self-evident even when the relevance of morality is affirmed. Its application is conditioned by various assumptions about human nature, both as scientifically established by the prevailing paradigm that has been constructed by current fashions in intellectual activity, and as influenced by the recall of decisive historical experiences. Some of the recent most perniciously influential social constructions bearing on the perception of war and morality are the various decontextualized readings by international relations specialists of 'the Melian Dialogue' in which a single incident in Thucydides' account of the Peloponnesian Wars, crystallized by reference to the line 'the strong do what they will and the weak do what they must', is generalized to validate a cynical view of the role of moral constraint in warfare, at least in the relations between unequal entities.[5] There are many ways to read and understand Thucydides' treatment of this incident. Unlike the various realist readings of the Melian Dialogue, even by such non-realists as Walzer and Hoffmann, it can be construed in a quite opposite manner, as pointing to one critical way station in the progressive weakening of Athenian morality that culminated in political as well as military disaster. In effect, I have understood Thucydides to be arguing that a decent respect for moral restraint is as much, if not more, of a necessity for the strong as for the weak, and that the decline of Athens was linked to their abandonment over time of such limits on their freedom of action.

There is also a relevant debate involving the interpretation of recent world history that is centred upon the prescriptive link between morality and international security, with various types of realists insisting that moral sensitivity (including deference to international law) and international security are negatively correlated in all situations of strategic conflict. Because realism has been ascendant in most elite circles since the end of World War II, autonomous claims about adherence to norms, whether moral or legal in nature, have been generally disregarded whenever serious security objectives have been at stake. In this view, morality is for the naive, whether weak or strong, as typically illustrated by reference to the Wilsonian outlook on international affairs that emerged after World War I and was later held significantly responsible for lulling the liberal democracies to sleep while new aggressor nations built their military machines that later produced World War II. Again the realist reading of this historical debate – 'the lessons of Munich', the rejection of 'appeasement' and of 'moralism' and 'legalism' – has dominated political consciousness with a dampening impact on the assertion of moral claims as serious constraints on behaviour as distinct from helpful rationalizations for recourse to force in foreign policy.[6] This realist domination of foreign policy discourse has been reinforced by an exaggerated dichotomy between the role of norms in domestic versus international space, a distinction that underlies structural arguments that are usually said to derive from Hobbes, but has resurfaced in recent decades in various forms, perhaps most famously in the phrase of Reinhold Niebuhr ('moral man in immoral society') and the parallel assertion generally made by American liberals that the United States is 'a Lockean nation in an Hobbesian world'.

My purpose in this essay is to examine the claims of morality in the sphere of global politics against this ideological and historical background. It seems useful to distinguish three types of moral relevance in the domain of global security, and to treat them for the sake of analysis as distinct, while recognizing their overlap in the minds of leaders and citizens:

Type I morality: a reliance on morality to constrain recourse to force as a source of security in international society;
Type II morality: the focus on a morality of means by which to realize most effectively the security goals of each country, given the character of conflict in a world composed of sovereign states;
Type III morality: the focus on a morality of ends by which one exerts control over the role of force in world politics through a combination of disarmament, demilitarization and an ethos of non-violence.

My orientation is Habermassian to the extent of believing that it is essential for the extension of democratic politics that the role of political violence as a basis for global security be drawn into serious question by a process of comprehensive reflection and debate that moral perspectives (a concern with what is right and proper) are integral to this process, but the policy outcome of such moral inquiry is inherently ambiguous as it depends more on 'which morality?' rather than upon the essentially false question of 'whether morality?'. Without a dynamic of continuous and unconditional democratic accountability, an undertaking made difficult by the use of secrecy and media manipulation as governing techniques even in a democracy, and especially with respect to national security, but without such accountability, I am sceptical about the overall benefit of bringing moral considerations explicitly to bear on the behaviour of states and other actors in relation to global security. Realist morality of what is identified here as Type I variety tends towards apologetics, while transcendent or Kantian morality tends towards utopian irrelevance.[7] It would be a mistake to attribute to moral considerations constraining pressures on the use of force that appear to reflect the impact of the narrowing of strategic interests in the current phase of global politics.[8] This strategic narrowing has been evident in recent debates about humanitarian intervention under the auspices of the United Nations in Bosnia, Burundi, Rwanda and elsewhere. In some respects it was the avowedly Type I moral pressures to use force that were being deflected by reference to an amoral calculus of geopolitical factors at stake.[9]

I share the outlook of Gabriel Kolko as developed in his powerful study of wars since 1914, *Century of War*, that the societal arrangements that caused so much human suffering through the recurrence of wars remain in place and cast a very dark shadow across the future prospects of humanity.[10] In this regard a people-oriented approach to global security, as distinct from statist or market-oriented approaches, proceeds from a trans-political moral claim, namely, that the social institution of war must be repudiated in a manner that implies a radical campaign against reliance for security upon war and its preparation, as well as against its cultural, social, economic and political support structures. From such perspectives, clear actions taken in self-defence and recourses to force by the United Nations and regional institutions might no longer seem morally acceptable even if the behaviour in question conforms to international law as impartially understood.

To consider this line of argument more fully, the historical dialogue on war will be considered in relation to the present global setting. Several illustrative instances of war will be briefly mentioned to exhibit their essential moral indeterminacy given the incoherence of the prevailing assumptions embedded in global security policy, and finally, the adoption of a stance of militant non-violence will be advocated as the most convincing available moral option with respect to sustainable global security, even though it too is not entirely free from moral dilemmas. In this fundamental respect, the human predicament seems sysiphean in nature as there is no enduringly satisfactory reconciliation between morality and global security available for application to concrete circumstances, and yet there is a permanent need to search again and again as occasions arise for that which is unattainable. And yet our inability to know what are the limits of the possible in political life validates a balancing of the imaginative faculties against the assessments of the rational faculties.[11]

II.   HISTORICAL FRAMING

Our understanding of the connections between morality and global security is framed by our collective short- and middle-term historical memory, occasionally reinforced by longer-term classical references to Athens and Rome. In this regard, the way the narrative of the past is most author-itatively (that is, politically effectively) told, especially in relation to allegedly costly failures of political leadership, shapes policy and decision in the present. With respect to the place of morality in global security policy, the narrative is heavily conditioned by the interpretation of the two world wars and the Cold War.

World War I was a disillusioning experience for the citizenry in Europe. The war was far more devastating and traumatic in its societal impacts than had been anticipated at the time by military and political elites. The war was widely condemned as a result of an amoral approach to inter-national relations by the rulers of Europe, creating a space for those who called for a more morally oriented approach.[12] In the aftermath of World War I, various conditions of acute alienation existed, most dramatically, in Russia, opening the way to the Bolshevik Revolution. Elsewhere in Europe the left leadership had largely been earlier compromised by its abandonment of political opposition under the sway of wartime patriotism, thereby forfeiting the opportunity to reconstitute the established order.[13]

The less analyzed impact of World War I was on shifts of opinion about the maintenance of global security, a consequence made far more salient because of the happenchance of Woodrow Wilson's moralizing, crusading leadership role, that is, a less visionary leader in the United States during the years 1918–20 would have altered the inter-war security debate. If the United States had not rescued the victorious powers from the quagmires of a disastrous war, Wilson's presence as US president would have mattered far less. And if Wilson had been Italian, or even British, his voice would not have counted. The diplomats representing the Great Powers of Europe, however cynical their actual convictions, were obliged, by the great wel-coming outpourings of enthusiasm by the peoples of Europe for Wilson, to listen and even to proffer a nominal acquiescence. Georges Clemenceau expressed vividly the Euro-scepticism of his era with his witty response to Wilson's celebrated '14 Points': 'Even the Good Lord had only ten!'.

But Wilson was the bearer of an anti-realist view of security for states and their peoples that was expressly couched in moral rhetoric and rested on a sharp critique of the balance of power mechanism as it operated in European history, and especially in relation to the breakdown of peace in the period leading up to World War I. Wilson's fervent plea centred on an insistence that it was possible and necessary to do better than realist geopolitics (to which he gave no Type II moral credence whatsoever), and that this doing better entailed the establishment of a global institutional authority that would substitute world community sentiments for unilateral governmental discretion to join competing alliances. The League of Nations was made responsible for upholding peace and security on the basis of adherence by states to the abstract rules set forth in the League Covenant. In essence, the Rule of Force would be superseded by the Rule of Law, and the pursuit of security by states acting on their own would be replaced by collective procedures. Such an approach was also interpreted by critics and advocates alike as expressive of an anti-war orientation that was to be complemented by drastic disarmament and a strict regulation of arms sales (whose operatives were then being widely defamed as 'merchants of death').

There is here a far more complex and multi-faceted story. The treatment of Germany as a defeated state was significant, as was the Euro-American opposition to the Russian Revolution, as was the isolationist refusal of the United States, despite Wilson, to join the League. But the essence of the relationship between morality and global security had to do with the insistence that flexible alliance arrangements designed to sustain balance among major states in earlier decades could not be relied upon to avoid destructive and useless wars; such a disposition toward power tended also to be wary about build-ups of national military capabilities, especially given the pre-Keynesian reluctance to devote public revenues to defence given the depressed economic conditions that prevailed in the 1930s.

As we know, what resulted was the rise of fascism as a political force determined to revise the established international order to the benefit of Germany, Japan and Italy. The leaders of these states believed that military might was the basis of all forms of power and prosperity in the world, and that war was an honourable and indispensable means to improve the relative position of a given country. Against this onslaught, European countries were psychologically and politically unprepared, and their leaders resorted to a variety of co-opting and delaying tactics at the diplomatic level, especially in relation to Hitler's Germany, while the United States was enjoying once more a return to its hallowed posture toward Europe of isolationist sleep. In light of what ensued, including the horrors of the Holocaust, this diplomacy between the two world wars was savagely attacked as an era of appeasement, of moralism and legalism, and of utopianism. The critical focus of these various realist readings of history was that the neglect of the logic of power and interest as the proper foundation for global security invited catastrophe, that the established order can be protected only by military means, and that in this sense, legal and moral rules of prohibition are futile, and even dangerous to the extent that they induce complacency. The American variant of the debate, drawing on America's supposed innocence, was inclined to bouts of excessive engagement followed by irresponsible withdrawal, inducing as a corrective the pronounced realist stress on the prudent identification and ardent pursuit of national interests, a series of fiercely argued positions, most influentially articulated by Morgenthau, Kennan, Acheson and Lippmann. Each of these interpreters was seeking to discredit the American impulse to do everything (reform the world) or nothing (isolationism), and instead, to ground policy upon an assessment of interests as a *via media*, selfishly and rationally conceived and upheld, and thus not subject to the grandiose imaginings associated with the alleged Wilsonian insistence on changing the world.

Against this background of experience and ideas, a realist consensus reemerged after World War II, especially given the widely shared conviction that the war against fascism was both a necessary and a just war, and not, like World War I, an essentially meaningless orgy of death and destruction. In this regard, the learning process of peoples and their leaders emphasized the constructive role of military capabilities and preparations for war. These realist tendencies were reinforced by the technological impact of nuclear weaponry that shifted attention from battlefield outcomes to deterrence capacities. In this security setting, mind games, decision logics and rational choice theory came naturally to the fore, and Type I morality, to the extent present at all, was ideologized as an instrument to be deployed in an essentially geopolitical encounter between East and West. Such a marginalization of morality doesn't imply that there were not crucial moral issues at stake in the Cold War, and that there was some sort of equivalence between the preferred public order systems of the two superpower rivals.[14] It does suggest, however, that global security was being safeguarded by essentially military means, including reliance on threats of nuclear retaliation, which by their exterminist character offended the most minimalist conceptions of Type I, but not necessarily of Type II morality, resting on the extreme assumption that the safeguarding of a particular government and way of life for a small minority of humanity was worth threatening the extinction of the human species and the breakdown of the biosphere.[15]

As with World War II, the Cold War ended with a triumphalist mainstream reading with respect to the security policies of the decades since 1945. As a result, despite the absence of strategic conflict, no determined effort to promote even nuclear disarmament has occurred in the years since 1989. There was the momentary pseudo-Wilsonian interlude associated with George Bush's efforts to mobilize support for the Gulf War by a call for 'a new world order', consisting essentially of reliance on the collective

security procedures of the United Nations Security Council to meet threats
of aggression directed at vulnerable countries. There was the related effort
to portray the response to Iraq's attack upon Kuwait as impressively robust
in contrast with the feebleness of the 1930s responses to Japan's aggression
against Manchuria, Italy's against Ethiopia, and Germany's against its
neighbours. But this flash in the pan for Wilsonian ideas was clearly oppor-
tunistic, rather than principled, and was rapidly abandoned by the United
States to the detriment of the United Nations which suffered a bad fall in
reputation from a shattering of raised expectations.

Such broad strokes do not purport to render the historical experience,
but merely to highlight aspects that illuminate the theme of the place of
morality in the pursuit of global security by states and their representatives. There are two features of this narrative that warrant special critical
comment. First of all, Wilson's conception of an alternative to traditional
balance of power geopolitics was not sufficiently comprehensive and
drastic to be credible; sovereignty and national military capabilities were
to be retained by states with no enforcing authority vested in the League.
In this sense, realist attitudes and structures were not being challenged by
Wilsonian ideas, except rhetorically and symbolically by the League as
either constitutional vision or political actor.[16] And secondly, despite the
repudiation of the alleged utopianism of the pre-1945 period, the essential
Wilsonian advocacy of the outlawry of war and the institutionalization of
security policy at the global level prevailed, and was carried several steps
forward in the conception and actuality of the United Nations. Articles
2(4) and 51 of the United Nations Charter incorporated the central moral
idea that force is an illegitimate and illegal instrument of statecraft unless
used in self-defence against a prior armed attack in a manner that is
adjudged, and then approved, by the Security Council.

But again, the United Nations was never psychologically, constitution-
ally, financially or politically empowered to become an alternative to
traditional geopolitics. Franklin Roosevelt's main expectation was that
the UN could provide a framework for the continuation of the alliance
that had won the war, and could now act to safeguard the peace. From the
time of its inception Cold War fissures fractured the great power solidarity that was embedded in the decision procedures of the UN by way of
the veto given to the permanent members of the Security Council. As 50
years of experience have now demonstrated, the UN cannot fulfil its
moral/legal mission of preventing aggression and protecting weak states
unless there happens to be a convergent geopolitical consensus among its
leading members. Such a consensus has existed only twice in UN history:
in the Korean War as a result of the fortuitous Security Council boycott

by the Soviet Union enabling a 'creative' interpretation of the Charter to treat the Soviet 'absence' as satisfying the requirement of Article 27(3) that decisions of the Security Council be supported by 'the concurring votes' of the permanent members; and then in the Gulf crisis when oil, Israeli security, and non-proliferation provided the strategic justification and there was no longer a political will by the Soviet Union or China to block collective action, although again the constitutional status of the undertaking depended on counting China's abstention from the crucial Security Council vote as a concurrence, although unlike Korea, China foresaw the outcome in the Gulf War and accepted the compromise as a way of establishing a global identity as neither partner nor adversary.

As subsequent developments have underscored, when strategic interests are absent or marginal, as mainly was the case in relation to Bosnia, Rwanda, Burundi, Haiti and Somalia, the normative commitments of the Charter are ignored, or at best, thinly acknowledged. In these circumstances, the self-help nature of international society has not been altered, and aggression against weaker states is tolerated so long as it does not infringe upon strategic interests of regional or global actors. To similar effect, the basic legal expectation that equals will be treated equally has not characterized UN responses to such salient questions as Israeli/Arab relations where double standards have been the order of the day.

What, then, is the historical conditioning for the relevance of morality to global security as the world nears the end of the millennium? In brief, as the next section will discuss, security policy remains largely in the domain of the Type II realist morality of geopolitics, retaining nuclear weaponry and military capabilities, implementing the non-proliferation regime, and resisting calls for financially autonomous international institutions with major war/peace responsibilities. In this regard, recent reliance on NATO rather than the UN in promoting peace for Bosnia accurately discloses the current disposition to prefer an alliance arrangement, a relic of the Cold War, to a community-based peacekeeping initiative even of regional scope.

III. WHICH MORALITY?

The dichotomizing of morality and power has been profoundly misleading in a number of respects. It has encouraged the impression that realists are amoral or immoral with respect to force, whereas when carefully considered the realist contention is that a *different* morality is appropriate when questions of global security are at issue. Further, to associate morality only with Wilsonian moralizing, passing moral judgment on the existing world order, without clearly comprehending the depth of adjustment required, is to misconceive, and in the end, discredit the claims of any authentic anti-war morality. The role of morality is to guide behaviour toward valued ends, given the characteristics of the relevant societal order; morality as a decontextulaized template can never itself be transformative. Even Shelley's famous assertion that poets were the unknown legislators of the world rests on the unspoken premise that poetry articulates the specific unconscious strivings of peoples in both their national and universal aspects, and is in this sense rooted morality.

Any genuine alternative, then, to realist morality must be predicated upon a comprehensive vision of global security. It must also satisfy the political preconditions for a transition from one security framework to another. The plausibility of transformative developments with respect to global security arise from several emergent trends: globalization in many aspects of international life; the alleged non-viability of war in relation to the resolution of strategic conflict; the growth of global civil society; the declining problem-solving capabilities of states; the potency of identities associated with ethnic, civilizational and religious characteristics.

But before considering alternatives to realism with respect to global security, it is important to grasp why different variants of realism exerted such a powerful impact on the political imagination in this century, and to appreciate that realists never advocated the abandonment of morality, but only its adjustment to the actualities of international political life. The prior section emphasized the relevance of historical conditioning, and it could usefully be supplemented by a section on the relevance of cultural conditioning. Western cultural development since the Renaissance has exhibited a cumulative tendency toward secularization and materialism that has marginalized deference to the relevance of religion, and with it, to any self-referential form of moral discourse, leaving morality as a bone for official and unofficial propagandists. The most influential practitioner of realism could be understood, in a manner opposite to their normal perception, as the rediscoverers of a moral discourse appropriate for a statist geopolitics that operates in secularized cultural space.

It was never E.H. Carr's intention to discard morality as irrelevant to statecraft, but only to refocus attention on its proper, and admittedly, marginal role in relation to global security. In Carr's words, '[i]n the international order, the role of power is greater and that of morality is less'.[17] Indeed, Carr points out that intellectual inquiry into political activity is inherently purposive, using the metaphor of 'the body politic' to suggest that the inquirer is seeking to cure its ills in a manner analogous to a medical doctor's concern with the human body.[18] With his rousing use of language Carr wanted to reorient thought about security in relation to self-interested states regarding their own well-being as the highest moral end, the pursuit of which would take precedence over other considerations such as the avoidance of war or the upholding of legal commitments. Carr was also clear that the juridical equality of states was misleading in view of their political and military inequality as it doomed efforts in the setting of vital interests to treat states equally and, therefore, confined the domain of law, and more generally, of rule-guided behaviour. Carr invites confusion to some extent by using 'morality' exclusively in its Kantian, Type I connotations of rule-governance in relation to right action rather than incorporating into morality the Machiavellian Type II connotations of right action as determined by systemic properties.[19]

Martin Wight once wrote that E.H. Carr's contribution was to restate Hobbes for his time, which in a sense is what Hedley Bull did in relation to Carr. The strength of Bull's achievement was to be very clear about what kind of morality applies to the use of force, the status of war, given the existence of a society of unequal, sovereign, states. As Carr was concerned with utopianism, really a special case associated with the Wilsonian phenomenon in his era, Bull emphasized more nuanced issues that related to the degree of cooperation among states that it was appropriate to achieve. In this regard, Bull was sceptical of efforts to promote what he called 'a Grotian conception of international society', which he felt exaggerated the existing strength of sentiments of solidarity among states. In this sense he questioned efforts to outlaw war, to punish political leaders for war crimes, and to invoke the United Nations so as to respond to violators of the peace. Bull believed that by raising expectations above the capacities for performance, there resulted an unwitting lessening of the specific morality of international relations: a shared commitment by great powers to keep conflict limited and the overall system stable, moderate and durable. By stigmatizing behaviour as immoral and illegal in a mobilizing sense, Bull believed that the effect was to encourage the erosion of limits and to inject a conflict-magnifying insistence on the unconditional surrender of the defeated side in international conflict and the criminal accountability of its leaders.[20]

Bull favoured benevolence by the great powers as an aspect of their stake in systemic stability. In this regard, Bull favoured meeting some of the equity demands for reordering international life that were being made two decades ago by the newly independent states of the Third World. He also explicitly realized that sentiments of solidarity could strengthen over time in such a way as to sustain more ambitious forms of international cooperation among states than was presently possible, although he rejected the role of 'globalization-from-below' and the potential agency of transnational democratic forces.[21] Of course, Bull was writing in the 1970s and earlier, that is, before the surge of transnational activism, but whether he would have regarded these developments as of sufficient weight to alter his statist assumptions about world order seems doubtful.

In this regard, the realist view of global security is heavily oriented around ideas of balance, deterrence and containment but also prudence and co-option to avoid dispositions by the aggrieved to adopt desperate strategies and pose radical challenges. John Mearsheimer has given a logical, if severe rendering of global security in the aftermath of the Cold War in which Bull's stress on addressing the grievances of challengers is ignored and replaced by the geopolitician's anxiety about unchecked power and power vacuums; in this extreme realist spirit, Mearsheimer, without Bull's emphasis on philosophy and history, actually suggests that denuclearization of security would be the worst imaginable future for Europe, and that an optimal security setting would include controlled proliferation that resulted in German acquisition of nuclear weaponry.[22]

Of course, there are many variations on the realist theme, but all rest on the proposition that what is moral for international relations is to privilege the part as against the whole and to regard the configurations of power as establishing the operative structures of order and the limits of meaningful cooperation. In these regards, rules, international institutions and transnational social movements are all categorized as more or less epiphenomenal when it comes to global security.[23] The deficiency in this conception of Type II morality is its foreshortening of normative horizons by its ahistorical conservatism about political potentialities. By realist reasoning the transformations of the Soviet Union and South Africa in the 1990s couldn't have happened, and by my reasoning, wouldn't have happened had not a morality of ends been treated as a necessary political project.

IV. TOWARD A TYPE III MORALITY OF ENDS

The position that I have argued up to this point is based on two broad ideas: (1) a moral template, Type I morality, cannot be effectively superimposed on global politics to improve the quality of security; this was the Wilsonian fallacy and the many variants of non-structural reformism;[24]

(2) realism provided a morality of means, Type II morality, by which to adapt political behaviour to the characteristics of an international society constituted by sovereign states and incorporating war as the ultimate means of conflict resolution. But this morality of means has many problematic aspects with respect to global security, including an accommodation of war, a failure to anticipate the extent of globalization from above and below, a disregard of ecological and equitable requirements for sustainable development, and an inability to foresee the emergence of an inchoate global civil society grounded on a human rights culture. To incorporate these dimensions of international political reality requires a morality of ends, a Type III morality, at this stage of world history, and as a consequence, a drastically revised conception of global security, that includes a depiction of normative horizons that relies on social activism, oppositional tendencies and transnational initiatives to give political weight to moral aspiration. Admittedly, the prospects for political implementation and intellectual acceptance in academic and policy constituencies are not currently favourable for a variety of reasons.[25] Global security seems effectively entrapped in the neo-realist paradigm, stressing hegemonic and great power managerial roles, for the indefinite future, with a high tolerance for abusive arrangements of state/society relations, including ethnic cleansing and genocidal onslaughts, so long as strategic interests are not seriously encroached upon. The tendency of such violent eruptions to generate massive refugee flows to countries unwilling to offer asylum may generate some perceptions of strategic interests. Such a perception seems to have largely accounted for the US willingness in 1994 to restore Aristide to power and dislodge the military junta that had been brutalizing the Haitian people for many months. But where such factors are not present, as in Burma, or even Chechnya, the tendency is to embrace politics of accommodation 'beautified' as 'constructive engagement'.

What, then, is the moral factor? It is mainly what has been in recent decades a systemic view of stability and moderation, as specified by the dominant state actors, with a certain display of humane concern for severe patterns of abuse and a degree of resistance to what comes to be regarded as 'cruel' or 'excessive' forms of force. What is not drawn into question is the continuing nature of self-help security, that includes a military option, with limits imposed either by great power initiatives or prudence. The current absence of strategic conflict among leading states creates a sense of geopolitical calm, a complacency that ignores the historic opportunity of the end of the Cold War to champion ambitious forms of demilitarization and denuclearization (comparable, say, to regional free trade negotiations or the step taken toward global economic governance by the establishment of the World Trade Organization). Pressures to achieve governance of a globalized world economy are currently far more formidable than pressures to transform the global security system.

To avoid rootless utopianism, a variant of the superimposed moral template, a serious and useful morality of ends with respect to global security must address the question of political agency at the outset. Accepting this mandate immediately suggests consideration of the Kantian political revival by way of the claims made on behalf of so-called democratic peace, namely, that democracies do not engage in wars against each other and thus the security rationale for militarism would be severely eroded.[26] The Clinton administration in its early period talked of its doctrine of enlargement, whereby it would encourage a peaceful world by promoting the spread of market-oriented democracies. Others foresaw that the near universal entry into the global market would inevitably generate a democratizing spillover as a by-product of prosperity and an expanding middle class. Among the likely benefits of such a world order scenario would be the disappearance of the impetus toward peacetime arms races arising from the inter-mixing of secrecy, the security dilemma and the fear of disabling surprise attacks. As well, a democratic political culture, in its present phase, is widely believed to be less war-prone under most circumstances and more inclined toward compromise and negotiation, as well as disposed to regard 'progress' more as a function of market shares and export opportunities than by way of draining military exploits to expand by means of territorial conquest.

This standard democratizing scenario of recent vintage, quite different from the actual characteristics of the Kantian antecedent, overlooks several serious problems with its expectations: the political culture of leading democracies has become more violent and war-prone; the re-emergence of strategic conflict in the next decade is quite likely (for example, in the form of renewed Sino-Russian alliance, with Japan as non-aligned, creating one of several possible formats for a new cold war more plausible than the Huntington 'clash' thesis); the disparities in world political and economic conditions is great and growing, whether conceived in relation to nuclear-haves and have-not states or with respect to rich and poor or even electronically empowered and disempowered; the conditions of economic and cybernetic globalization are likely to generate 'enforcement' missions in relation to potential challengers (for example, as in the Gulf War).

A more coherent and credible democratization scenario, as developed especially in the recent work of David Held, couples domestic democratic patterns with ambitious, cumulative regional and global democratizing developments.[27] In effect, a democratic structure of global, or as Held prefers, 'cosmopolitan' governance, with participatory procedures for the peoples of the world and effective accountability extended to sites of economic, as well as political, power. Would cosmopolitan governance qualify as a Type III morality of ends such that global security would be re-embedded in a non-realist framework of reference? It would depend, in my view, on whether leading political actors, including international institutions, effectively renounced war as their major instrument for achieving security. It needs to be noted that a morality of ends does not escape from 'the moral dilemma' arising from the intrinsic character of knowledge as necessarily situated; as moral purposes, ends reflect a variety of ontological, epistemological, anthropological and historicist assumptions, and hence an array of alternative candidates for privileged ends is always present, including those advocating retention of the war option, and even nuclear weapons, on moral grounds. This debate between contending moral claims can never be resolved through argument or analysis.[28] What is called for, then, is dialogue and a politics of conviction; the latter being fraught with danger as a general position because it cannot be assumed to imply a renunciation of instrumental violence by all participants.[29]

Another approach to the issue of political agency is to emphasize the radicalizing potential of those constituencies being disrupted by globalization, including disempowerment via exclusion from cybernetic interconnectedness. Robert Cox, for instance, enumerates the following 'social forces' as oppositional: 'National capital, those sections of established labour linked to national capital, newly mobilized nonestablished workers in the Third World, and social marginals in the poor countries are all in some way or another potentially opposed to international capital, and to the state and world order structures most congenial to international capital.'[30] From such tensions Cox envisions as 'remotely possible' the emergence of 'a counter-hegemony based on a Third World coalition against core-country dominance and aiming toward the autonomous development of peripheral countries and the termination of the core-periphery relationship'.[31] Such a development doesn't imply anything more than a realignment of relative forces in relation to global security, but elsewhere Cox looks sympathetically at the emergence of what he calls 'the new multilateralism', the impact of transnational social movements giving birth to a rudimentary global civil society, a set of tendencies that calls militarism into question, although it is not yet clearly abolitionist with respect to the war system.[32]

V. CONCLUSION

Realist morality continues to underpin global security, providing widely acceptable moral rationalizations along Type II lines for recourse to force and stretching the law in the relations among states both by the hegemonic leading states and by dissident states. These include opposing aggression, preventing nuclear proliferation, upholding a balance within a given region or protecting a particular state, containing or promoting the spread of Islam, ending Western domination and secularization, resolving ethnic and territorial grievances, and promoting independence and justice. Humanitarian morality, embodied in various ways in different Type I constructions of 'a human rights culture', exerts only a marginal influence, one that is uneven, media dependent, and generative of shallow commitments; in this regard, except to disavow superfluous suffering, global security structures and processes give only lip service to humanitarian morality.

For humanitarian morality to underpin global security it would be necessary for drastic shifts in world order to occur, a reining in of state/market forces and a rise of those transnational social forces that embody a non-violent ethos in their world-view. Tendencies in this direction cannot be ruled out, although their present prospects appear to be in virtual eclipse. It is possible, however, that within the next decade or so, the economic, ecological and cultural pressures of inadequately regulated globalization-from-above will generate acute alienation of sufficient magnitude as to create new revolutionary opportunities, including those that would mount a Type III challenge to realist morality as the basis of global security. Although unfocused and primarily agitated by fears of environmental and health concerns, the widespread grassroots protests against French nuclear tests in the Pacific (1995–6) bear witness to the existence of human constituencies that reject statist authority to manage world order on the basis of realist morality. Whether this witness will turn into a Type III movement in the next century dedicated to the drastic reform of global security, including an insistence on humanitarian morality, is neither assured nor precluded at this point.

Notes

1.   For influential formulations of the case for an expanded notion of security see Jessica Tuchman Matthews, 'Redefining Security', *Foreign Affairs* 68(2): 162–77 (1989); Richard Ullman, 'Redefining Security', *International Security* 8(1):129–53(1983); for a well-reasoned rejection of arguments for an expanded conception of security see Daniel Duedney, 'The Case Against

Linking Environmental Degradation and National Security', *Millennium* 19(3):461–76(1990).

2. There are other concerns present: to what extent does the UN Charter prohibition on the use of force presuppose that the collective enforcement provisions of Chapter VII have been implemented? How then, should the prohibition be adapted to the reality of non-implementation?

3. This failure to promote enforcement ignored the Security Council responsibility as set forth in Article 94 of the UN Charter.

4. See Thomas Franck: *Judging the World Court* (New York: Priority Press 1986, 35–76).

5. Thucydides, *History of the Peloponnesian Wars* (London, Penguin 1956, 400–8), see the use of the Melian Dialogue by Michael Walzer in *Just and Unjust Wars: a Moral Argument with Historical Illustration* (Glasgow: HarperCollins, 1992) and Stanley Hoffman in *Duties Beyond Borders: On the Limits and Possibilities of Ethical International Politics* (Syracuse, NY: Syracuse University Press, 1981)

6. For classic critiques along these lines see especially E.H. Carr, *The Twenty Years' Crisis. 1919–1939: An Introduction to the Study of International Relations* (New York, Harper & Row, 2nd edn, 1946, reprinted 1964); George F. Kennan, *American Diplomacy 1900–1950* (Chicago: University of Chicago Press, 1951).

7. A distinction adapted from the very important work of the Finnish jurist Martti Koskenniemi (ed.), *International Law* (Aldershot: Dartmouth, 1992); see also Freidrich Kratochwil, 'Sovereignty as *Dominium*: Is There a Right of Humanitarian Intervention?' in Gene M. Lyons and Michael Mastanduno (eds), *Beyond Westphalia? State Sovereignty and International Intervention* (Baltimore, MD: Johns Hopkins University Press, 1995, 21–43, at 33–41).

8. But for the sort of Type II realist or geopolitical morality articulated by Hedley Bull as a matter of systemic moderation, such a narrowing would be appropriate given the character of international society: see discussion of Bull's approach in Section II.

9. The actually emergent policy was in many respects an unsatisfactory compromise, amounting to 'a geopolitics of gesture', that made superficial concessions to the Type I moral claims through such steps as sanctions on former Yugoslavia, an arms embargo, and the establishment of a war crimes tribunal in The Hague, but for Type II reasons withheld peacekeeping efforts needed to protect the victims of war crimes and ethnic cleansing or the integrity of the Bosnian state.

10. Gabriel Kolko, *Century of War: Politics, Conflicts and Society since 1914* (New York: The New Press 1994).

11. See important discussion of these concerns in Timothy Dunne and Nicholas J. Wheeler, 'Hedley Bull and the idea of a Universal Moral Community: Fictional, Primordial or Imagined?' in B.A. Robertson (ed.), *The Structure of International Society* (Pinter, 1996).

12. Semantics are confusing as 'morality' is used as counterrealism and geopolitics, ignoring the realist position on morality which is to condition the relevance of values to the character of the societal matrix, the sort of moral approach worked out so effectively by Hedley Bull in *The Anarchical Society* (New York: Columbia University Press, 1976).

13. Kolko, note 10, at 139–79.
14. See Myres S. McDougal and Harold D. Lasswell, 'The Identification and Appraisal of Diverse Systems of Public Order', in McDougal and Associates, *Studies in World Public Order* (New Haven, CT: Yale University Press, 1960).
15. cf. E.P. Thompson, 'Notes on Exterminism, the Last Stage of Civilisation', *New Left Review* 121 May–June 1980, 3–31; J. Schell, *The Fate of the Earth*; Robert Jay Lifton and Richard Falk, *Indefensible Weapons: The Political and Psychological Case Against Nuclearism* (New York: Basic Books. rev. 2nd edn, 1992).
16. For one of several far more coherent challenges see Grenville Clark and Louis B. Sohn, *World Peace Through World Law* (Cambridge, MA: Harvard University Press, rev. 3rd edn, 1966); by shifting war-making capabilities to the reformed UN it remains doubtful that such a system could on its own satisfy requirements for a Type III morality as specified in the next section.
17. Carr, 168.
18. 'Desire to cure the sickness of the body politic has given its impulse and purpose to political science.' Carr., p. 3.
19. Kant, as world order thinker, rather than a philosopher of ethics, is also best understood as a Type II or even Type III moralist.
20. Hedley Bull, 'The Grotian Conception of International Society', in Herbert Butterfield and Martin Wight (eds), *Diplomatic Investigations: Essays in the Theory of International Politics* (Cambridge, MA: Harvard University Press, 1966 at 51–73) and *The Anarchical Society*, note 12: see also Martin Wight, 'Western Values in International Relations', in Butterfield and Wight, 89–131.
21. See Dunne and Wheeler, note 11; Falk, *Explorations at the Edge of Time: The Prospects for World Order* (Philadelphia, PA: Temple University Press, 1992).
22. John J. Mearsheimer, 'Back to the Future: Instability in Europe After the Cold War', in Michael E. Brown, Sean M. Lynn-Jones and Steven E. Miller (eds), *The Perils of Anarchy: Contemporary Realism and International Security* (Cambridge: MIT Press, 1993, 78–129, at 105–8).
23. Again see Mearsheimer's 'The False Promise of International Institutions', in Brown, Lynn-Jones and Miller, note 22, 332–76.
24. A prominent recent example is the report of the Commission on Global Governance, *Our Global Neighbourhood* (New York: Oxford, 1995); for critique along these lines see Falk, 'Liberalism at the Global Level: The Last of the Independent Commissions?', *Millennium* 24(3): 563–76 (1995).
25. Part of the explanation can be found in Ethan B. Kapstein, 'Is realism dead? The domestic sources of international politics', *International Organization* 49(4)(1995) 751–74.
26. See Bruce Russett, *Grasping the Democratic Peace: Principles for a Post-Cold War World* (Princeton University Press, 1993); Michael Doyle, 'Kant, Liberal Legacies, and Foreign Affairs', Parts I and II, *Philosophy and Public Affairs* 12(3 & 4): 205–35, 323–53; for critique see John Mearsheimer, note 22, at 121–4; Christopher Layne, 'Kant or Cant: The Myth of Democratic Peace', *International Security* 19(2): 5–49 (1994).

27. See, especially, David Held, *Democracy and the Global Order: From the Modern State to Cosmopolitan Governance* (Cambridge, UK: Polity, 1995).
28. This position is well articulated by Hugh Gusterson, 'Exploding Anthropology's Canon in the World of the Bomb: Ethnographic Writing on Militarism', *Journal of Contemporary Ethnography* 22(1): 58–79(1993).
29. That is, non-violence is but one of several Type III possibilities.
30. Robert W. Cox, 'Social Forces, States and World Orders: Beyond International Relations Theory', in Robert O. Keohane (ed.), *Neorealism and its Critics* (New York: Columbia University Press, 1986, 204–54, at 237).
31. Idem., at 238
32. Cox, 'Future World Order and the UN System', paper presented at the Conference on the UN and Japan in the Age of Globalization, Yokahoma, Japan, 30 Nov.–3 Dec. 1994; for more general discussion along these lines see Falk, *On Humane Governance: Toward a New Global Politics* (Cambridge, UK: Polity, 1995).

Part II
Normative Questions in European Integration

3 Ideals and Idolatry in the European Construct
Joseph Weiler

THE EUROPEAN *FIN-DE-SIÈCLE* CRISIS OF MEANING

I

The Europe I shall talk about is 'Europe' – the European construct, the 'Union', the 'Community', 'European integration' – amorphous as polity, as concept, as ethos and as telos but, ontologically, very present.

There is little euphoria in this *fin-de-siècle* Europe. The triumphalism and newly discovered self-confidence of American 'end of history' contrasts sharply with European self-doubt and soul searching. In the universe of European integration, of Community and Union, the Maastricht saga signalled the entering into doldrums from which the Union has not yet emerged. The precarious fate of Economic and Monetary Union, the lifeless, listless preparations for the 1996 Intergovernmental Conference and the distinct lack of enthusiasm regarding enlargement towards the East are the current manifestations of a malaise which began with the deliciously sceptical manner in which Maastricht itself was received by general public opinion.

A subtle change has occurred in the positioning of the idea of European integration in public discourse. The political scientists of the various realists schools never tire of telling us that the evolution of European integration was driven by national self-interest and cold calculations of cost and benefit to its participating member states. But in its formative years, and for a considerable while after that, the very idea of the Community was associated with a set of values which, it seems to me, could captivate the imagination and mobilize broadly based political forces. Supporting the Community was to 'do the right thing'. It was a happy state in which one could believe that long-term self-interest coincided with higher values.

The cool to hostile reception by the public of the Maastricht Treaty was the writing on the wall: could it be that at this end of the century 'Europe' has become an ideal which has lost its mobilizing force? A force which has lost its mobilizing ideals?

We are forced thus to face squarely the ends of European integration, often neglected in what seems to be the more urgent debate of means – the instruments and mechanisms, political and economic, for achieving the specific objectives of the Treaties.

The first part of this chapter is an attempt to (re)introduce a discourse on ideals into the current debate on European integration.

II

A disquisition focusing explicitly on ideals is not an easy task, and this for two reasons.

First, much of the social science of European integration has been dominated by the realist and neorealist schools of international relations. Notions of ideals, ethics and the like have a very limited place in both their explanatory and normative apparatus of state behaviour and transnational behaviour. In non-international relations theories of integration, such as critical social theory, ideals are often there to be exposed as sham, as a mask to be lifted and debunked. All in all, ideals, like religion and spirituality are almost embarrassing topics, to be reconceptualized as ideology and treated with the reductive methodologies of psychology, sociology and the like.

Second, a twentieth-century phenomenology of ideals is hard to construct. We should not confuse ideals with ideology or morality. Ideals are usually part of an ideology. Morality is usually part of ideals. But the terms do not conflate. Ideologies, in relation to which theories abound, often include or are premised on some ideals. But they are much more than that. Ideology is part an epistemology – a way of knowing and understanding reality – in part a programme for changing that reality to achieve certain goals. Ideals, in and of themselves, constitute neither an epistemology nor a programme for realization, and are often the least explained elements of any given ideology. Morality, practical reason, the good life, will inform ideals, but ideals have a social reality which practical reason necessarily does not – though it can be an ideal to live the good life. It is not surprising that, for example, the *Macmillan Encyclopedia of Philosophy* has no separate entry for ideals.

It is surprising, however, that there appears to be no systematic analysis of the ideals – as distinct from the objectives – of European integration and the European Community. If this, indeed, is the case, one may wonder if there is no good reason for this absence. Could it be that a low 'pay-off' is the explanation? I think not. I think the pay-off could be high and that the reason for the absence lies rather with the disciplinary 'misfit' of ideals as an object for enquiry.

What then would be the interest, the intellectual 'pay-off', in exploring the ideals of European integration and the European Community?

I propose to answer this question after describing first one of the Community's foundational ideals, which, in turn, will serve as a means for a general phenomenological reflection and as a tool to explain the utility of exploring the ideals of European integration.

Peace, in the immediate wake of World War II, was the most explicit and evocative of ideals for which the would-be-polity was to be an instrument. Nowhere is this captured better than in the oft repeated phraseology of the Schuman Declaration of 9 May 1950.

> World peace cannot be safeguarded without the making of constructive efforts proportionate to the dangers which threaten it ....

> The gathering of the nations of Europe requires the elimination of the age-old opposition of France and the Federal Republic of Germany; The first concern in any action undertaken must be these two countries ....

> [This] solidarity ... will make it plain that any war between France and the Federal Republic of Germany becomes, not merely unthinkable, but materially impossible ....

Peace, at all times an attractive desideratum, would have had its appeal in purely utilitarian terms. But it is readily apparent that in the historical context in which the Schuman Plan was put forward the notion of peace as an ideal probes a far deeper stratum than simple swords into ploughshares, sitting under ones' vines and fig trees, lambs and wolves – the classic biblical metaphors for peace. The dilemma posed was an acute example of the alleged tension between grace and justice which has taxed philosophers and theologians through the ages – from William of Ockham (pre-modern), Friedrich Nietzsche (modernist) and the repugnant but profound Martin Heidegger (postmodern).

These were, after all, the early 1950s with the horrors of war still fresh in the mind and, in particular, the memory of the unspeakable savagery of German occupation. It would take many years for the hatred in countries such as The Netherlands, Denmark or France to subside fully. The idea, then, in 1950, of a Community of Equals as providing the structural underpinning for long-term peace among yesteryear's enemies, represented more than the wise counsel of experienced statesmen.

It was also a call for forgiveness, a challenge to overcome an understandable hatred. In that particular historical context the Schumanian notion of peace resonates with, is evocative of, the distinct discourse, imagery and values of Christian love, of grace – not, I think, a particularly astonishing evocation given the personal backgrounds of the founding fathers – Adenauer, de Gasperi, Schuman, Monnet himself.

III

I will use peace as a springboard for a more general reflection of ideals. I would like to develop four principal considerations which inform ideals as a concept and as a social construct: the idyllic, the demonic, the virtuous and the idolatrous. If my understanding of peace as an ideal is valid and typical it would enable me to illustrate all four considerations.

The idyllic

In upholding or subscribing to an ideal, one is in part putting forward a desired state of affairs (material or spiritual) in which one would like to exist. It can be peace, it can be justice, it can be power or grandeur. It is usually, but not necessarily futuristic. It is usually a state of affairs the desirability or appeal of which is self-evident in both an essentialist worldview and/or because they correspond to deep-seated social constructs.

The altruistic

A simple desirable state of affairs – an idyllic state: 'If I were a rich man' – does not in and of itself qualify as an ideal. Often it can be almost a counter-ideal. What prevents us from making all our fantasies of desired – idyllic – states IDEALS, is that so often they are selfish, self-serving. We perceive these desiderata, in fact, as an expression of desire, greed, jealousy, of our Hobbesian side. In the words of Genesis: for the imagination of man's heart is evil from his youth (Gen: viii.21).

Ideals then involve not simply putting forward a desired state of affairs – material or spiritual – but a recognition of our demonic tendencies. Ideals must represent a challenge to the demonic in us, a call to our better half. Ideals, and this is a central part of their allure, contain an altruistic component.

In my view this challenge accounts for the huge appeal of the great ideals. First, there is the *per se* attractiveness and satisfaction of sacrifice: things that demand sacrifice are cherished more than things that come easily. Sacrifice invests things with value. Additionally, the combination of the idyllic and the altruistic in ideals explains their abiding centrality to all human culture: the call to overcome the demonic ennobles our self-interest – it legitimates our desires.

The desire for peace is frequently not an ideal. Like riches it is a very comfortable state of affairs – for the sake of peace I will not fight my battles, not stand up for my values, turn my gaze, avert my eyes. (This is not the place to engage the altogether more serious claims of neutrality or even pacifism in international relations.)

What brings the message of peace in the formation of the Community into the realm of ideals, what connects it to so deep a fountain as Christian love, is the historical context of justified hatred and fear. The infamous *Peace In Our Time* approach of the 1930s which saw the sacrifice of Czechoslovakia was a counter-ideal: the idyllic, the comfortable, without the altruistic. In the EC of the early 1950s and somewhat beyond, there is a context where peace has both the idyllic and the altruistic – we have to overcome our feelings of revenge, which were given full vent after World War I, but at the same time the comfort of peace is being offered. It was not then the fear of war (between say, France and Germany) which rendered peace an idealistic desideratum in 1950. It was the psychological and spiritual demand that it made that so rendered it.

The virtuous

The idyllic and the demonic elements have been explained in linguistic and behaviouristic terms: they correspond to what we normally mean when we use the word, or think of, ideals; they imply a certain understanding of the human psyche and what appeals and motivates us.

They are also value-free and ahistorical. They do not differentiate between the 'ideals' of Adolph Hitler or Mother Theresa. One can, after all, desire evil or mistake it for virtue, and make great sacrifices to achieve it.

I would add therefore a third consideration: the grounding of ideals in ethics. I can justify this consideration in two ways. First, as a reflection of social reality: when ideals have been put forward as a social phenomenon, as part of a programme of action, they have always been presented as being so grounded. But, I would also add this consideration as an unashamedly normative layer to ideals discourse: a refusal on my part to discuss ideals in purely behaviouristic terms, even if I am mindful of the fashionability of moral relativism, and the manipulability of ethics. Even peace can pose considerable ethical dilemmas. Few of us, after all, are total pacifists.

I shall explain the fourth and final consideration later in this chapter.

IV

Before we turn to examine the other ideals of European integration in its formative years I shall reflect now more deliberately on the interest in exploring ideals in general and European integration ideals in particular.

I see three distinct interests:

1. A large, the largest, part of EC studies is instrumentalist: Actor–Interest–Result, Structure–Power–Process. Trying to explain why things are the way they are. The disciplines – political science, economics, law – will shift the 'thing' which is being explained, and will privilege one kind of explanation over another, or, alternatively, try to be interdisciplinary or even challenge the disciplinary divide altogether and adopt an holistic approach.

From this instrumental perspective, the value of looking at ideals is evident: ideals can be part of the matrix which explains socialization, mobilization and legitimacy. In an analysis as to why certain elites, or masses, support or tolerate or oppose European integration in general or this or that policy in particular, ideals should clearly have a place. To deny the mobilizing force of ideals is folly.

2. There can be interest in ideals (and the ideals of European integration) from a perspective which is more indifferent to the specific story of European integration but acknowledges it, and its rhetoric, as part (important or otherwise) of social intercourse. This perspective has as its focus the individual as such and 'society' (national society, regional society, transnational society). The interest here then is in the 'social'. In particular I have in mind our 'modern' understandings of constitution of the self – individual and collective, the shift from fate to choice in self-understanding and self-positioning.

Ideals are a principal vehicle through which individuals and groups interpret reality, give meaning to their life, and define their identity – positively and negatively. The idyllic in ideals refers in this context to social space, the demonic to individual self. In what kind of society do I live, what does our society 'stand for' – can only be given an answer by reference, at last partially, to ideals. Likewise, what kind of person am I, can only be given an answer by reference to ideals. What kind of society should I live in, aspire to; what kind of person should I be is similarly premised on the existence of ideals. Even the rejection of ideals (a pseudo-Machiavellian approach to life) is just that: a rejection of ideals. You cannot do without them as a referent for value and meaning.

If we are, then, interested in the European persona, in a European polity, we will profit by understanding the world of ideals which is part of the polity. Can there be a psychological understanding of the individual without a reference to one's conflict with ideals? Can there be an appreciation of the political culture of a polity without reference to its values and ideals? In the tension between eros and civilization, our discourse of civilization is in substantial part a discourse of values and ideals.

Where one might have strong disagreements is the importance that European integration ideals have had in society. Some would argue that until recently their importance was marginal. Others will disagree.

3. There is a third interest in ideals – an interest in ideals as a locator in the history of ideas. They are part (and with the passage of time an important part) of cultural history and cultural identity of an epoch. They are, sometimes, the deepest residue – or at least the most visible – that history leaves. Even educated women and men will probably be more fluent with the *values* of antiquity (notably the 'declared values' rather than their realization!) or of the age of enlightenment than with their respective political or social histories.

It appears to me that, even to a body of social scientists, it is a totally serious, and possibly longer lasting enterprise, to try to define European integration in terms of its ideals and not only in terms of its structural, processual and material components. It is an enterprise which will help locate the idea of the Community in the flow of European intellectual history.

V

We may return now to the history of the Community. In its foundational period, alongside peace, I would identify two other principal ideals: prosperity and supranationalism.

Prosperity is the second value for which the Community was to be instrumental. Max Kohnstamm used to say: 'The twin dilemmas for Monnet were "What do we do with Germany?"' – I translate the answer given as the peace ideal in the European Construct – 'and How to rebuild Europe' – and I translate that as the ideal of prosperity. This is captured in, among other places, Article 2 of the Treaty of Rome.

> The Community shall have as its task ... to promote throughout the
> Community a harmonious development of economic activities, a contin-
> uous and balanced expansion, an increase in stability, an accelerated
> raising of the standard of living ...

The focus on prosperity should not come as a surprise. After all, the economic reconstruction of the devastated continent was intimately connected
with the notion of peace. Each was the means for the other. Indeed in the
biblical passage, frequent in the book of Judges, peace and prosperity are
linked: the vineyard and the fig tree being a symbol for both.

The idyllic, the desired state of affairs is self-evident. But at first blush
it is hard to capture the altruistic, non-hedonistic dimension of the quest
for prosperity. Are we not here in the presence of pure self-interest, something to be almost ashamed of – the very antithesis of altruism, challenge,
sacrifice which are essential parts of idealistic narrative? Where is the
virtuous and where is the challenge to the demonic which, I argued, were
essential components of ideals discourse?

There was an idealistic dimension, nuanced to be sure, to the quest for
prosperity which mediated its utilitarian aspects. Its virtue appears when
set against a backdrop of destruction and poverty. In these conditions
(individual and social) prosperity assumed an altogether different
meaning: dignity – both personal and collective. In an Enlightenment-
bound vision of the individual, poverty resonates with the embarrassment
of dependence on others, with the humiliation bred by helplessness, with
the degradation of lack of autonomy. There is, thus, nothing shameful in
aspiring to prosperity when it comes to mean dignity. There, then, is its
virtue.

Second, the Community's quest for prosperity in its formative years
took place in a period which inextricably linked it with widespread
(re)construction, with visible (re)generation, with palpable effort and toil.
Bread gained with the sweat of one's brow is a matter for pride rather than
embarrassment, shame and degradation.

Last but not least, linking prosperity to a cooperative enterprise
inevitably blunted the sharp edges of avidity feelings. The Community in
its reconstructive effort was about collective responsibility: it was a
regime which attempted to constrain unchecked search for economic
prosperity by one member state at the expense of others. To be sure, there
was an economic theory of open markets, level playing field and all the
rest which informed the Common Market. But the elements of transnational economic solidarity are an undeniable part of the discourse at
the time and of the Treaty itself. This solidarity is the element which

appeals to the better self. It is the control of the demonic at the statal economic level.

Put in this way, we also detect here, as with the peace ideal, the deeper roots of the Community notion of prosperity as an ideal: it links up with, and is evocative of, a different but no less central strand of European idealism since the mid-nineteenth century, be it socialism, fabianism, communism, or Welfare Statism all sharing an underlying ethos of collective societal responsibility for the welfare of individuals and the community as a whole.

VI

The third ideal is that of *supranationalism* – for want of a better word. A word of caution would be necessary here. There is no fixed meaning to the term supranationalism. Indeed, from its inception there seem to have been two competing visions of its realization through the Community: a Unity vision – encapsulated in those who favoured a United States of Europe – and a more attenuated Community vision. The two strands (which, of course, overlap) have continued to co-exist. But it is my reading of the historical map – the rejection of the European Defence Community and the European Political Community in the 1950s and the articulation of supranationalism in, especially, the Treaty of Rome, that the Community vision prevailed in the formative years of the EC. But clearly, even more than everything else in this essay, the construction of supranationalism and its virtues follows my understanding with no pretence to a commonly 'received knowledge'.

In trying to explain the ways in which the Community is, or has become, supranational, most discussion over the years has tended, interestingly, to focus on its relation to the 'state' rather than the 'nation'. This conflation of nation/state is not always helpful. Supranationalism relates in specific and discrete ways to nationhood and to statehood. Indeed, in my understanding and construction of supranationalism its value system is actually wrapped up with the value system of European ethno-national liberalism of the nineteenth century. In that respect supranationalism will be seen to have the same, Janus-like, quality as peace and prosperity: looking to the future while affirming the past – a radical conservatism.

To see the relationship between supranationalism, nationhood and statehood, I propose to focus in turn on nationhood and statehood and try to explore their promise and their dangers. This will be then related to the ends of supranationalism. Naturally, in discussing nation and state, I shall only give a few pointers and headlines of what would otherwise have to be an extremely elaborate analysis.

First, then, nationhood.

It seems to me that, at least in its nineteenth-century liberal conception, two deep human values are said to find expression in nationhood: belongingness and originality. (It should immediately be stated that nationhood is not the only social form in which these values may find expression.)

Belongingness is inherent in nationhood, nationhood is a form of belonging. Nationhood is not an instrument to obtain belongingness, it is it. Form and substance here conflate, the way they do, say, in a love sonnet by Shakespeare: the value of the sonnet does not lie in, say, its message of love; we do not think of the sonnet as an instrument for the conveyance of the idea. Take away the form and the message is banal. What gives the sonnet its timeless value is the inextricable way in which the substance and the form were woven together by Shakespeare.

What are the values embedded in belonging, in national belonging, beyond the widely shared view that belonging is pleasant, is good? We can readily understand a certain basic appeal to our human species which is, arguably, inherently social: the appeal that family and tribe have too. Part of the appeal is, simply, the provision of a framework for social interaction. But surely one has to go beyond that: after all, much looser social constructs than nationhood, let alone tribe and family, could provide that framework. Belonging means, of course, more than that. It means a place, a social home.

The belonging of nationhood is both like and unlike the bonds of blood in family and tribe and in both this likeness and unlikeness we may find a clue to some of its underlying values.

It is like the bonds of blood in family and tribe in that those who are of the nation have their place, are accepted, belong, independently of their achievements – by just being – and herein lies the powerful appeal (and terrible danger) of belonging of this type – it is a shield against existential aloneness. In, for example, the tradition of the Jewish nation, a tradition worthy of some consideration given the continuity of Jewish national survival for over three millennia, we find a normative expression to this form of belonging: 'Even though he has sinned, he remains Israel' (Talmud Sanhedrin, p. 44:2) The power of this belongingness may be understood by the drama and awesomeness of its opposites: isolation, seclusion, excommunication.

But nationhood transcends the family and tribe and maybe here lurks an even more tantalizing value: nationhood not only offers a place to the familyless, to the tribeless, but in transcending family and tribe it calls for loyalty – the largest coin in the realm of national feeling – towards others which goes beyond the immediate 'natural' (blood) or self-interested social unit.

And, indeed, belongingness of this type is a two-way street. It is not only a passive value: to be accepted. It is also active: to accept. Loyalty is one of those virtues which, if not abused, benefits those on both the giving and receiving ends.

The other core value of nationhood, in some ways also an instrument for national demarcation, is the claim about originality. On this reading, the Tower of Babel was not a sin against God but a sin against human potentiality; and the dispersal that came in its aftermath, not punishment, but divine blessing. The nation, with its endlessly rich specificities, co-existing alongside other nations, is, in this view, the vehicle for realizing human potentialities in original ways, ways which humanity as a whole would be the poorer for not cultivating. (How one decides the self which qualifies as a nation is a tantalizing issue which is not necessary to explore here).

It is here that one may turn from the nation to the modern state. It is worth remembering at the outset that national existence and even national vibrancy do not in and of themselves require statehood, though statehood can offer the nation advantages, both intrinsic as well as advantages resulting from the current organization of international life which gives such huge benefits to statehood.

I would argue that in the modern notion of the European ethno-national nation-state, the state is to be seen principally as an instrument, the organizational framework within which the nation is to realize its potentialities. It is within the statal framework that governance, with its most important functions of securing welfare and security, is situated. The well-being and integrity of the state must, thus, be secured so that these functions may be attained. That is not a meagre value in itself. But to the extent that the state may claim, say, a loyalty which is more than pragmatic, it is because it is at the service of the nation with its values of belongingness and originality. (This conceptualization underscores, perhaps exaggerates, the difference with the American truly radical alternative liberal project of the non-ethno-national polity, and of a state, the republic, the organization of which, and the norms of citizenship behaviour within, were central to its value system.)

It is evident, however, that in the European project, boundaries become a very central feature of the nation-state.

There are, obviously, boundaries in the legal-geographical sense of separating one nation-state from another. But there are also internal, cognitive boundaries by which society (the nation) and individuals come to think of themselves in the world.

At a societal level, nationhood involves the drawing of boundaries by which the nation will be defined and separated from others. The categories of boundary drawing are myriad: linguistic, ethnic, geographic, religious and so on. The *drawing* of the boundaries is exactly that: a constitutive act, which decides that certain boundaries are meaningful both for the sense of belonging and for the original contribution of the nation. This constitutive element is particularly apparent at the moment of 'nation building' when histories are rewritten, languages revived, and so on. Of course, with time, the boundaries, especially the non-geographical ones, write themselves on collective and individual consciousness with such intensity that they appear as natural – consider the virtual interchangeability of the word international with universal and global: it is hard not to think, in the social sphere, of the world as a whole without the category of nation (as in international).

Finally, at an individual level, belonging implies a boundary: you belong because others do not.

As evident as the notion of boundaries is to the nation-state enterprise, so is the high potential for abuse of boundaries.

The abuse may take place in relation to the three principal boundaries: the external boundary of the state; the boundary between nation and state; and the internal consciousness boundary of those making up the nation.

- The most egregious form of abuse of the external boundary of the state would be physical or other forms of aggression towards other states.
- There abuse of the boundary between nation and state is most egregious when the state comes to be seen not as instrumental for individuals and society to realize their potentials but as an end in itself. Less egregiously, the state might induce a 'laziness' in the nation – banal statal symbols and instrumentalities becoming a substitute for truly original national expression. This may also have consequences for the sense of belongingness whereby the apparatus of the state becomes a substitute for a meaningful sense of belonging. An allegiance to the state can replace human affinity, empathy, loyalty and sense of shared fate with the people of the state.
- There can be, too, an abuse of the internal boundary which defines belongingness. The most typical abuse here is to move from a boundary which defines a sense of belonging to one which induces a sense

of superiority and a concomitant sense of condescension or contempt for the other. A sense of collective national identity implies an other. It should not imply an inferior other.

The manifestations of these abuses are a living part of the history of the European nation-state which are so well known as to obviate discussion.

VII

A central plank of the project of European integration may be seen, then, as an attempt to control the excesses of the modern nation-state in Europe, especially, but not only, its propensity to violent conflict and the inability of the international system to constrain that propensity. The European Community was to be an antidote to the negative features of the state and statal intercourse; its establishment in 1951 was seen as the beginning of a process that would bring about the elimination of these excesses.

Historically there have, as mentioned above, always been those two competing visions of European integration. While no one has seriously envisioned a Jacobin-type centralized Europe, it is clear that one vision, to which I have referred as the Unity vision, the United States of Europe vision, has really posited as its ideal type, as its aspiration, a statal Europe, albeit of a federal kind. Tomorrow's Europe in this form would indeed constitute the final demise of member state nationalism replacing or placing the hitherto warring member states within a political union of federal governance.

It is easy to see some of the faults of this vision: it would be more than ironic if a polity set up as a means to counter the excesses of statism ended up coming round full circle and transforming itself into a (super) state. It would be equally ironic if the ethos which rejected the boundary abuse of the nation-state gave birth to a polity with the same potential for abuse. The problem with this Unity vision is that its very realization entails its negation.

The alternative vision, the one that historically has prevailed, is the supranational vision, the Community vision. At one level aspirations here are both modest compared to the Union model and reactionary: supranationalism, the notion of community rather than unity, is about affirming the values of the liberal nation-state by policing the boundaries against abuse. Another way of saying this would be that supranationalism aspires to keep the values of the nation-state pure and uncorrupted by the abuses I described above.

At another level the supranational community project is far more ambitious than the Unity one and far more radical. It is more ambitious since, unlike the Unity project which simply wishes to redraw the actual political boundaries of the polity within the existing nation-state conceptual framework, albeit federal, the supranational project seeks to redefine the very notion of boundaries of the state, between the nation and state, and within the nation itself. It is more radical since, as I shall seek to show, it involves more complex demands and greater constraints on the actors.

How, then, does supranationalism, expressed in the community project of European integration, affect the excesses of the nation-state, the abuse of boundaries discussed above?

At the pure statal level supranationalism replaces the 'liberal' premise of international society with a community one. The classical model of international law is a replication at the international level of a liberal theory of the state. The state is implicitly treated as the analogue, on the international level, to the individual within a domestic situation. In this conception, international legal notions such as self-determination, sovereignty, independence and consent have their obvious analogy in theories of the individual within the state. In the supranational vision, the community as a transnational regime will not simply be a neutral arena in which states will seek to maximize their benefits but will create a tension between the state and the community of states. Crucially, the community idea is not meant to eliminate the national state but to create a regime which seeks to tame the national interest with a new discipline. The idyllic is a state of affairs which eliminates the excesses of narrow statal 'national interest'. The challenge is to control at societal level the uncontrolled reflexes of national interest in the international sphere.

Turning to the boundary between nation and state supranationalism is meant to prevent abuses here too. The supranational project recognizes that at an inter-group level nationalism is an expression of cultural (political and/or other) specificity underscoring differentiation, the uniqueness of a group as positioned *vis-à-vis* other groups, calling for respect and justifying the maintenance of inter-group boundaries.

At an intra-group level nationalism is an expression of cultural (political and/or other) specificity underscoring commonality, the 'sharedness' of the group *vis-à-vis* itself, calling for loyalty and justifying elimination of intra-group boundaries.

But, crucially, nationality is not the thing itself – it is its expression, an artefact. It is a highly stylized artefact, with an entire apparatus of norms and habits; above all it is not a spontaneous expression of that which it signifies but a code of what it is meant to give expression to, frequently even translated into legal constructs. Nationality is inextricably linked to citizenship, citizenship not simply as the code for group identity, but also as a package of legal rights and duties, and of social attitudes.

Supranationalism does not seek to negate as such the interplay of differentiation and commonality, of inclusion and exclusion and their potential value. It is a challenge to the codified expressions in nationality. Since, in the supranational construct with its free movement provisions which do not allow exclusion through statal means of other national cultural influences and with its strict prohibition on nationality/citizenship based discrimination, national differentiation cannot rest so easily on the artificial boundaries provided by the state. At inter-group level then it pushes for cultural differences to express themselves in their authentic, spontaneous form, rather than the codified statal legal forms. At the intra-group level it attempts to strip the false consciousness which nationalism may create instead of belongingness derived from a non-formal sense of sharedness.

Supranationalism at the societal and individual, rather than the statal level, embodies, then, an ideal which diminishes the importance of the statal aspects of nationality – probably the most powerful contemporary expression of groupness – as the principal referent for transnational human intercourse. That is the value side of non-discrimination on grounds of nationality, of free movement provisions and the like. It is precisely the absence, in the pre-Maastricht conceptualization of the Community, of a European citizenship, which is symbolically important: essential relationships are to be defined despite citizenship. In its intra-Community manifestation the ideal is the relative irrelevance of the formal category of citizenship.

It is not difficult to identify the idyllic and the demonic and the deep idealistic well-spring with which this ideal resonates.

Hermann Cohen, the great neo-Kantian, in his *Religion der Vernunft aus den Quellen des Judentums*, tries to explain the meaning of the Mosaic law which calls for non-oppression of the stranger. In his vision, the alien is to be protected, not because he is a member of one's family, clan, religious community or people, but because he is a human being. In the alien, therefore, man discovered the idea of humanity.

We see through this exquisite exegesis that in the curtailment of the totalistic claim of the nation-state and the reduction of nationality as the principle referent for human intercourse, the Community ideal of supranationalism is evocative of, and resonates with, Enlightenment ideas, with the privileging of the individual, with a different aspect of liberalism which has as its progeny today the liberal notions of human rights. In this respect the Community ideal is heir to Enlightenment liberalism.

VIII

The ideals of peace, prosperity and supranationalism which animate the Community in its foundational period are, on my reading, a new expression to the three principal strands of European idealism which the twentieth century inherits. They tap into core values of Christian grace, social responsibility (for want of a better term) and the Enlightenment.

At this point a critical proviso would be in order. My claim is not, decidedly not, that the Community in its foundational period actually lived these ideals, realized their virtues (whatever these may be) or vindicated their promise. I am agnostic on this issue. To explain the ideals of the French Revolution, of the American Revolution or of the October Revolution is not to claim that post-monarchist France, Republican America or the Soviet Union lived up to the aspirations which animated these social revolutions. We are all familiar with analyses which tell a very different story of the ensuing reality of the Community.

But the reality of the ideals themselves works, nonetheless, at all three levels I explained before:

1. First, mobilization, socialization and legitimacy. European integration, it has often been claimed, was elite driven. Ideals discourse may be part of the explanation of the mobilization of these elites. It was a construct which was safe, appealing to values inculcated deeply in a generation which grew up in this century.

The idea of Europe and the ideals of Europe may also be a part explanation for mobilization at mass level, through national party structures. All principal political forces and parties in post-World War II continental Europe regarded themselves as the true inheritors of European idealism as explained above. The socialists and social-democrats, the lay parties, decidedly do not turn their back to the Church. Christian Democrats embrace the Welfare State.

The vision of European integration as explicated above may explain, in part, how it was that the Community only rarely becomes the focus of party politics in continental Europe. All parties can embrace it, because of, if you want, the appeal or the blandness (take your pick) of its idealistic superstructure. The Community, like other political forces in post-war Europe, embraces both liberalism and social democracy so as to avoid – at the level of rhetoric – the actual choices which exist between these programmes. Historically, one cannot speak of mass mobilization for Europe. But as years of Eurobarometer surveys show, it was an acceptable idea always easy to support.

2. At a second level we may turn to ideals as a vehicle for constitution of the self – individual and social. Consider first the generation of the so-called founding fathers who saw their world fall apart in the horrors of World War II – a negation of the very values of Christian love, of solidarity, of the Enlightenment project. European integration presents itself on my analysis as very alluring: it is not only a new political and economic architecture for post-war Europe which radically supplants the old Versailles model of post-World War I. It is a vision which, while being innovative and radical, is also deeply conservative, since it re-affirms their old *Weltanschauung*, indeed, it gives a new lease of life to ideals for which there are no available (meaning acceptable) substitutes at the time.

It was a *par excellence* way of affirming one's identity on well-known terrain and avoiding the deep dislocations which the breakdown of civility in the war may have created.

It provided, for individuals and societies, a comfortable way of dealing with the recent past: this past need not call into question fundamental values and ideals: only the political structure and technology for their real-ization. Europe could re(define) itself as Christian, socially responsible, a worthy successor of the Enlightenment.

It is interesting here to consider the perception and self-perception of bureaucracies. Already in the early 1950s the renewed Frankfurt School, back from exile, develops its profound insight of the state as adminis-tration, governance as management. The personification of the New Frankfurt school's conceptualization is, I would think, the state func-tionary – in Germany, in France, in Italy (each with a specificity of patho-logy which is altogether original in the different states ...). To become a *Beamte* or a *funzionario dello Stato* is desirable, since it gives power and security, and it is also the *par excellence* expression of blind state loyalty internally, of a vindication of the national interest externally. But service in the public administration is hardly conceived in the language of ideals for these very same reasons, neither by its practitioners nor by the public. The pursuit of power and security are understandable to all, but hardly put on a pedestal.

Service in the Community administration, in its earlier period, was, instead, conceived as living the Community ideals – it too provided secu-rity and some power (increasing) but its 'supranational' dimension, formally defying loyalty to the state and countering the national interest in favour of the community (and Community) interest, redefined it in idealistic terms. The meeting of a Community official and a member state official of the same nationality was at some level a meeting of a 'superior' supranational idealist with an 'inferior' state realist. The Community official may have been earning a lot more than his or her national counterpart and enjoying working conditions and a social package which was the envy of all national administrations, but he or she was also occupying the high moral ground: a true public servant.

What I am talking about, of course, is perception, not reality. In reality there may not have been any difference between the two public servants. But if there is any truth in my claim of differing perceptions, this truth will have been rooted in an image of the Commission and a self-image of its officials, as seen through the mirror of the Community ideals.

3.   As for the history of ideas – we can evaluate European integration in that epoch as being at the cusp, the very end brink of modernism. The Community idea on this reading is quintessentially European, embracing the core of European classical idealism. It was not simply a reflection of these ideals, but, as explained above, it became a vehicle for their rejuvenation, lending them a new, temporary perhaps, credibility and outlet, a mask, in some eyes, to their vacuity, a rearguard action before their final collapse. Be that as it may, importantly, indeed crucially, as pretender to the inheritance of classical idealism, Europe of the Community was placed not as an end in itself, but as a means for the realization of higher ennobling values.

IX

There is a final element to my discussion of the formative ideals which tries to pull all three ideals together.

Let us first consider another set of ideals. It is, for example, certainly a great ideal for an individual to seek, say, to live a life of internal and external truth and integrity. Likewise, to give another example, we consider noble, and rightly so, those academics who pursue the life of scholarship for its own sake, unswayed by consideration of prestige or advancement or career. But one feels, surely, an intuitive difference of kind between these ideals and those of the European Community.

Whence the difference? What is special about the type of ideals which the European Community encapsulated is in fact their *community* nature – they are the type of ideals which depend for their realization on being shared by a group of persons; definitionally they are beyond the reach of a lone individual. Further, it is not only that they cannot be achieved by any one individual, that they require a community for their practice, in fact they are constitutive of a community – they create the community on whose existence they depend.

That this is so in relation to peace is self-evident: it takes, as the saying goes, two to tango. It is only slightly less self-evident in relation to the supranationalism cluster. The invitation to pierce the veil of nationality is at one level to celebrate the individual as an autonomous being, a universe unto himself or herself, an end not a mere instrumentality. But it is also, at the same time, with all the richness of paradox, evocative of the two-sidedness of Enlightenment liberalism, a cry for community which transcends the artificial barriers of nationality and emphasizes the commonality of shared humanity.

It is least evident in relation to the Market, the Community vehicle for prosperity. There is a powerful strand in the political theory of markets which idealizes them as a neutral arena in which by giving freedom to individuals to pursue vigorously individual economic self-betterment aggregate prosperity will be enhanced. The caricature of this view is the 'invisible hand'; its modern hallmarks are passivity of government, unshackling the individual from pervasive regulation and vigorous individual competition. Arguably, it was a variant of this idea which informed and explained government mobilization behind the Single European Act. There is much power to this idea and it is certainly dominant in current discussions. It is also, just as certainly, at odds with the community notion I have been discussing. But there is a complementary view of the market place, with no less an impressive pedigree – Thomas Paine in his *Rights of Man* would be a good place to start – which emphasizes the social dimension of the market. Under this view, when government sets out actively to create or expand a market, against the backdrop of, say, historical agrarian autarchy and feudalism or, closer to us, national protectionism, it is not only economic goals which can be achieved. The market on this view is a forum for personal intercourse, for social interaction, for widening of horizons, for learning about and learning to respect others and their habits. It is community too and, I believe, this view was as strong in the formation of the Community as the purely economic one.

In this light we may, indeed, return briefly to the 1992 programme and the Single European Act. As mentioned above, like Maastricht, here too there was a discrepancy between the reaction of government, Community and member states, and of the population at large: coolness by the former, enthusiasm by the latter. Could it be, perhaps, that whereas government conceived the Single Market in pure economic terms, in the street that same Single Market was perceived not simply, or even primarily as a vehicle for economic betterment but as a metaphor for the creation of a European society encapsulated in the slogan of a Europe without Frontiers?

X

What has become of ideals discourse in the Europe at the end of the century? What values, as opposed to interests, can be associated with European Union 1997?

It is decidedly not my intention to join in that favourite game of Euro-bashing. But this does not mean that we cannot engage in a sober assessment of the ideal structure. The narrative here is short: the Treaties up to and including Maastricht – emblematic of the current stage of European integration – can no longer serve as a vehicle for the foundational ideals; and not much has been offered in replacement. The current documents of the IGC 96 offer little that is new.

To say that the European Union can no longer serve as a vehicle for the foundational ideals is not necessarily condemnation: in some measure, as I shall try to show, this is so because of the very success of the Community.

Peace, reconciliation between France and Germany 'and all that' has been achieved, thanks perhaps to the Community. To continue to posit *intra-Community* peace as a Maastricht ideal does not have much conviction. That this is so is, paradoxically then, a sign of a remarkable success of the Community. It is also, perhaps, part of the very phenomenology of peace itself: it is an ideal during, and in the immediate aftermath, of war: for then it demands the triumph of grace. After a long period of peace, it becomes a comfort, an excuse for inaction even in the face of moral imperatives. It can, thus, be an extremely potent mobilizing force. The electorate may well prefer a platform which guarantees peace at any cost. But it is often far from an ideal.

If peace has any place in European discourse today, it is the peace of Munich, of Chamberlain, of peace in our time, which saw 50 years ago the dismemberment of Czechoslovakia and witnessed the destruction of Bosnia until, boringly again, the US cavalry came to the rescue. Again, it is not that peace within the Community has become a less attractive notion; that it should not be pursued and safeguarded; that it cannot even be an element of mobilization. But for peace to re-emerge as an ideal it has to be a challenge, a demand on the self and on society. The kind of demand that the threats in Eastern Europe and the former Soviet Union so clearly pose. Instead, the way peace is presented now is the opposite:

passive, the status quo, preserving the existing comforts, looking after our-selves while watching, largely scared and detached, the horrors so close to our borders. How did Europe respond, not for the first time, to the 'ethnic cleansing' of a religious minority so close to its historical centre? With words and palliatives. And the Maastricht provisions on a Common Security and Defence Policy have been shown up for what they are. Peace can mobilize: who in Europe wants war? But one can hardly evoke the current peace discourse as a mobilizing *ideal*.

In a more serene manner, it is not then that peace itself has lost its rele-vance. My argument is that if this particular ideal is to remain part of the ethos of the European Union, the way it is construed requires considerable re-tooling.

Prosperity too has lost its idealistic bite, thanks perhaps to the Community: in large measure, as with peace, intra-Community prosperity has been achieved. It was the move from poverty to prosperity which was virtuous. Today, even during a recession, the move is from prosperity to even more prosperity. This too can capture votes and support – pocket-book politics always has. But there is no pretence even at casting this discourse in the language of ideals.

The obsolescence of the Community as a vehicle for the foundational ideals was personified in the figures of two leading European politicians waging their European battles.

There was something altogether pathetic in the ageing figure of the late M. Mitterand preaching Franco–German peace to an incredulous electo-rate in 1992. And there was something equally pathetic in Mr Major's technocratic and shopkeeper's 'what's in it for us' approach to all European problems.

What then of supranationalism: was not Maastricht, at least in its aspira-tions and rhetoric, a definite clarion cry for further supranationalism? To believe that is to misunderstand supranationalism. From this perspective too Maastricht was a deception. It may or may not have advanced the structure and processes of European integration. One has learnt to be cautious and non-dismissive of these steps in Community evolution. But its symbolism was very clear. In its rhetoric Maastricht appropriated the deepest symbols of statehood: European citizenship, defence, foreign policy – the rhetoric of a superstate. We all know that these are the emptiest and weakest provisions of the Treaty, but they undermine the ethics of supranationalism. In its statal aspect supranationalism was a move away from statism to a new uneasy relationship between Community and its member state. Community was a fine word to capture that value. Now the operational rhetoric is Union, not Community. We have come full circle. The deep irony is that the full circle has come on the ideological level, since in practice, Maastricht, as we now know, constituted an empowerment of the member states and in at least some significant aspects (such as the legislative gags imposed on the Community in some of its new policies) a weakening of the Community.

In its individual aspect supranationalism was about the diminution of nationality as a referent for transnational intercourse. Under the rhetoric of Maastricht, the Us is no longer Germans or French or Italians and the Them is no longer British or Dutch or Irish. The Us has become European and the Them, non-European. If Europe embraces so earnestly at the symbolic level European citizenship, on what moral ground can one turn against French National Fronts, German Republicans and their brethren elsewhere who embrace member state nationalism? On the ground that they chose the wrong nationalism to embrace? The irony, if it needs spelling out, is that while the idealistic moral ground has been shattered, perhaps even lost, in reality, in these areas, Maastricht offers very little by way of tangible prospects. On this reading, Maastricht has thrown out the supranational water without waiting for the baby to get in the bath.

XI

The Europe of Maastricht no longer serves, like its grandparents the Europe of Paris and Rome, as a vehicle for the original foundational values. This, if my analysis is correct, represents, too, a rupture with an earlier pre-modern and modern historical continuity of ideas.

The explanation for rupture may not however lie simply at the feet of the Community, and at the changed historical conditions which have rendered the Community an obsolescent vehicle for the foundational ideals. It may, too, be a reflection of a rupture in European society as such. On this reading Maastricht becomes the mirror of the society which it is supposed to serve, a reflection of *fin-de-siècle* Europe, in which those classical ideals have lost in and of themselves their pull.

Consider afresh the Maastricht Treaty and its double structure: EMU and political union. There is a symbolism in this double structure and the relative weight given to each. It is a commonplace that Economic and Monetary Union constitutes the heart of the Treaty; that the Political Union IGC was more rhetorical than substantive, lip service paid to the need to increase accountability and strengthen the powers of the European Parliament. The symbolism is that of the Roman circus: a scale of values which privileges the economic: wealth and prosperity; which de-privileges control, autonomy and responsibility.

The language of symbols is just that – symbolic. And thus not too much should be read into it. But the notion that the problem of Maastricht is in the drafting, in its prolix style, in its incomprehensibility should perhaps be questioned. Maybe its message is all too apparent. And, to the extent that Maastricht is a reflection, a mirror of its polity, the interesting datum is not in the size of the opposition, but in the impressive support the Treaty has evoked. In this respect Maastricht is simply a creature of its time.

The personification of this symbolism is to be found in the Commission no longer occupying that high moral ground, more likely in search for a plausible justification for privilege. It is almost, but only almost, as if the tables have turned in that meeting between the Community official and his or her national counterpart. It is no secret that there is a deep crisis of morale in the Commission, emblematic of the fortunes of Europe. To be sure, the cool reception of Maastricht and the current uncertainty in an IGC which has few captivating themes is part of the explanation. But the low morale may have an additional explanation in synch with the theme of this chapter, namely the loss of the deeper *raison d'être* of the enterprise, the disconcerting realization that Europe has become an end in itself – no longer a means for higher human ends. No measure of information, explanation or structural tinkering can remedy this.

XII

Assuming that there is some merit to my analysis, there could be a tendency to take it as an indication of a bleak future for Europe. That tendency should be resisted. Europe may or may not have a bleak future, but a causal nexus to the theme of this essay is tenuous. Pragmatic and utilitarian politics can be highly successful, in both mobilization and result. Providing welfare and security may be all we wish from public authority in the postmodernist age. Indeed, this is the place to mention the fourth and last element – ideals as idolatry. An unstated premise of this narrative was that ideals give meaning, ennoble existence, refine materialism. But, as Simone Weil in her anorexic state warned already in the 1940s, and as our own experience will often indicate, ideals are not only a promise but always, at the same time, a danger. For the move from, the change of, ideals to idolatry – a blinding enslavement to supposedly higher values in the name of which all manner of barbarism is committed, is almost pre-determined. European history is replete with such examples:

the savagery of the Crusaders was committed in the name of Christian love, collective responsibility was the justification for the ghastliness of the Gulags, and the brutality of European colonialism was committed under the flag of the Enlightenment. *Fin-de-siècle* Europe may, thus, be not a reflection of emptiness, but the sign of a healthy suspicion of ideals as idolatry.

There is, however, an alternative and more sobering consideration in this regard, whereby European Union may be seen not simply as having suffered a loss of its earlier spiritual values, but as an actual source of social *ressentiment*.

Consider, chillingly, the turn to fascism in Italy, France and Germany at the beginning of the century. In a most profound comparative analysis of the cultural–political roots of the phenomenon the common source is identified as a reaction to some of the manifestations of modernism.

At a pragmatic level the principal manifestations of modernism were the increased bureaucratization of life, public and private; the depersonalization of the market (through, for example, mass consumerism, brand names) and commodification of values; the 'abstractism' of social life, especially through competitive structures of mobility; rapid urbanization and the centralization of power. At an epistemological level modernism was premised on, and experienced in, an attempt to group the world into intelligible concepts making up a totality which had to be understood through reason, science – abstract and universal categories.

On this reading, fascism was a response to, and an exploitation of, the angst generated by these practical and cognitive challenges.

Eerily, at the end of the century, European Union can be seen as replicating, in reality or in the subjective perception of individuals and societies, some of these very same features: it has come to symbolize, unjustly perhaps, the epitome of bureaucratization and, likewise, the epitome of centralization. One of its most visible policies, the Common Agriculture Policy, has had historically the purpose of 'rationalizing' farm holdings which, in effect, meant urbanization. The single market, with its emphasis on competitiveness and transnational movement of goods, can be perceived as a latter day thrust at increased commodification of values (consider how the logic of the Community forces a topic such as abortion to be treated as a 'service') and depersonalization of, this time, the national market. The very transnationalism of the Community, which earlier on was celebrated as a reinvention of the Enlightenment idealism, is just that: universal, rational, transcendent: wholly modernist.

That the Union has ceased to be a vehicle for its foundational ideals and has thus become a contingent being and experience removed from a normative framework just gives a fashionable 'postmodernist' twist to modernist anxiety.

I am not suggesting that Europe is about to see a return to fascism, nor most certainly should this analysis, if it has any merit, give joy to *fin-de-siècle* chauvinists, whose wares today are as odious as they were at the start of the century. But I am suggesting that the crisis of ends might be worse than simply a rupture with the past. It might be an unwelcome connection to another worrisome past, and, in this light, the possible turn away from community to unity in the Maastricht project is simply sad.

COMMUNITY AND STATE – EROS AND CIVILIZATION

XIII

And yet, at the core of the Maastricht Unity project – the provision for a European Citizenship – there is the possibility of constructing a new departure, addressing one of the most challenging problems facing Europe as a whole in the post-Cold War era, once again a way in which Europe could, as it did after the World War era, provide fresh and imaginative departures and a new ideal for humanity in the cold world of the market.

Earlier I poured scorn on this notion of European citizenship introduced by Maastricht. One can add: citizens constitute the demos of the polity. The collective side of the citizenship coin is peoplehood – demos. But what is this European demos? And who are to be the citizens of the European polity? How are we to define the relationships among them? A demos, a people, cannot, after all, be a bunch of strangers. How should we understand, then, and define the peoplehood of the European demos if we insist that the task remains the ... ever-closer union among the peoples of Europe? Does not, indeed, the introduction of citizenship constitute a change in the telos of European integration?

I wrote above:

If Europe embraces so earnestly at the symbolic level European citizenship, on what moral ground can one turn against French National Fronts, German Republicans and their brethren elsewhere who embrace member state nationalism? On the ground that they chose the wrong nationalism to embrace? The irony, if it needs spelling out, is that while the idealistic moral ground has been shattered, perhaps even lost, in reality, in these areas, Maastricht offers very little by way of tangible prospects. On this reading, Maastricht has thrown out the supranational water without waiting for the baby to get in the bath.

Is this not an inevitable result of introducing citizenship and demos into the politcal vocabulary of Europe? Can one reconcile the idea of the Peoples of Europe as resting at the core of the European telos and, at the same time, introduce citizenship?

One way to reconcile is denial – by rejecting the notion of a European demos. The implications of this No Demos thesis, espoused, among others, by the German Constitutional Court, is to deny any meaningful democratization of the Union at the European level, to reassert the implicit underpinning of the Community legal order in international law, and if one is to be intellectually consistent, to negate likewise any meaningful content to European citizenship. Space does not permit full elaboration but a few hints will suffice.

Under this view, the nation, which is the modern expression of demos, constitutes the basis for the modern democratic state: the nation and its members constitute the polity for the purposes of accepting the discipline of democratic, majoritarian governance. Both descriptively and prescriptively (how it is and how it ought to be) a minority will/should accept the legitimacy of a majority decision because both majority and minority are part of the same demos, belong to the nation. That is an integral part of what rule-by-the-people, democracy, means on this reading. Thus, nationality constitutes the state (hence nation-state) which in turn constitutes its political boundary. The significance of the political boundary is not only to the older notion of political independence and territorial integrity, but also to the very democratic nature of the polity. A parliament is, on this view, an institution of democracy not only because it provides a mechanism for representation and majority voting, but because it represents the nation, the demos from which derive the authority and legitimacy of its decisions. To drive this point home, imagine an *anschluss* between Germany and Denmark. Try telling the Danes that they should not worry since they will have full representation in the Bundestag. Their screams of grief will be shrill not simply because they will be condemned, as Danes, to permanent minorityship (that may be true for the German Greens too), but because the way nationality, in this way of thinking, enmeshes with democracy is that even majority rule is only legitimate within a demos, when Danes rule Danes.

Turning to Europe, it is argued as a matter of empirical observation that there is no European demos – not a people, not a nation. Neither the subjective element (the sense of shared collective identity and loyalty) nor the objective conditions which could produce these (the kind of homogeneity of the organic national–cultural conditions on which peoplehood depends such as shared culture, a shared sense of history, a shared means of communication(!)) exist. Long-term peaceful relations with thickening economic and social intercourse should not be confused with the bonds of peoplehood and nationality forged by language, history, ethnicity and all the rest.

For some the problem is temporal. Although there is no demos now the possibility for the future is not precluded *a priori*. For others, the very prospect of a European demos is undesirable. It is argued (correctly in my view) that integration is not about creating a European nation or people, but about the ever-closer Union among the peoples of Europe.

The consequences of the No Demos thesis for the European construct are interesting. The rigorous implication of this view would be that without a demos, there cannot, by definition, be a democracy or democratization at the European level. This is not a semantic proposition. On this reading, European democracy (meaning a minimum binding majoritarian decision-making at the European level) without a demos is no different from the previously mentioned German–Danish *anschluss* except on a larger scale. Giving the Danes a vote in the Bundestag is, as argued, ice cold comfort. Giving them a vote in the European Parliament or Council is, conceptually, no different. This would be true for each and every nation-state. European integration, on this view, may have involved a certain transfer of state functions to the Union but this has not been accompanied by a redrawing of political boundaries which can occur only if, and can be ascertained only when, a European people can be said to exist. Since this, it is claimed, has not occurred, the Union and its institutions can have neither the authority nor the legitimacy of a demos-cratic state. Empowering the European Parliament is no solution and could – to the extent that it weakens the Council (the voice of the member states) – actually exacerbate the legitimacy problem of the Community. On this view, a parliament without a demos is conceptually impossible, practically despotic. If the European Parliament is not the representative of *a* people, if the territorial boundaries of the EU do not correspond to its political boundaries, than the writ of such a parliament has only slightly more legitimacy than the writ of an emperor.

XIV

What, however, if the interests of the nation-state would be served by functional cooperation with other nation-states? The No Demos thesis has an implicit and traditional solution: cooperation through international treaties, freely entered into by High Contracting Parties, preferably of a contractual nature (meaning no open-ended commitments) capable of denunciation, covering well-circumscribed subjects. Historically, such treaties were concluded by heads of state embodying the sovereignty of the nation-state. Under the more modern version, such treaties are concluded by a government answerable to a national parliament often requiring parliamentary approval and subject to the material conditions of the national democratic constitution. Democracy is safeguarded in that way.

And citizenship? Citizenship on this view must remain in the exclusive domain of the member states through whose authority the Community and Union may function with legitimacy.

Is there an alternative to this view? How, then, could and should European citizenship be constructed? What should be the political attributes which forge the linkages which must flow, at the European level, from citizen to public authority? How should European demos be understood? Does it exist? Can it exist? What are its implications for European identity?

Let us consider again the Maastricht citizenship provisions:

Article 8
Citizenship of the Union is hereby established.
Every person holding the nationality of a Member State shall be a citizen of the Union [...]

The introduction of citizenship to the conceptual world of the Union could be seen, as I argued above, as just another step in the drive towards a statal, unity vision of Europe, especially if citizenship is understood as being premised on statehood.

But there is another more tantalizing and radical way of understanding the provision, namely as the very conceptual decoupling of nationality from citizenship and as the conception of a polity the demos of which, its membership, is understood in the first place in civic and political rather than ethno-cultural terms. On this view, the Union belongs to, is composed of, citizens who *by definition* do not share the same nationality. The substance of membership (and thus of the demos) is in a commitment to the shared values of the Union as expressed in its constituent documents, a commitment, *inter alia*, to the duties and rights of a civic society covering discrete areas of public life, a commitment to membership in a polity which privileges exactly the opposites of nationalism – those human features which transcend the differences of organic ethno-culturalism. On this reading, the conceptualization of a European demos should not be based on real or imaginary trans-European cultural affinities or shared histories nor on the construction of a European 'national' myth of the type which constitutes the identity of the organic nation. The decoupling of nationality and citizenship opens the possibility, instead, of thinking of co-existing multiple demoi.

One view of multiple demoi may consist in what may be called the 'concentric circles' approach. On this approach one feels simultaneously as belonging to, and being part of, say, Germany and Europe; or, even, Scotland, Britain and Europe. What characterizes this view is that the sense of identity and identification derives from the same sources of human attachment albeit at different levels of intensity. Presumably the most intense (which the nation, and state, always claims to be) would and should trump in normative conflict.

The view of multiple demoi which I am suggesting, one of truly variable geometry, invites individuals to see themselves as belonging simultaneously to two demoi, based, critically, on different subjective factors of identification. I may be a German or Italian – and even French – national in the inreaching strong sense of organic-cultural identification and sense of belongingness. I am simultaneously a European citizen in terms of my European transnational affinities to shared values which transcend the ethno-national diversity. So much so, that in the a range of areas of public life, I am willing to accept the legitimacy and authority of decisions adopted by my fellow European citizens in the realization that in these areas I have given preference to choices made by my outreaching demos, rather than by my inreaching demos.

On this view, the Union demos turns away from its antecedents and understanding in the European nation-state. But equally, it should be noted that I am suggesting here something that is different from simple American Republicanism transferred to Europe. First, the values one is discussing may be seen to have a special European specificity, a specificity I have explored elsewhere but one dimension of which, by simple way of example, could most certainly be that strand of mutual social responsibility embodied in the ethos of the Welfare State adopted by all European societies and by all political forces. But the difference from American Republicanism goes further than merely having a different menu of civic values and here it also goes beyond Habermassian Constitutional Patriotism. Constitutional Patriotism is set forth as an alternative to the classic romantic basis for national myth and national identification. I question whether it can answer the existential yearnings to which romantic nationalism so effectively responds. Americanism was, too, after all, about nation-building albeit on different premises. Its end state, its myth, as expressed in the famous Pledge of Allegiance to the American Flag – One Nation, Indivisible, Under God – is not what Europe is about at all: Europe is precisely not about One Nation, not about a Melting Pot and all the rest, for despite the unfortunate rhetoric of Unity, Europe remains (or ought to remain) committed to '… an ever closer union among the peoples of Europe'. Likewise, it is not about indivisibility nor, blessedly, about God.

But where, then, in this concept of European demos, would be the sense of feeling 'at home' so central in the national, organic understanding of demos and a source of its appeal and legitimating power? A partial answer would be in the assertion that the rationality of civic and political commitment can have at least as much normative legitimation and at least to some a high degree of psychological attachment. I will say more on this below. The metaphor of feeling 'at home' may, however, be useful in explicating my preference for the variable geometry version of multiple demoi. I want to suggest two ways of feeling 'at home'.

In the organic concept of demos, the sense of feeling 'at home' derives from affinity and closeness to landscape and classical culture and a feeling of social similarity. I am at home when the mountains or lakes or beaches I behold are familiar, when the language and literature, the music and the poems, the food and aromas are shared, when people are, naturally, not exactly like each other, but *the* people are 'mine'. I am 'at home' because of similarity and familiarity. The surroundings, physical and social, by merely being there are home. It is a captivating feeling.

But there is, surely, a different way of feeling 'at home'. I can feel 'at home' when I am in a strange place, where the mountains and lakes and beaches are different, where the language and food and dress seem strange, where *the* people are not mine but people are like me and they *make me feel at home*. I am 'at home' despite lack of organic similarity and familiarity but because of a civic and political culture. This too is a captivating feeling – to those who give and those who receive.

The co-existence of the two is another dimension of the multiple demoi.

The Treaties on this reading would have to be seen not only as an agreement among states (a Union of States) but as a 'social contract' among the nationals of those states – ratified in accordance with the constitutional requirements in all member states – that they will in the areas covered by the Treaty regard themselves as associating as citizens in this civic society. We can go even further. In this polity, and to this demos, one cardinal value is precisely that there will not be a drive towards, or an acceptance of, an over-arching organic-cultural national identity displacing those of the member states. Nationals of the member states are European citizens, not the other way around. Europe is 'not yet' a demos in the organic national-cultural sense and should never become one.

One should not get carried away with this construct. Note first that the Maastricht formula does not imply a full decoupling: member states are free to define their own conditions of membership and these may continue to be defined in Volkish terms. (But then we know that the conditions of nationality and citizenship differ quite markedly from one member state to another.) Moreover, the gateway to European citizenship passes through member state nationality. More critically, even this construct of the European demos, like the Volkish construct, depends on a shift of con-sciousness. Individuals must think of themselves in this way before such a demos could have full legitimate democratic authority. The key for a shift in political boundaries is the sense of feeling that the boundaries surround one's own polity. I am not making the claim that this shift has already occurred. Nor am I making any claims about the translation of this vision into institutional and constitutional arrangements. I am making, however, the following claims: A. We don't know about public consciousness of a civic polity based demos because the question has to be framed in this way in order to get a meaningful response. B. This shift will not happen if one insists that the only way to understand demos is in Volkish ways. C. That this understanding of demos makes the need for democratization of Europe even more pressing. A demos which coheres around values must live those values.

XV

There is one final issue which touches, perhaps, the deepest stratum of the No Demos thesis. It is one thing to say, as does Maastricht, that nationals of member states are citizens of the Union. But are not those nationals also citizens of their member state? Even if one accepts that one can decouple citizenship and nationality and that one can imagine a demos based on citizenship rather than on nationality, can one be a citizen of both polities? Can one be a member of not one but also a second demos? We have already noted the great aversion of this strand of German constitutionalism to multiple citizenship.

I want to address this question in two different ways. One is simply to point out the fairly widespread practice of states allowing double or even multiple citizenship with relative equanimity. For the most part, as a matter of civic duties and rights this does not create many problems. This is true also in the Community. It is true that in time of, say, war the holder of multiple citizenship may be in an untenable situation. But cannot even the European Union create a construct which assumes that war among its constituent member states is not only materially impossible but unthinkable? The sentiment against multiple citzenship is not, I think, rooted in practical considerations.

Instead, at a deeper level the issue of double citizenship evokes the spectre of double loyalty. The view which denies the status of demos to Europe may derive thus from a resistance to the idea of double loyalty. The resistance to double loyalty could be rooted in the fear that some flattened nondescript unauthentic and artificial 'Euro-culture' would come to replace the deep, well-articulated, authentic and genuine national version of the same. It could also be rooted in the belief that double loyalty must mean that either one or both loyalties have to be compromised.

On the first point I do not believe that any of the European organic national–cultural identities is so weak or fragile as to be risked by the spectre of a simultaneous civic loyalty to Europe. I have already argued that the opposite is also likely. Unable to rest on the formal structures of the state, national culture and identity has to find truly authentic expressions to enlist loyalty which can bring about real internally found generation. What is more, the existential condition of fractured self, of living in two or more worlds can result not in a flattening of one's cultural achievement but in its sharpening and deepening. Can anyone who has read Heine, or Kafka, or Canetti doubt this?

But what about the political aversion to double loyalty? This, paradoxically, is most problematic especially in a polity which cherishes organic national–cultural homogeneity as a condition of membership. It is hard to see why, other than for some mystical or truly 'blood thicker than water' rationale, say, a British citizen who thinks of herself as British (and who forever will speak with an English accent) but who is settled in, say, Germany and wishes to assume all the duties and rights of German citizenship could not be trusted in today's Europe loyally to do so. Moreover, we have already seen that European citizenship would have a very different meaning from German citizenship. The two identities would not be competing directly 'on the same turf'. It seems to me that the aversion to double loyalty, like the aversion to multiple citizenship itself, does not seem to be rooted primarily in practical considerations. It rests I think in a normative view which wants national self-identity – identified with the state and its organs – to rest very deep in the soul, in a place which hitherto was occupied by religion. The imagery of this position – turning to Fate – is occasionally evocative of those sentiments . The reason for this, I think, derives from the recognition of the greatest pull of nationalism. It is by evoking fate and destiny that nationalism can respond to the deepest existential yearning, that of giving meaning and purpose to life which extend beyond mere existence or selfish fulfilment. Religion, with greater legitimacy, occupies itself with these deeper recesses of the human spirit and, consequently, makes these claims for exclusivity. The mixing of state loyalty and religion risks, in my view, idolatory from a religious perspective and can be highly dangerous from a political one. Historically, it seems as if Volk and Staat, Blood and Soil, did indeed come to occupy these deepest parts of the human spirit to the point of being accepted 'über alles' with terrifying consequences. My view of the matter is not that the very idea of Volk and Staat was murderous or even evil though, as I think is clear from this essay, my preference is for multiple loyalties, even demoi within the state. It is the primordial position which Volk mixed with Staat occupied, instilling uncritical citizenship which allowed evil, even murderous designs to be executed by dulling critical personal faculties, legitimating extreme positions, subduing transcendent human values and debasing one of the common strands of the three monotheistic religions that human beings, all of them, were created in the image of God.

The European construct I have put forward, which allows for a European civic, value-driven demos co-existing side by side with a national organic-cultural one (for those nation-states that want it), could be seen as a rather moderate contribution to this goal. Maybe in the realm of the political, the special virtue of contemporaneous membership in an organic national–cultural demos and in a supranational civic, value-driven demos is in the effect which such double membership may have on taming the great appeal, even craving, for belonging and destiny in this world which nationalism continues to offer but which can so easily degenerate to intolerance and xenophobia. Maybe the inreaching national–cultural demos and the outreaching supranational civic demos by continuously keeping each other in check offer a structured model of critical citizenship. They might even induce us to look for meaning and purpose not simply or primarily to statal structures at either European or state levels.

The national and the supranational encapsulate on this reading two of the most elemental, alluring and frightening social and psychological poles of our cultural heritage. The national is Eros: reaching back to the pre-modern, appealing to the heart with a grasp on our emotions, and evocative of the romantic vision of creative social organization. But we know that darkness lurks too. The supranational is civilization: confidently modernist, appealing to the rational within us and to Enlightenment neoclassical humanism. Here, too, we are aware of the frozen and freezing aspect this humanism might take. Martin Heidegger is an unwitting ironic metaphor for the difficulty of negotiating between these poles earlier in this century. His rational, impersonal critique of totalistic rationality and of modernity remain a powerful lesson to this day; but equally powerful is the lesson from his fall: an irrational, personal embracing of an irrational, romantic pre-modern nationalism run amok.

On this reading supranational citizenship is the context in which nationality and statism may thrive, their daemonic aspects under civilizatory constraints.

4 Moral Choice and European Integration
Bill McSweeney

War is unthinkable between France and Germany. This is probably the commonest expression of the consequences of European integration, not only among lay theorists, but also among professionals in the academic and policymaking arena. As an affirmation of fact, it is seen as the effect and the cause of integration, not just between the two central states, but between the members of the wider Community in which France and Germany form the core relationship.[1] The transformation of their old conflictual association, in which war was chronically triggered as the outcome of their competitive relations, into a security community, is viewed as the cause and the consequence of their solidarity, and of the solidarity of the Community as a whole. As war becomes unthinkable, so the participants are motivated to integrate their interests and institutions even further, and thus to strengthen the new relationship between them.

It seems clear that the origins of the European Union lay, in part, in a deliberate policy of key individual actors, accepted by state leaders, to initiate a process by which the relationship between them would be transformed into one in which the structural constraint would favour the peaceful resolution of conflict rather than war. Throughout the century, state leaders had made the connection between war and the anarchy of self-seeking states. British Prime Minister Lord Salisbury, in 1897, wrote of a 'Federation of Europe' as 'our sole hope of escaping from the constant terror and calamity of war', while his successor in office, Winston Churchill, looked forward in 1942 to 'a United States of Europe in which the barriers between the nations will be greatly minimized ... and the economy of Europe studied as a whole'.[2]

That peace was a conscious motive stimulating the integrative initiative of the six founding states – France, West Germany, Italy and the three Benelux countries – is not the issue in evaluating the popular theory about European integration. After all, war is seldom the motive in the process by which some states bring about a conflictual relationship in which war is made a likely occurrence. If a 'security dilemma' is the unintended consequence of interaction in some regions, leading to a conflictual association which it was not in anyone's interest to construct, so a security community does not have to be traced to the altruistic motives of any of the actors involved.

The urge to dismiss the normative factor in favour of narrow self-interest as the only force driving the integration process is misconceived by some political analysts and historians, whose work is premised on the assumption that moral values exclude self-interest, and that self-interest is an observable and unproblematic fact. Thus Milward rejects the idealist view which 'attribute(s) the movement towards integration to human idealism fortunately triumphing at specific moments over the narrow anachronistic realism of national governments'. Integration must not be seen, he writes, as 'a victory of higher ideals' over national government bureaucracies but rather as the product of 'narrow self interest' on the part of those very 'cohorts of government and bureaucracy whose task it was and is to define and uphold the national interest before all else'.[3]

If the European Union is a political structure 'in which there is real assurance that the members of that community will not fight each other physically but will settle their disputes in some other way' as Deutsch expressed it,[4] it cannot have emerged and endured through the accident of the convergence of 'narrow' self-interest, any more than it can be the consequence of 'international altruism'. The convergence of self-interest with the interests of others is an accomplishment of actors who know what they are doing. What matters is to analyze the structure which their actions create in terms of the values which it embodies – for war or for peace, for mutual antagonism or cooperation. All social structures are the carriers of human values, whether designed by visionary idealists or bureaucrats. While they have unintended consequences, they are the product of intended actions, the overall design of which can only be inferred, not observed.

What is required to support the idea that war within the European Union is unthinkable is an objective indicator of a community of interests, which allows us to infer that the states involved are structured to see themselves as cooperative, rather than self-help, actors, even if in other areas of international relations they are egoistic or self-help entities. Thus a state may form part of a conflictual relationship in one area and a security community in another. Its identity as a cooperative actor is not necessarily one that determines its relations in all its activities. Identity is not unitary. Just as individuals can have multiple identities – position themselves in different ways with respect to the different structures of their relations – so with states. Just as an individual's relations may be cooperatively structured within the family, but conflictually structured in the workplace, so a state may demonstrate a commonality of interests in one community and opposition of interests in another.

Britain may be seen as an example of such a state, with multiple and conflicting identities in respect of its community with the United States, on the one hand, and its community with the European Union, on the other. In neither case do we need to infer the motives of the individual state actors whose decisions entered causally into the process of constructing the relationships, in order to view the one as cooperative and the other as self-oriented – and both as moral, or normative, choices.

To claim that war is unthinkable between France and Germany, and the other Community members, is to imply that no interest is conceivable in which violence as a means of pursuing it would be less costly to the states concerned than peaceful negotiation. The structure established at its origins, and voluntarily embraced by the founding members, is one that conditions the way in which states perceive their self-interests. War remains clearly possible, but unthinkable.

Of the major powers invited to participate in the initial step of the European Coal and Steel Community,[5] only Britain declined. Since then, despite becoming a member in 1973, Britain has been consistent in its opposition to deepening the level of integration and in its support for the view that the Community is primarily a vehicle for economic cooperation. Why does every state not behave like Britain? The obvious answer is that they have different interests: unlike the continental powers, Britain is mainly interested in the deregulation of trade, in the maintenance of a strong American defence identity in Europe, in the protection of its separate identity from migration, an important part of which is expressed and symbolized in its sovereignty. Britain thus exercises the option, open to all actors in the EU structure, to define itself in relation to the Community more as a self-help than as a cooperative actor.

The idea that Britain behaves as it does simply because it 'has' different interests is warranted neither by empirical data nor by philosophical analysis. States do not *have* interests, in the way that they have territorial boundaries. Interests are chosen – within the constraints of structures – not bestowed. Contrary to Palmerston's famous quip,[6] states have interests in exactly the way they have friends – as a consequence of choice within a structure of constraint. Britain was once at war with America, just as Finland with Sweden, France with Germany. If today the relations between the United States and Britain constitute a security community – less integrated, but structured in regard to their common security – it is not just because the material world changed, but because Britain and the US interpret it differently.

Behind the interests which motivate our action lies the identity – the sort of person or collectivity we are – which formulates interests of such a kind. In a logical sense, our wants or interests derive from our character as this or that sort of individual, or group. Our identity accounts for our behaviour. If Britain perceives its interests differently, it is because it is a different kind of entity to the other members of the Community. But this raises the ontological question in regard to identity also. Like interests, identity is a choice, not solely an inheritance or a discovery.

What made the states of the European Union choose to be cooperative, rather than egoistic, and therefore to perceive their own interests in terms of the interests of all in the region, rather than the self? How do we explain the process by which a region of conflictual relations and self-regarding identities became transformed into a network of interlocking political and economic institutions and interests, to form a security community? Two different attempts to explain this process will be discussed.

As in most accounts of the social order, a self-fulfilling dynamic links theory and practice in our attempts to explain European integration. How we understand integration theoretically significantly influences the range of policies deemed appropriate to address it, which tend, in turn, to validate our theories and explanations. If we judge that integration is a function of a convergence of the fixed and unchangeable interests of the individual states, expressed in terms of economic criteria alone, it is sensible to assess each proposal for further cooperation only in terms of its immediate economic benefit to the state and to resist attempts to advance or even to sustain integration on the basis of long-term political benefits or idealistic appeals to community. British historian, Milward, erects a policy barrier to all proposals for further integration which do not meet the criterion of state economic interests – a position reflecting historical attitudes on the part of political leaders in his own country and one which appears to command increasing popular support there in recent years.[7]

If we favour an older and alternative theory of neofunctionalism, on the other hand, quite different policies will be deemed appropriate. At least in its classical formulation, neofunctionalism postulates a structural mechanism which determines the outcome of the integration process, making it irrational, and contrary to the interests of the states, to retard it.

A third approach will be presented, based on a revision of the neofunctionalist idea. This view sees European integration as a social construction and thus a consequence of human agency as well as structural constraints, and it opens up a wider range of policy options. No structural mechanisms are forcing the member states towards an ever-closer union; no laws of the international order are preventing them from achieving it. Integration is a normative project, in the sense that it is the product of moral purpose and choice with respect to the structure which achieves it. As Haas expresses it:

> The units and actions studied provide a living laboratory for observing the peaceful creation of possible new types of human communities ... and of the processes which may lead to such conditions.[8]

The objective of this chapter is to make the case for conceiving of European integration as a security policy embodied in an integrated security community. This is accomplished, it is argued, through the reconstruction of identities and interests, and is consequent upon a moral choice of the actors involved. Following initial comments on security policy and community, a discussion of the two principal theories of integration sets the background for developing a third approach. This account of the integration process will then be set in the context of particular events illustrating the choices and decisions of three member states.

Our view of the possibility of normative integration is determined by the assumptions and theories we bring to bear on the nature of states and their capacity for cooperative or competitive relations. Whether integration is advanced or weakened is a consequence of policy choices arising from how we understand it; and how we understand integration is, in part, determined by our normative assumptions about states and their relations. European integration, it is argued, can be seen as a process and a policy – something which happens to states because they choose to make it happen. As policy, it has the property of a social action, which is directed towards its ends by the intentions of the actor, including the pursuit of self-interest. As process, it has the character of a social project, managed to ensure the convergence of intended and unintended consequences of action in the form of a security community.

In this sense, European integration can be understood as a security policy, designed to bring about the transformation of the relationship between states in a region of conflictual association. This is to understand security in terms of a wide, but unitary, concept, embracing the negative dimension of military defence against threat, the middle range of policies oriented to managing or resolving conflict, and the positive dimension which addresses the conflict of identity and interests underlying threat. The positive aspect of security policy draws attention to the dynamics involved in what is conventionally termed a 'peace process', bringing us back to a terminology familiar to the founders of the European Union. Like a positive security policy, a peace process can be envisaged as a managed project by which states learn to perceive their interests and identity in terms of cooperation rather than conflict, in a manner which becomes progressively more costly to unravel.

A peace process does not imply some ideal relationship of equality between the parties to it. Nor does it require us to hold that the parties are drawn to participate in it by motives of goodwill and the altruistic sacrifice of perceived interest in favour of others. As in the case of Northern Ireland, the reality of power, unequally distributed, may be as much a contributory factor to the success of a peace process as it is to an international regime of competitive relations as traditionally conceived.[9] Indeed, it is difficult to conceive the project of a peace process, or security community, acquiring the necessary momentum without the push and stabilizing force of a hegemonic party. In the European Union, a coalition of France and Germany and, in earlier periods, the United States, provided the push towards integration without which the process would scarcely have begun.

THE NEOFUNCTIONALIST ACCOUNT OF INTEGRATION

Neofunctionalism, the best-known and most elegant attempt to explain European integration, declined for over two decades before its qualified revival in 1989. First developed in the early 1950s, it offered an attractive alternative to the realist focus on the autonomy of the state.[10]

The theory is centred on the concept of spillover, the structural mechanism which supplies it with powerful explanatory and predictive promise. Integration is driven by a logic which Haas defined as the consequence of 'policies made pursuant to an initial task and grant of power [which] can be made real only if the task itself is expanded'.[11] This 'expansive logic of integration', as he called it, is activated by the trigger of spillover, which Lindberg saw as a function by which

> a given action, related to a specific goal, creates a situation in which the original goal can be assured only by taking further actions, which in turn create a further condition and a need for more action, and so forth.[12]

As integration progressed at the technical–economic level towards greater complexity, the technical spillover described would prove inadequate to the problems of integration and would yield to the demand of interest groups for a higher level of political control at the centre. Functional spillover would inevitably cause political spillover, which Haas defined as:

the process whereby political actors in several distinct national settings are persuaded to shift their loyalties, expectations and political activities towards a new centre, whose institutions possess or demand jurisdiction over the pre-existing national states.[13]

Unlike traditional negotiations between states, which produce agreement on the basis of minimum common denominator, neofunctionalists saw integration proceeding on the basis of upgrading the interests common to member states: problems of cooperation in one sector would stimulate cooperation in others.[14] This gradual expansion of tasks, enmeshing the participating states ineluctably into an ever-tighter web of integration, depended on the key role of the Commission in managing the process to that end.

Neofunctionalism provided a seductive and powerful way of grasping the complexities of integration in the early years of enthusiasm for the project. Instead of identifying the unit actors as the source of integration in the manner of classical diplomatic analysis, or the structure of the international system in the way of neorealism, it attributed causal power to the process of interaction itself. Cooperation created a learning process in which state actors, constrained by the existing web of relationships in which their interests were engaged, learned to identify themselves and their interests with higher levels of cooperation. Non-state actors, in particular the Commission, played a vital role in managing the process and ensuring that spillover and the reconstruction of state interests and identity were progressive and incremental. The theory attempted to explain how incentives for personal gain at different levels of society could be managed by covert forces to bring about the consequence of integration, conditional upon voluntary acceptance of a change of identity.

There is some ambiguity about the automaticity of spillover in the writings of the early theorists. Haas and Lindberg emphasized the political dimension of integration and the contingency of political spillover, in opposition to classical functionalist views which saw the process more as self-propelling.[15] Nonetheless, the overall tone of optimism, the weight of tight, formal analysis, and the general scientific objectivism of the theory made neofunctionalism hostage to the facts which it purported to control, and gave to it an economic determinism which helped to bring down the whole intellectual edifice in the early 1970s. Optimism was underpinned by several claims which would later be retracted in the light of the long period of inertia in the Community – 'the functional logic which may lead, more or less automatically, from a common market to political unification'.[16] By the end of that decade, the Community had patently not

responded to the economic and political challenges in the manner predicted. Insufficient attention to the impact on integration of events in the
wider international arena were also noted as major defects of the theory.[17]

In 1967 Haas admitted that the 'high politics' of de Gaulle had challenged his theory.[18] In an important retraction of his earlier view, he
acknowledged that spillover is not automatic: the incremental process is
'always subject to reversal' and, he now postulated, a certain level of
integration is necessary to withstand the resistance of powerful political
intervention:[19]

> the very success of the incremental method becomes self-defeating as
> important elites recognise that welfare can be safeguarded without a
> strong Commission and overt political unity ... If integration has gone
> very far by then, no harm is done to the union but in Europe it had not
> gone far enough before the national situation improved once more.[20]

Haas now saw integration and disintegration 'as two rival social processes
... simultaneously at work'.[21] This makes the theory untestable, since any
failure can be ascribed to the disintegrative intrusion of national
consciousness.

In the classical formulation of neofunctionalism, the process of interaction, through which states learn to construct interests, effectively
removes the voluntary dimension of agency which it purports to preserve.
States become determined in their interests by the supranational agencies
which manage that process. Neofunctionalist spillover reflects an over-
socialized conception of state behaviour. They become the cultural dupes
of the integration process, parallel to the individual actor *vis-à-vis* the
central value system in the theory of structural functionalism, fashionable
in sociology in the heyday of neofunctionalism.

INTERGOVERNMENTALISM AND THE REVISION OF NEOFUNCTIONALISM

For almost two decades following the decline of neofunctionalist theory,
attempts to account for European integration took an atheoretical turn
under the label of 'intergovernmentalism'.[22] Students of integration displayed no particular interest in the classical intergovernmentalism of international relations theory, which had provided the intellectual basis for
Stanley Hoffman's realist critique of neofunctionalism.[23] The term 'intergovernmentalism' was for the most part employed as shorthand for the

rejection of the idea of grand theory which would explain the integration process as a whole, and as justification for the enterprise of piecemeal, empirical analysis. Keohane and Hoffman reflected:

> It seems unfortunate to us that many of the accounts of European Community politics have discarded older theories, such as neofunctionalism, without putting anything theoretical in their place: recourse is had to mere description of processes and events. Attempts to avoid theory, however, not only miss interesting questions but rely implicitly on a framework for analysis that remains unexamined precisely because it is implicit.[24]

Against Haas's view that the institutions of the EC could not endure a messy equilibrium and a collapse of legitimacy would result,[25] inter-governmentalists argued that the mixed institutional structure of the mid-1970s was likely to continue indefinitely.[26] It was only with the dramatic and quite unanticipated progress towards the achievement of the internal market in 1988–9 that theorists revisited and revived elements of the discredited neofunctionalism.

Sandholtz and Zysman, in 1989, marked the beginning of this revision, stressing the importance of domestic politics, international institutions and the international economy, and laying particular emphasis on international factors as a stimulus to closer integration.[27] Echoing some tenets of the long-abandoned theory, they identified business interests and the Commission as having 'together bypassed national governmental processes and shaped an agenda that compelled attention and action'.[28] But this, in their view, was consistent with the claim that 'the Community remains a bargain among governments'.[29] They resurrected the concept of spillover as a useful analytical device to focus on likely areas of expansion to monetary union and defence, but without the deterministic tone of old.

Stanley Hoffman revisited neofunctionalism in a similar overall analysis, while stressing the international factors which stimulated the inter-governmental bargain on the 1992 project.[30] For Keohane and Hoffman, reviewing the theory in the same period, the idea of spillover 'has ... not been discredited: in the wake of an intergovernmental bargain ... actors can have incentives to promote task expansion into new sectors in order to protect gains already achieved'.[31] But it was *governments* which took the final crucial steps leading to negotiation and ratification of the Single European Act. Explanation must begin with recognition that *governments* took decisions to revive supranational decisionmaking in their own interests.

To say this is not to declare that a state-centric perspective will provide a satisfactory explanation of the Single European Act, only that such an explanation must *begin* with governmental actions, since these actions are what we observe leading directly to the Act.[32]

A renewed attack on neofunctionalism came with Andrew Moravcsik's much-cited riposte to its revision and to the claim that regional integration theory had been 'unjustly consigned to the dustbin'.[33] His work is particularly germane to the concerns of this chapter because it explicitly raises the question of the source of state interests and preferences, and – by implication – of state identity. And this raises the question of moral choice: whether states have options and can choose a cooperative identity and interests with integrative outcome, or define their interests at the self-help end of the spectrum, with disintegrative consequences.

While his principal focus is the negotiations on the Single European Act, Moravcsik's explanation of what drove them to their successful conclusion is implicitly an account of the integration process in general, not one tied to the particular case of the SEA. It claims a radical break with neofunctionalism as 'the sole attempt to fashion a coherent and comprehensive theory of European integration'.[34]

His focus on the domestic arena as the source of state interests marks a break with the neorealist tradition to which his analysis is otherwise sympathetic. The Single European Act was the consequence of a convergence of domestic conditions around the interest of deregulation in the Big Three member states of the Community – France, Germany and Britain. Integration is a process of lowest common denominator bargaining rather than the upgrading of common interest; there are clear limitations to the pooling of sovereignty, rather than the incremental spillover from functional to political levels; and the key actors are the major governments, independently facilitating or inhibiting the significant agreements which further the process, and doing so in their own domestic interests.

> The primary interest of governments is to maintain themselves in office; in democratic societies, this requires the support of a coalition of domestic voters, parties, interest groups and bureaucracies, whose views are transmitted, directly or indirectly, through domestic institutions and practices of political representation. Through this process emerges the set of national interests or goals that states bring to international negotiations.[35]

What Moravcsik calls 'intergovernmentalist institutionalism' rejects the central role of supranational organizations and the mechanical operation of spillover as the forces which push member states to ever-higher levels of integration. While spillover has a role *within a given sector*, it plays 'a minimal role in the process of opening new issues, reforming decision-making procedures, and ratifying the accession of new members.'[36] The main actors in the integration process are not supranational agencies, steadily eroding the sovereignty of states, but the heads of governments, to whom Moravcsik accords the function of initiating and negotiating institutional reforms and major steps in the integration process. Interstate bargaining reflects the interests of the major states, and their successful outcome is inevitably the consequence of a drift to the lowest common denominator among the interests of the large states. These interests are determined by domestic political preferences, not by the process of negotiating agreements.

Moravcsik emphasizes the separation of the two levels of the domestic and the intergovernmental and the dependence of the latter upon the former in the integration process: '...governments *first* define a set of interests, *then* bargain among themselves in an effort to realize those interests'; we understand the process 'through the *sequential* analysis of national preference formation and intergovernmental strategic interaction'.[37] On the familiar question of the effect of integration on state power, Moravcsik rejects the thesis that supranationalism is in a zero-sum relationship to statehood. Strong supranational institutions serve the purpose of strengthening the nation-state's control over domestic affairs, permitting it to attain goals which are otherwise unachievable.[38] Rather than eroding the power of the state, European integration strengthens it:

> In the intergovernmentalist view, the unique institutional structure of the EC is acceptable to national governments only insofar as it strengthens, rather than weakens, their control over domestic affairs, permitting them to attain goals otherwise unachievable.[39]

The theoretical starting point on which his analysis depends is, thus, that state interests and preferences are given prior to, and independently of, the process of interstate negotiation. Governments do not learn or construct interests; they 'emerge' through the domestic process and are then in some way aggregated or collected as 'national interests or goals that states bring to international negotiations'.[40] How these competing preferences are constructed into the national interest is not a problem to which Moravcsik attends other than to insist that they constitute the independent variable in the sequence of interstate negotiation to be explained.

The same conclusion is drawn from a different perspective by Alan Milward. For Milward, the state does not become a different kind of state – implying a changed identity – with different interests. It is the environment which changes to allow the same state to pursue the same interests to better or at least different effect. Economic self-interest is the perennial motivating force of foreign policy; the state is a self-help actor by nature – its international and domestic identity are fixed in unwavering commitment to the pursuit of narrow national interest by the anarchic structure of the environment in which it lives. Identity and interests are assumed to be given; behaviour is a variable conditioned by the shifting configurations and economic inducements of international relations at any time.

THE CRITIQUE OF INTERGOVERNMENTALISM

Different theoretical assumptions about the nature of social interaction are at work in these explanations of integration. Neofunctionalism claims that states come to negotiations open to acquiring a new form of cooperative identity and to upgrading their interests to a community level. Moravcsik's liberal intergovernmentalism claims that states come to negotiations with interests and identity established prior to interaction. In opposition to realism (and Milward) however, these interests are not constant for all or for any particular state. They are determined by the domestic political process of substate bargaining and aggregated by governments independently of, and prior to, their interaction with other governments in the community. The social interaction of state leaders and representatives within the integration process is not given any role within his general schema, other than the minor one noted, 'within a given sector'.

Empirical inquiry of itself cannot decide which view is correct in regard to the relation between the fundamental attributes of the actor and the behaviour which logically flows from these attributes. If we approach a particular empirical problem like the Single European Act from a neorealist perspective, the consequence will be to close off inquiry into the possibility that the actor's fundamental attributes – what kind of actor it is, and what interests motivate its relations with other actors – may be influenced by interstate interaction, and to focus exclusively on changes of actor's *behaviour*. The observable evidence can only confirm the theoretical assumption. If, like Moravcsik, we start from the theoretical standpoint of 'intergovernmental institutionalism', the assumption about state interests and preferences opens up to investigation the influence of sub-state groups on state interests, but it closes off the inquiry into the influence of interstate interaction. In both cases, the theoretical starting point conditions the interpretation of the available evidence.

The response of Sandholtz to Moravcsik[41] concedes much to the inter-governmentalist case: 'Community decisions are bargains that reflect state interests', and raises the question: Where do state interests come from? Sandholtz addresses this as simply an empirical question – they are 'shaped in part by membership in the EC', in his view – but without credible evidence to support his inference.[42] As long as this dispute is conducted in terms of a methodology which views empirically observable facts as unproblematic, then 'governmental actions' will be privileged, since – to cite Keohane and Hoffman again – 'these actions are what we observe leading directly to ... [integration]'.[43]

For Moravcsik, the demand for integration comes solely from domestic calculation of cost and benefit.[44] 'Groups articulate preferences; governments aggregate them.'[45] But this is to raise a further question in addition to that of Sandholtz. Where do *domestic* interests and the process of aggregation or selection into an idea of the 'national interest' come from? Moravcsik reduces government preferences to domestic interests, making these interests an independent variable and excluding international inter-action as a causal factor. But he also ignores the role of government in manipulating domestic interests, leaving such interests to emerge mysteriously from the well of public opinion and domestic competition.

The action of government cannot be reduced to that of the mouthpiece of domestic interests. Governments are actors within a twofold structure of interaction: with substate groups within the domestic arena, and with other governments internationally. Governments systematically manage do-mestic interests, as they manage public opinion, through their capacity to control the public perception of costs and benefits in the interest of a wider constituency which can also help sustain government in office. Neither the domestic nor the interstate structures can be privileged *a priori* with respect to their influence on the view of the world which determines government behaviour.

Governments are a fulcrum on which communication between the inter-national and the domestic turns. Their articulation of domestic interests is only the observable endpoint of a complex interactive process in which governments manage as well as articulate group interests, and in which governments reproduce and are constrained by the process of integration. Which of these variables is the more independent one depends upon the case under inquiry. None can be denied a causal role in the abstract.

To return to the point raised in the introduction to this chapter about the relation of theory to policy, our view of what drives the motor of integration has important policy implications for the future of the European Union. If the classical neofunctionalist account were to be accepted, the policy implications would be clear. Since integrative decisions of governments are viewed as the inevitable consequence of spillover, managed and manipulated by the supranational institutions of the community in conjunction with the political elites in member states, the task is to strengthen these institutions and to cooperate with the progressive enlargement and deepening consequent upon spillover. There is no pressing need to attend to problems of collective identity formation, largely ignored by neofunctionalists until they yielded to the pressure of events too hastily – to abandon the entire framework. Haas elevated the importance of elite socialization to the neglect of public opinion, regarding public opinion surveys as 'impracticable' and 'unnecessary':

> It suffices to single out and define the political elites in the participating countries, to study their reactions to integration and to assess changes in attitude on their part.[46]

If Moravcsik is correct, on the other hand, it follows that such a course is counter-productive both for the community and for its member states. Any policy which threatens the domestically generated interests of the state, as articulated by governments, must be resisted. Supranational institutions play an important role in improving the efficiency of interstate bargaining and reducing their domestic political cost; but they are the creature and the servant of the states themselves, not their hidden manipulator.[47] Personified in the actions of government, the state is supreme *vis-à-vis* the interstate arena, and is the more-or-less passive voice of competing interests in regard to the domestic.

There are competing assumptions at work in these rival accounts of integration. In the intergovernmentalism of Moravcsik, governments are agents of domestic interests only in the superficial legal sense – persons who act on behalf of the interests of others. They are not social agents, acting under the constraints, and by virtue of the intersubjective ideas and norms, of an interstate structure.[48] In neofunctionalism, states are collective actors within an interstate structure which determines how they construct a view of the national interest and through which they learn an identity consonant with their interests. The concept of spillover is based on this assumption, it is central to neofunctionalist theory, and its revision in the light of a more adequate social theory of agency and structure helps to make more sense of the problem of identity-formation, the neglect of which Haas noted as a factor in the decline of theoretical relevance.

SPILLOVER AND IDENTITY

The question at issue as to where a state positions itself – and is positioned – in terms of its security relationship with other states (conflictual or community) is the question of identity and interests (self-help or cooperative). A reinterpreted concept of spillover can help in making sense of change, and the source of change, in the identity and interests of states relevant to their security and security policy.

The philosophical and theoretical problems of agency and identity are relevant to two points which relate the concept of spillover to a sociology of security.[49] The first concerns the core idea of spillover itself, sometimes expressed in the French *engrenage*, or the more colloquial 'enmeshment'; secondly, the interrelation of identity and interests.

The lesser-used metaphor of 'enmeshment' is preferable to the base metaphor of 'spillover': it denotes the entanglement in a web of relationships which is at the root of the neofunctionalist idea, rather than the mechanical and material connotations of 'spillover'.[50] Enmeshment hints at conspiracy, at the conscious manipulation of others' identities and interests, and it hints also at human agency – influenced, but not determined, in its role as co-conspirator. Enmeshment also points to the processual character of the concept envisaged, rather than the discrete moment suggested by the term 'spillover'.

For neofunctionalists, that which becomes gradually entangled in a web of relationships, over time, is the interests of states *and* of people and interest groups within and across states, so that their loyalties, their allegiance, becomes refocused on the Community. For 'loyalties', or 'allegiance', we can read 'identity'. The gradual expansion of tasks consequent upon functional cooperation would persuade states not only to 'upgrade' their interests to those common to other member states, but persuade domestic actors also 'to shift their loyalties, expectations and political activities towards a new centre'.[51] This move is better expressed as a change in identity (loyalties) and interests (expectations and political activities). It is difficult to make sense of the qualitative change implied in the shift from technical to political spillover without incorporating the concept of identity to express it.

The strategy of conscious management of the enmeshment process to the end of achieving such a shift towards a more collective identity and interests is fully compatible with the 'sovereign' choice of the actors to cooperate with, or to resist, enmeshment. In respect of European integration, it is part of the learning process, whereby agents become enmeshed with constraints of structure and learn to reconstruct their interests and identity, under the tutelage of the Commission, *while remaining agents with the choice to do otherwise.* Where the process is successful, the new identity and interests are not perceived as the sacrifice of self in favour of others, but as the realization of a different and superior conception of the national self and the national interest. Where the process is resisted – as in the case of unionists in Northern Ireland and Britain in the EU – the prospect on offer with integration is deemed to entail the denial of self.

The processual character of 'enmeshment' draws attention to its temporal dimension as a social project. This should be understood as a continuous flow of action on the part of human agents – as individuals and as state leaders – initiated and managed by an elite or institutional body, but accomplished by actors who may not intend, or be fully aware of, the consequences of their actions. The reconstruction of an *individual's* identity is conceivably an intended outcome of his or her agency. It is inconceivable that *collective* identity be reformed on the basis of intended action alone. The 'imagined community' which directs British interests in the European Union, and the quite different identity which guides Germany, is neither the intended action of their respective populations, nor is it the imposition of a determinative structure or political elite. It is the accomplishment of both. A security community could never be accomplished without the enmeshing of individuals' *choices* in a project consciously managed by a leadership elite.

The concept of spillover, secondly, offers insight into the relation of identity and interests, which can enrich the sociological or 'constructivist' approach to international relations theory.

If we understand identity as a structure, and interests as the action element within the framework of this structure, then the idea that interests are formed as the effect of identity suggests a structural determinism at odds with the social theory underlying 'constructivism'. It is also at variance with the strong emphasis on the causal role of interests in neo-functionalism, and with an intuitively plausible view of how identities – individual, as well as collective – come to be formed and changed in practice. The apparent fact that national identities are formed and reformed as the consequence and instrument of the pursuit of elite interests is supported in the social constructionist literature on nationalism and national identity.[52] Likewise in neofunctionalism, the shift in loyalties and attitudes (identities) is mainly seen as the *result* of the upgrading of interests, while allowing that the relationship is a dialectic one in practice.

Identity and interests cause each other. Spillover points to a dynamic of identity and interest, which locates the source of identity- and interest-formation in the learning process of interstate cooperation – in the 'co-ordination reflex' which integration literature attributes to individual officials who are professionally engaged in the process; and it locates the source of identity construction in the pursuit of interests, or wants. Such a conception of the dynamic is consistent with a more adequate theory of social action, which underlines the agency of the individual and the element of choice in the formation of individual and collective identity. We are who we want to be.

THE MORAL CONSTRUCTION OF EUROPEAN INTEGRATION

The relationship between France and Germany is central to a theoretical interpretation of the integration process, as it is to the popular understanding of what integration has accomplished. This is expressed in the everyday theory which attributes to European integration the fact that 'war is unthinkable' between France and Germany. As noted, however, war is clearly not impossible between them, or between the US and Britain, or Sweden and Finland – all once on opposite sides of violent confrontation. It is the cognitive factor in their relations which makes it unthinkable.

What is it about France and Germany, and about the European Union as a whole, which justifies the claim that the member states have created a security community, giving confidence in its long-term capacity to generate peaceful relations between them and to survive the inevitable tensions and conflicts without disintegrating or resorting to violence? The claim rests on the argument that a change of identity, not just one of behaviour, is the basis of such a community. Member states continue to pursue their own interests, but the image of self which selects interests and preferences in the international arena is cooperative, rather than self-regarding, and the interests chosen are those which take into account the longer-term benefits of pursuing common interests rather than those which exclude the interests of others. This cannot be adequately analyzed in terms of a motivational distinction between altruism and egoism, but in terms of the range of options open to an actor which seeks to pursue its own best interests. What kind of actor a state is, conditions the choice of interests which it will pursue. But the reverse is also true. The experience over time of choosing those interests which take into account the interests of others, influences the development of an identity – the choice of a principle of choice, one might say.

States have always been open to cooperation with others, even with others who are identified as potential enemies in other respects. Balancing alliances, trade agreements, functional cooperation in terms of specific common interests, are familiar forms of strategic cooperation which do not imply permanence, or justify the inference that they are indicators of anything more profound than a shift in behaviour. If the European Union is assumed to be merely a vehicle of strategic cooperation of that kind, our attitude, and that of state leaders, to EU negotiations will inevitably serve to validate this assumption. Theory and practice, structure and agency, identity and interests – each of these pairings must be seen as a duality, the one constituting the other in an inseparable relation. For this reason, how we conceptualize the European Union, discursively or implicitly, is not an abstract problem which can be left to academics interested in that sort of thing, while the rest tackle the practical questions of what to do next. Philosophical reflection, conceptual analysis and theory are of the utmost relevance to deciding such practical questions.

How would we know that France and Germany have changed their identity, and not merely their behaviour? At the philosophical level, the problem is one which links with the discussion of behaviourism in general.[53] Even if we reject a radical behaviourism, the question arises in relation to states: is the identity of states (and, so, their interests) fixed and determined by forces outside their influence? Analytically, this position can be shown to rest on, and be reducible to, a general proposition about the determination of human nature and identity. Robert Gilpin summed up the assumption which connects Morgenthau with Waltz, Mearsheimer, and Gilpin himself:

> I believe that political realism must be seen as a philosophical dis-
> position and set of assumptions about the world ... [it] is best viewed as
> an attitude regarding the human condition ... founded on a pessimism
> regarding moral progress and human possibilities.[54]

No empirical evidence could be adduced which would falsify this assumption. Whatever the state of the world appears to be, and however long some states may cooperate in specific or general institutional sectors, time will tell, human nature will out, and reassert itself in the nature of states as egoistic and self-help actors in a determinative structure of anarchy.[55]

At the empirical level, time is an important factor in providing support for the assumption that states can shift on a continuum of identity and interests. As stated in regard to neofunctionalism, it is the experience over time of the benefits of redefining interests in terms which respect the interests of others, which is critical to the shift of loyalties, the reconstruction of identity. More is involved in the experience of cooperation than the passage of time, however. We know intuitively that the theory of the Franco–German relationship is based on something more than its age; war between China and Russia is not so 'unthinkable', though its non-occurrence is of similar duration. States which have cooperated across a wide range of intersecting areas over a long period are constrained by the consequence of their choices and the integration of their interests. The same structural indicators which allow us to predict the likelihood of war between states in a conflictual association permit us to judge its 'unthinkability' in an integrated security community. To the extent that the cooperative relationship is institutionalized and the change of identity is reflected not just at the level of state leadership, but at the level of domestic or national identity also, we can have confidence that cooperation is based upon a more secure foundation than the calculation of immediate costs and benefits to each state.[56]

Assuming the malleability of state identity and interests, against neorealism, some evidence can be advanced in support of the idea that the European Union is more than a collection of cooperating states, by looking at the choices made in situations of conflicting interests. It suggests that the degree of enmeshment, or process of state socialization, was a significant factor in influencing state decisions at key junctures.

Germany perceived its interests and chose to define its identity in terms of integration within a security community, while Britain chose to define itself as a marginal European and to emphasize its transatlantic and Commonwealth links in opposition to integration. This marks the historic choice at the origin of the Community in 1951, and continues to structure their different relationship with the Community at the end of the 1990s. Like many other countries in Europe after World War II, they both faced the same problem which individuals and collectivities routinely address at critical junctures in their lives, but which now posed itself with unprecedented starkness: who are we?

Who are the Germans? The question they addressed in the immediate aftermath of the war continues to arouse debate at every level of German society today and in the societies of its European neighbours. It was essential for the legitimacy of Adenauer's post-war foreign policy that a formal, speedy resolution of the question be adopted. But the identity of a society committed to cooperation and integration with its democratic neighbours was not there for Adenauer or anyone else to *discover*. History had provided different packages from which to select an answer – the Germany of Kant, Nietzsche, Marx or Herder offered a range of options, a variety of recipes from which Adenauer and the German people could select appropriate ingredients.

This choice was not, and could not be, made in a vacuum of external pressures and competing domestic interests. While these factors limited the freedom of choice, they did not determine it. Both at that time, and increasingly throughout the post-war period, Germans struggled to find adequate and credible expression of the cooperative democracy which they chose, and to distance themselves from other options which history offered as candidates. In particular, their choice of self-containment within a West European identity was a voluntary strategy to limit their freedom to choose, in the future, the Germany of Nazism and the Holocaust.[57]

In opting to subordinate the various nationalist identity-kits in favour of a European Germany, Adenauer and his successors were not abandoning national interest in a spirit of self-sacrifice for the good of others. They were choosing, from an array of competing German interests, that self-interest which served a new identity, repudiated the romantic nationalism of their past, and which converged with the interest of European integration. The choice of an integrationist foreign policy was, in effect, a choice of a cooperative rather than a self-help identity. Were they in the future to choose, under the pressure of foreign stereotypes or native nostalgia, to re-identify themselves with past romanticism, a quite different set of policies would emerge to mark their new interests.

The core issue leading to the Monnet/Schuman proposal for the reconstruction of Europe was the Franco–German relationship. How to transform this conflictual association into a security community was the problem answered by both states in terms of integration. Coal and steel were the critical instruments of war, and as such they were the obvious choice for the limited economic integration which the European Coal and Steel Community achieved.

French concerns in the reconstruction of Europe were centred on what was conceived as the overriding national interest at the end of World War II: the problem of containing Germany in a manner which would guarantee French security and recreate a French identity – shattered by the war – as a major power in Europe. Perhaps for longer than in Britain, the state in France has pursued a national vision of itself at odds with its achievements, which today takes on the pathos of a nation in decline from past grandeur. The history of French participation in the European Community, from de Gaulle's cunning in seizing the opportunities of Britain's self-imposed exclusion, to his successors' management of the Franco–German

Alliance, manifests the significance of this vision of itself and the manner in which French interests were made to converge with those of its major partner.[58]

In Britain, the historic choice made in the early post-war years was similarly conditioned by the pressures of interests and identity, though the outcome was quite different. Britain chose to distance itself from the Community because other economic and strategic interests coincided with the demands of post-war identity articulated by policymakers in successive governments during the 1950s.[59] While, again, one cannot separate out the material self-interest from the moral choice in respect of identity, the British case sharpens the focus on identity even more than the German. The idea that Britain was in Europe, but not of it, and must disentangle itself from the legacy of wartime involvement with the European allies in order to reassert its role as a major world power, proved a powerful motive for rejecting the Schuman Plan for European integration. Arguably, the case for short-term material self-interest should have led Britain in 1952 to the same decision made in 1961, when application was finally made for membership of the Community. But this appeared to the political leadership of the time to entail the surrender of a centuries-old tradition of imperialism and independence to the uncertain benefits of integration with the 'lesser' states of Europe.

An interesting case study is presented in David Cameron's examination of the response of France and Britain to the 1992 crisis of the Exchange Rate Mechanism.[60] The attempt to predict the response of Britain and France to the crisis fails the test of evidence if we approach it from the domestic politics perspective of Moravcsik. One would expect that French domestic interests, were they paramount in the government's decision, would have driven France out of the ERM, while British interests would have ensured that Britain remained in. That the opposite actually happened poses a problem for liberal intergovernmentalism. It allows Cameron to claim that it was long interaction within the regime of the ERM and within the Franco–German Alliance which determined the position of the French government against domestic interests, while the absence of such a history of 'shared norms, convergent preferences and cooperation' influenced Britain's departure from the regime.[61]

One can also cite the actions of the Chirac government in pressing for tighter monetary controls against the widespread protests of most of the voting public in France in November/December 1995 as another case in point. Like Mitterrand and John Major in 1992, Chirac's behaviour was more in line with the neofunctionalist than the intergovernmentalist model. Faced with the threat of failing to meet the Maastricht criteria for monetary union and the consequent damage to long-term French interests in European integration, the Chirac government resisted domestic pressure to maintain the level of public expenditure, opting instead for maintaining France's partnership with Germany as the motor of integration. With the evidence of the Maastricht referendum providing a domestic warning of growing apathy towards the EU and record levels of his unpopularity in the French polls to guide him, Chirac would be expected to be sensitive to French domestic interests and, if we follow Moravcsik, to express these interests in relation to the EU. Such a course should have led to the hardening of French attitudes consistent with the Chirac pragmatism towards the EU on which he had campaigned during the presidential election. Yet, within 12 months as president, Chirac had become the new Mitterrand in respect of the EU, leading *Le Monde* to compare him with Monnet and Schuman as a future prophet of a Europe of shared sovereignties.[62]

These examples run counter to the predictions of the general theory of intergovernmentalism, which rests on unexplained properties of the state as principal actor, deriving from untested assumptions about the international order. They are consistent with a sociological view which allows a causal influence to the process of intergovernmental interaction, and human agency. They emphasize the point that the enmeshing of identities and interests in an integrated community facilitates state choice as well as constrains it. How spillover functions, and whether it is sustained, developed, or abandoned, depends upon what states make of it.

What states make of it as international actors – the identity they choose in respect of interstate cooperation – depends in turn on the *domestic* process of identity-formation. The neglect of this arena of identity construction was revealed particularly in the post-Maastricht period, manifesting the gap between the identity of states and the identity of their populations. In Denmark and France, in particular, and to a lesser extent reflected in the trend in other countries, the neofunctionalist policy of managing the enmeshment process in respect of elites only failed the test of the popular referendum.[63] This serious weakness in the structuring of the relationship which constitutes the Community is revealed in the gap between the identity of the state as actor in the external forum and the state as a structure *vis-à-vis* the society. The reconstructed identity of the French, German, Danish or Swedish state-as-actor is displayed in the co-ordination reflex which upgrades their interests in the Community, while – hidden until the critical test of the referendum – their human agents sustain a self-image with a different policy outcome.

Integration of sovereign states into a security community requires the reconstruction and management of the two dimensions of identity – the societal and the state – into a self-image compatible with the level and pace of cooperation being pursued. The sharp lesson delivered to state leaderships in the post-Maastricht period – that neofunctionalists got it wrong, and that identity needs to be built from below – should not be misinterpreted. It is true that 'the legitimacy of moves towards closer integration cannot be imposed from above but has to be built up from below'.[64] But there are two dimensions of identity, and governments are the principal agents of both. If public loyalties and allegiance are to shift towards the Community, they will do so only under the constructive management of powerful agents – if not the government, then other interests of party, media or business. Whichever agency influences the outcome, it is still a moral choice, not a structural or mechanical inevitability, which determines who we are and whether our own best interests are defined in terms of community or self.

Notes

1. I use the term 'Community' as a general expression of the European Union (EU) throughout its history, employing strictly accurate labels only when the context necessitates it.
2. Both cited in Harold Macmillan, *Tides of Fortune, 1945–1955* (London: Macmillan, 1969), p. 151 and Appendix 1.
3. Alan Milward, *The Reconstruction of Western Europe 1945–1951* (London: Methuen, 1984), pp. 492/3. See also his *The European Rescue of the Nation-State* (London: Routledge, 1992), Ch. 6. Desmond Dinan, in his otherwise excellent historical analysis, *Ever Closer Union? An Introduction to the European Community* (London: Macmillan Press, 1994), p. 10, similarly opposes 'narrowly defined national interest' to 'international altruism'.
4. Deutsch Karl *et al.*, *Political Community and the North Atlantic Area* (Westport: Greenwood Press, 1955), p. 5.
5. The Treaty of Paris, which established the European Coal and Steel Community, was signed on 18 April 1951.
6. It has since become an aphorism of *realpolitik* that states do not have friends, they only have interests.
7. Alan Milward, (1984), *op. cit.*
8. Ernst Hass, 'The study of regional integration: reflections on the joy and anguish of pretheorizing' in L. Lindberg and S. Scheingold (eds) *Regional Integration: Theory and Research* (Cambridge, MA: Harvard University Press, 1971), p. 4
9. For discussion of the Northern Ireland case, see Bill McSweeney, 'Security, identity and the peace process in Northern Ireland', *Security Dialogue*, 27/2, 1996, pp. 167–78.
10. The principal texts of the neofunctionalist school include Ernst Hass, *The Uniting of Europe: Political, Social, and Economic Forces* (Stanford: Stanford University Press, 1958); L.N. Lindberg, *The Political Dynamics of*

European Economic Integration (Stanford: Stanford University Press, 1963).

11. Ernst Haas, 'International integration: the European and the universal process', in *International Organization*, XV, 1961, p. 368.

12. Lindberg, (1963), *op. cit.*, p. 10.

13. Ernst Haas, (1958), p. 16.

14. P.C. Schmitter, 'Three neofunctionalist hypotheses about international integration', *International Organization*, 23, 1969, p. 162ff.

15. Haas, (1958), *op. cit.*; Lindberg, (1963), *op. cit.*

16. Ernst Haas, 'The uniting of Europe and the uniting of Latin America', *Journal of Common Market Studies*, 5/4, 1967, p. 324/5.

17. Stanley Hoffman 'Obstinate or obsolete? The fate of the nation-state and the case of Western Europe', *Daedelus*, No. 95, 1966, pp. 862–915.

18. Hass, (1967), *op. cit.*, p. 325.

19. Hass, (1967), *op. cit*, p. 328.

20. Hass, (1967), *op. cit*, p. 331.

21. Hass, (1967), *op. cit*, p. 315.

22. Carole Webb 'Theoretical perspectives & problems' in Wallace H., Wallace W. and Webb C. (eds), *Policy-making in the European Community*, 2nd edition (Chichester: Wiley, 1983), pp. 1–42.

23. Stanley Hoffman 'The European process at Atlantic crosspurposes', *Journal of Common Market Studies*, 3, 1964/5 pp. 87–91, and Hoffman, (1966), *op. cit.*

24. Robert O. Keohane and Stanley Hoffman 'Conclusions: community politics and institutional change' in William Wallace (ed.), *The Dynamics of European Integration* (London: Pinter, 1990), p. 284.

25. Ernst Hass, 'Turbulent fields and the theory of regional integration' in *International Organization*, 30, 1976, p. 203/4.

26. William Wallace, 'Less than a federation, more than a regime: the Community and the nation-state', in Wallace, Wallace and Webb, (1983), *op. cit.*; Donald Puchala 'Domestic politics and regional harmonization in the European Communities', *World Politics*, 1975, pp. 496–520.

27. Wayne Sandholtz and John Zysman, '1992: Recasting the European bargain', *World Politics*, 42/1, 1989, pp. 1–30.

28. Sandholtz and Zysman, (1989), *op. cit.*, p. 100.

29. Sandholtz and Zysman, (1989), *op. cit.*, p. 108.

30. Stanley Hoffman, 'The European Community and 1992', *Foreign Affairs*, 68, 1989, pp. 27–47.

31. Robert O. Keohane and Stanley Hoffman 'Conclusions: community politics and institutional change' in Wallace (1990), *op. cit.*, p. 289.

32. Keohane and Hoffman (1990), *op. cit.*, p. 284. The view that 'what we observe leading directly' to an act of integration lends it priority over non-observable factors comes strange from authors who complain of the theoretical poverty of other accounts of integration in the same volume.

33. Andrew Moravcsik, 'Negotiating the Single European Act', in Robert O. Keohane and Stanley Hoffman (eds), *The New European Community* (Boulder: Westview Press, 1991), p. 75.

34. Moravcsik, (1991), *op. cit.*, p. 75.

35. Andrew Moravcsik, 'Preferences and power in the European Community: a liberal intergovernmentalist approach', *Journal of Common Market Studies*, 31/4, 1993, p. 483.
36. Moravcsik, (1991), *op. cit.*, pp. 75, 67.
37. Moravcsic, (1993), *op. cit.*, pp. 480/481, emphasis added.
38. Moravcsic, (1993), *op. cit.*, p. 507ff.
39. Moravcsic, (1993), *op. cit.*, p. 507.
40. Moravcsic, (1993), *op. cit.* – see text to note 34.
41. Wayne Sandholtz, 'Choosing Union: monetary politics and Maastricht', *International Organization*, 47, 1993, pp. 1–39.
42. Sandholtz, (1993), *op. cit.*, p. 3.
43. Keohane and Hoffman, (1990), *op. cit.*, p. 284.
44. Moravcsik (1993), *op. cit.*, p. 496.
45. Moravcsik (1993), *op. cit.*, p. 483.
46. Haas, (1958), *op. cit.*, p. 17.
47. Moravcsik, (1993), *op. cit.*, pp. 507ff; and (1991) *op. cit.*, p. 75.
48. The attribution of agency to collective entities is problematic. Agency properly belongs only to individuals. Collective actors may be treated as 'agents', however, in respect of the properties of individual actors representing them.
49. For more detailed discussion of agency, identity and security see Bill McSweeney, *Security and Identity in International Relations Theory*, forthcoming, n.d., Chs 6 and 7.
50. See Paul Taylor, 'Supranationalism' in A.J.R. Groom and Paul Taylor (eds), *Frameworks for International Cooperation* (London: Pinter, 1990). In the same volume, Harrison speaks of integration by stealth – 'incremental, concrete, economic achievements which build up *de facto* "engrenage" or enmeshment of one national political and economic system with another.'
51. Haas, (1958), *op. cit.*, p. 16.
52. Ernest Gellner, *Nations and Nationalism* (Oxford: Blackwell 1983); E.J. Hobsbawm, *Nations & Nationalism since 1780* (Cambridge: Cambridge University Press, 1993); Benedict Anderson, *Imagined Communities: Reflections on the Origins and Spread of Nationalism* (London: Verso Press, 1989).
53. Are concepts to be understood in terms of their operational definition alone? Is time simply what a watch keeps? Is human nature what we observe in human behaviour? For well-known statements of the behaviourist philosophy see Gilbert Ryle, *The Concept of Mind* (London: Hutchinson, 1949) and J.B. Watson, *Psychology from the Standpoint of a Behaviourist* (London: Pinter, 1983).
54. Robert Gilpin, 'The richness of the tradition of political realism', in Robert O. Keohane (ed), *Neo-realism and its Critics* (New York: Columbia University Press, 1986), p. 304
55. For a contemporary Waltzian expression of such realism, see John Mearsheimer, 'The false promise of international institutions', *International Security*, 19/3, 1995, pp. 5–49 and his earlier 'Back to the future: instability in Europe after the Cold War', *International Security*, 15/1, 1990, pp. 5–56.

56. The problem of judging a change of identity in collective actors is only a more complex variant of the same problem in regard to individuals. The weight we give to time and the weight we give to indicators of the structuring, or institutionalization, of interests in the cooperative behaviour of collective actors are a problem no different from that of weighing the indicators of change of identity in interpersonal and family relationships.

57. On German self-containment, see Wolfram Hanrieder, *Germany, America, Europe: 40 Years of German Foreign Policy* (Newhaven: Yale University Press, 1989); Alfred Grosser, *The Western Alliance: European–American Relations Since 1945* (London: Macmillan, 1980); Anne Deighton, *The Impossible Peace: Britain, the Division of Germany & the Origins of the Cold War* (Oxford: Oxford University Press, 1993).

58. Robert Tombs (ed.), *Nationhood & Nationalism in France: from Boulangism to the Great War 1889–1918* (London: HarperCollins, 1991); Rogers Brubaker, *Citizenship & Nationhood in France & Germany* (Cambridge, MA: Harvard University Press, 1992).

59. See Milward, (1984), *op. cit.*; Deighton, (1993), *op. cit.*; Stephen George, *An Awkward Partner: Britain in the European Community* (Oxford: Oxford University Press, 1990); Peter Hennessy, *Never Again: Britain 1945–1951* (London: Jonathan Cape, 1992).

60. David Cameron, 'British exit, German voice, and French loyalty: defection, domination and cooperation in the 1992–93 ERM crisis', European Community Studies Association paper, Washington, May 1993.

61. Cameron, (1993), *op. cit.*, p. 61.

62. Cited in *The Economist*, 11 May 1996.

63. There were other factors involved in the decline of support for the EU in 1992, not least the collapse of communism, which had provided a significant cement to the solidarity of the Community throughout its history.

64. Leader, *The Guardian*, 20 February 1997.

Part III
Moral Challenges in Negotiating an Ever Closer Union

5 The Compatibility of EU Membership with Neutrality
Walter Carlsnaes

INTRODUCTION

A foreign policy such as neutrality can be analyzed in at least two ways: as a *doctrine* underlying and justifying the pursuit of a particular kind of foreign policy; or with reference to the *substance* of interstate political actions in real time and space. Quite obviously it makes a significant difference which of these approaches one chooses, since the former refers to a cognitive realm populated exclusively by logical entities – what Karl Popper called the world of ideas to distinguish it from both the inanimate and psychological worlds – whereas the latter focuses on an empirical and dynamic reality containing actors, structures *and* ideas.

Neutrality has far too often been treated exclusively as a doctrine, which has tended to make discussions of it arid and, surprisingly often, without any real relevance to the actual world of international relations. I here speak from personal experience, since discussions of Swedish foreign policy were for many years one of the more somnolent topics in the Swedish press, in research reports and in parliamentary debate. Raising it in polite dinner conversation was sure to stamp you forever as an utter bore. And the reason for this was that it was almost invariably discussed as a doctrine, and a very sanctified and untouchable one at that, with the mandarins of the Foreign Office both its high priests and theologians. What was happening outside our borders, and our responses to this, seemed to have little to do with this doctrine, the main tenet of which was doctrinal consistency with the established canon. And I think this has to a large degree been the same in the other Euro-neutrals – Finland, Austria and Switzerland – although here I speak with less authority.

Thus it will come as no surprise to you that I will here forego the dubious pleasures of the doctrinal approach. Instead I will focus on neutrality as foreign policy in action – as something political and hence more than just a logically self-contained body of ideas. In short, I want to discuss the topic in 'high politics' terms, since my assumption is that all foreign policy worth its salt is part of the world of power in some sense or other.

Furthermore, the purpose of this article is not to assess the compatibility of neutrality with EU membership in any general or abstract sense, but rather to focus on the particular variants of neutrality of the Euro-neutrals and to discuss and to assess the compatibility of these with membership. This will entail a concentration on past policies rather than on future possibilities, as well as a total avoidance of its juridical aspects as expressed in the rights and obligations of neutral states during war as stipulated in the Hague Conventions of 1907. What I will thus focus on are the peacetime policies of these states after the Second World War, usually but not accurately denoted by the term 'neutrality', which strictly speaking should be reserved only for wartime conditions.

THE POLITICS OF POST-WAR NEUTRALITY

A conceptual starting point

Although the notion of power is both ubiquitous in the literature and frequently contested as an essential tool for understanding interstate relations, this is not the proper place to enter into an extensive discussion of its analytic merits in the study of foreign policy. Instead, I shall forthwith accept Felix Oppenheim's assumption that 'this notion is indispensable for political analysis, not only in its own right but also ... because it belongs to a network of other key notions such as influence, deterrence, coercion, punishment, authority, legitimacy, and also unfreedom and freedom'.[1] The trademark of the contemporary conception of power is the notion of causality, in contrast to the traditional view of power – stretching from Niccolò Machiavelli to Hans Morgenthau – postulated as an innate or acquired property of the power holder. David A. Baldwin has epitomized this contemporary conception in his assertion that when discussing power 'it is essential to specify or at least imply who is influencing whom with respect to what; in short, both scope and domain must be specified or implied'.[2] Following Harold and Margaret Sprout, Baldwin has also referred to this necessary specification of the causal parameters of power in terms of the broader notion of a 'policy–contingency framework', signifying the essentially contextual nature of all social manifestations of power.[3]

However, given the complex nature of the notion of power, the concept is in need of at least one further step of elaboration before it can be utilized for our specific purposes. The immediate question here is the following: what type of power relationship is implied when speaking of neutrality? Following the main outline of Oppenheim's discussion of the inclusive concept of social power, it is here suggested that pursuing a policy of neutrality is an instance of *exercising influence* in international relations rather than exerting power in a more straightforward manner.

Although the purpose of this chapter is not to argue for or against the merits of neutrality, or to engage in policy recommendations of any far-reaching kind, I will nevertheless end with a brief conclusion of a *normative* nature, namely, that a certain type of neutrality is not only compatible with membership of the European Union, but also that it may in fact benefit both the EU and Europe as a whole.

Furthermore, before applying the conceptual logic of the above discussion to an analysis of contemporary neutrality, two additional concepts need to be clarified as well, since they refer more specifically to how power relationships are constitutive of international relations. These are the notions of 'sovereignty' and 'autonomy', perhaps the two most crucial terms in the conceptual repertoire of International Relations as a discipline. To define these concepts and hence to clarify the distinction between the two is, as William Wallace has pointed out, 'not a straight-forward task: economists, lawyers, politicians and political scientists all have their own preferred definitions'.[4] However, he then cites a set of definitions – appropriated from Fred Hirsch – which he finds useful in this connection: '*Formal sovereignty* concerns legal rights. *Effective sovereignty* concerns the practical power to exercise those rights. *Autonomy* concerns the results achieved by their exercise'.[5] A similar distinction is to be found in Richard N. Cooper's conception of sovereignty as 'the formal ability of a nation to act on its own rather than under the instruction of another nation', in contrast to national autonomy, which 'is the ability of a nation to attain its objectives through unilateral action'.[6] Thus whereas the sovereignty of a state – or aspects of it – can be specified in an either/or sense, autonomy refers to the ability of a state to achieve the objectives that it has set for itself within a given issue area, and is as such a highly relative and dynamic notion. As noted above, this follows from the view that sovereignty concerns the power *to* exercise rights, while autonomy pertains to the effects *of* this exercise. Thus, while both concepts refer to a power relationship, the former implicates power in the formal sense of *rights* (which a state has or has not been able to appropriate), whereas the latter does this in terms of *causality* – the 'production of intended effects', to cite Bertrand Russell's classic and felicitous definition of power.[7]

The conceptual logic of the above discussion can be illustrated by means of three simple figures (Figure 5.1) intended to represent

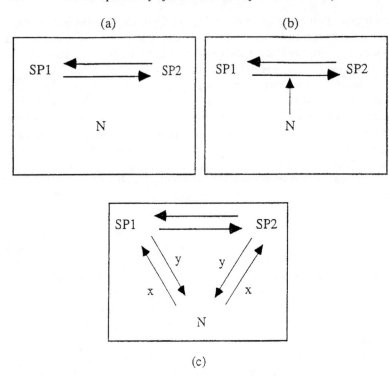

Figure 5.1   Three types of peacetime policies of neutrality

(i) peacetime relationships among three actors in a (ii) bipolar international system of the post-World War II kind, two of which are involved
in a bipolar power relationship with each other (the two superpowers SP1
and SP2), while the third (the neutral actor N) is neither aligned to, nor in
conflict with, the other two.

Figure 5.1(a) represents the case of a non-aligned state whose policy it
is to remain neutral in the 'pure' meaning of not in any politically
significant sense partaking in international power relations *per se*, either
vis-à-vis specific actors or within the system as a whole. The rationality
underlying this type of policy is essentially premised on a strategy of
defensive neutrality, of not basing national security on the calculation of
exogenous behaviour but, instead, aspiring to be defensively as self-
sufficient as possible in this respect. In an exclusionary system of this kind
no external power is exercised, hence the lack of any causal arrows of
influence *from* N. As I shall argue below, the contemporary practice of

Swiss neutrality conforms to the logic of this model of foreign policy aloofness.

Figure 5.1(b) represents an instance of a non-aligned state attempting to affect the external conditions of her neutrality – and international relations more broadly – by trying to exercise influence on the conditions determining the interaction patterns of these bipolar actors, and hence the structural aspects of the international system itself. Using a term from Jon Elster's discussion of rationality, this can be called a *parametric* policy of neutrality, a view equating the pursuit of national security with the pursuit of conditions favouring peace, that is, with a policy aimed at maintaining or changing the given structural and operational principles of the larger regional or world system in order to lessen international tension and hence, ultimately, to prevent war.[8] If we disregard the very special origins of both *Austrian* and *Finnish* neutrality, I will argue below that their practice has conformed closely to the logic exemplified in this model.

In contrast to a parametric policy, Figure 5.1(c) illustrates a quintessentially *strategic* approach to international relations.[9] From the point of view of a state pursuing a neutral foreign policy (N), the purpose of x in each instance is to influence both SP1 and SP2 to do y, that is, to refrain from violating state N's neutrality in the event of war. Its function is to indicate that not only must we in this connection think in terms of a power relationship between the neutral state and *both* of the superpowers *at the same time*, but that *two* types of interaction patterns are involved in each such reciprocal, asymmetrical relationship. *Sweden*, in my view, has uniquely exemplified this form of neutrality in practice.

Neutrality in practice

Switzerland: the politics of defensive neutrality

Switzerland's policy of neutrality is unarguably the oldest of the four considered here, and also the easiest to characterize in formal terms. Its roots go back at least to the sixteenth century, and since the Congress of Vienna Switzerland has been guaranteed – at her own request – the status of a 'perpetual' or 'permanent neutral' state, a status (?) which was diplomatically reaffirmed in the Peace Treaties following World War I, now also elaborated with reference to the juridical terms of the Hague Conventions of 1907. It has always been restrictively interpreted by the Swiss, who have given it a doctrinaire rigour which – as we shall see below – is absent from the other types of neutrality in post-war Europe. In the words of one commentator, speaking of his own country, the 'Swiss are neutrality perfectionists'.[10]

One result of this rigorously conceived nature of her policy is that Switzerland joined the League of Nations only after receiving confirmation on the continued validity of the guarantees received in 1815, as well as a special exemption from taking part in military actions (though not from participation in economic and financial sanctions). Due, in part, to her negative experiences as a member of the League (she left it in 1938), Switzerland did not join the United Nations after the Second World War; and as late as in 1986, the Swiss people rejected – by a vote of 75 per cent, with all cantons voting against – a proposal to seek such membership. Although the Swiss did vote to join the International Monetary Fund (IMF) in 1992, later the same year the country rejected seeking membership of the European Economic Area (EEA). This, at least for the time being, has put a stop to any plans of joining the other Euro-neutrals in the European Union.

It is always possible to give up even a policy strictly adhered to once it becomes sufficiently obvious that it is politically no longer in a country's interest to stick to it. However, in the Swiss case it is not in the first place the doctrinaire nature of her neutrality *qua* foreign policy which has made membership impossible, but rather the deep-rooted domestic embeddedness of this doctrine. As Clive Church notes, 'it has been claimed that, save perhaps in wartime, the Swiss have no foreign policy, only a domestic policy'.[11] The fact is that the domestic setting of Swiss politics is fundamentally different not only from that of the other Euro-neutrals, but also from that of all the other members – small and large – of the European Union. This is, I would argue, one of the major consequences of pursuing a foreign policy of defensive neutrality as adamantly as Switzerland has done for so long: being a consistently inward-looking and exclusionary policy, it has *ipso facto* become a policy which forms and sustains the political culture and identity of a state. This has been the case in particular after the Second World War, the period with which we are mainly concerned here.

Church identifies seven major reasons why Swiss neutrality is so fundamental to her domestic politics: historically it has solved internal conflicts, pacifying and integrating the very diverse cantons and peoples of Switzerland; it has provided a shield behind which the Swiss have been able to establish their own particular form of democracy, involving a unique combination of federalism and the active use of a local plebiscitary system; it has become essential to the definition of her political culture and national identity, particularly as a result of her wartime experiences, when she was forced to rely wholly on her own resources; it underwrites the cohesive effects of the Swiss army – the socializing rope, it is said, which holds Switzerland together; it provides the internal order which has been necessary for the particular Swiss contribution to Europe, in both the nineteenth and twentieth centuries; it helps to justify Swiss economic advantages, both in her role as a major banking and trading nation but also by distinguishing clearly between political and economic neutrality and totally rejecting the latter; and, finally and more broadly, it effectively symbolizes Swiss national interests, defined in terms of its role in defending independence, internal equilibrium and prosperity.[12] Both individually and collectively, these factors have not only proved a formidable constraint on Swiss foreign policy, but have also contributed to an un-usually weak foreign policy ministry and elite. 'Indeed,' Church writes laconically, 'many Swiss have often questioned the need for such a policy, and see little reason why the Minister of Foreign Affairs should travel abroad.'[13] In other words, precisely because of its crucial role in domestic politics, Swiss neutrality has had a very delimiting or constraining effect on her international relations. This, as we shall see below, is in glaring contrast to the other Euro-neutrals, for which neutrality has foremost been a characteristic of, and dynamic force behind, their foreign relations rather than their domestic politics.

In view of this extreme domesticity of her neutrality, it is thus not difficult to understand why the Swiss continue to find it so difficult to conceive of changing their relations with Europe, as exemplified in the 1992 vote against even joining a very unpolitical European Economic Area: it would mean not only a change in how she conducts her foreign policy, but, exceedingly more important, also of the whole Swiss domestic structure and its socio-political dynamics and underlying rationale.

Finland and Austria: a parametric policy of neutrality

Although Austrian and Finnish neutrality are rarely treated together, I will do so here, and this essentially for three reasons: both came into exist-ence after the Second World War and at about the same time; both were tied formally to superpower agreements in some form or other; and, most importantly here, and as I shall argue below, as foreign policies in action they both conform closely to my second model above, that is, to an essentially parametric type of neutrality.

As noted by Harto Hakovirta in his important study of European neutrality, the 'establishment of Austrian neutrality in 1955 and Finland's transition from a relatively passive policy of non-involvement to an open policy of neutrality in 1955–6 constituted what has been the most dramatic expansion and diversification of post-war European neutrality'.[14] Let us briefly look at how each was established before considering their similarities and in what sense they can be said to exemplify a similar form of foreign policy practice.

In the *Austrian* case, her neutrality was the result of three major developments during the early post-war period: the Austrians themselves, through her two major parties, the Christian Democrats and the Socialists, were open to the possibility – and perhaps even desirability – of such a foreign policy reorientation once full independence had been re-established; the Soviet Union's sudden willingness to decouple the German question from Austria's future status on condition that she acquiesced to a Swiss type of permanent neutrality; and the acceptance by the three other Allied powers of the agreement reached between Austria and the Soviet Union in May 1955.[15] The State Treaty signed at this time does not, however, contain any provisions with regard to neutrality, since the Austrians wanted to avoid creating the impression that the country had been neutralized, that is, that neutrality had been imposed by the four Great Powers. Instead, on the very first day of being fully restored as a sovereign state the Austrian National Council, the Lower House of Parliament, enacted a constitutional amendment to the effect that Austria of her own free will declares herself permanently neutral.[16] Although this means that she is not free to modify or abandon her neutrality at will but must abide by the rules governing neutrality as stipulated in the Hague Conventions, it also means that, on the level of public international law, permanent neutrality was not imposed upon her. It was a political choice which she made – the price, so to speak, of escaping the fate of Germany, that is, continued occupation and partition.[17] Subsequently it has become obvious that, from the point of view of the Austrians themselves, as measured by means of opinion polls over the years, this was a price very well worth paying.

Finland's neutrality is perhaps the most difficult of all four to pin down, since it has neither an historical pedigree nor was it established with the flourish of a signature or two. Rather, as Hakovirta notes in the passage cited above, it came into being through a transitional process, the starting point of which is the Finnish–Soviet treaty of 1948, in which, paradoxically, Finland bound herself to limited military cooperation with the Soviets. However, the conditions under which she did so were very special, as were the circumstances under which she would engage in such cooperation (essentially in the unlikely event of German aggression). This was not regarded by either party as constituting any form of alliance, and the treaty itself explicitly prohibited any form of alignment with the Western powers. Finland has also always emphasized that the preamble to the treaty recognizes the Finnish desire to remain outside Great Power conflicts. As a consequence, as noted by Hakovirta, 'For Finland itself, the compatibility of the treaty with its policy of neutrality is ... a doctrinal truth'.[18] However, both J.K. Paasikivi (the first post-war president) and the Soviet Union refrained from using the word 'neutrality' to characterize Finnish foreign policy during the early Cold War years; this did not come about until Urho Kekkonen succeeded Paasikivi and Stalin's heirs had initiated less conflictual relations with the West.

Both Austria and Finland experienced some choppy waters during the early days of their neutrality. However, they both succeeded in navigating through them more or less unscathed, as a result strengthening the general acceptance of them as *bona fide* neutral European states. Hakovirta has characterized these developments as follows:

> Both Austria and Finland thus passed their tests, and by the mid-1960s the expanded and more diversified constellation of European neutrality was an irreversible fact, though in the Finnish case there was still widespread doubt about the adequacy of the label of neutrality. While it is obvious that the early Austrian and Finnish difficulties largely resulted from aggravated East–West tensions, their positions have not been similarly challenged within the context of the 'new Cold War' of the 1980s. In other words, once a state's neutrality has gone through an initial test-phase, its sensitivity to variations in East–West tensions decreases.[19]

It is also after this point – the mid-1960s – that these two states come into their own as international bridge-builders between the East and the West.

With regard to Austria Neuhold thus notes that 'as a newcomer to the exclusive club of the European neutrals, Austria felt it had to be particularly active in order to shape a specific 'neutrality profile', and that 'Austria can point to a rather impressive record in this respect in the East–West context. Its main contributions have consisted of good offices through the hosting of negotiations between East and West and of humanitarian service.'[20] He here points in particular to Austria's hosting of the SALT negotiations (together with Finland), her activities with regard to the Conference on Security and Cooperation in Europe (CSCE) – once again together with Finland – and the use of the Austrian capital as the venue for two US–Soviet summits: between Kennedy and Khrushchev in

1961 and Carter and Brezhnev in 1979 (when the latter two also signed the SALT II agreements).

Similarly, Hakovirta writes that 'Bridge-building ambitions played a particularly important role in Finnish policy in the 1960s. The idea that Finland's geographical location and history could make it a bridge-builder between East and West was first suggested by President Kekkonen in 1961. Towards the end of the 1960s, the idea had become one of the leading themes in the Finnish policy of neutrality and peace.'[21] In 1963, the Finnish president thus proposed a nuclear-free zone in Northern Europe, and was active in supporting the convening of a security conference in Europe, a policy which culminated in the signing of the Final Act of the CSCE in Helsinki in 1975. As we have seen above, Finland was also very active with respect to the SALT discussions.

These policies of active neutrality are distinct from those pursued by the other two Euro-neutrals. As noted by Hakovirta, 'Swedish, Swiss and Irish foreign policy bridge-building has never figured as a topical issue'.[22] This is also why, in my view, they should be clearly demarcated *qua* foreign policies from those of the latter two. In the case of Switzerland, such a demarcation is certainly not difficult to justify, given the extremely inward-oriented nature of her neutrality. In the case of Sweden, as I shall argue below, neutrality serves a different and essentially strategic purpose as a single-minded *security* policy, and should hence not be confused or conflated with her generally active policies on a number of other international arenas. In the Finnish and Austrian cases the roots of neutrality – a policy in neither case freely chosen but accepted under severe constraints not of their own provision – were historically less glorious and hence not the stuff which forms and sustains strong feelings of national self-identity on the international arena. Such identity could, however, be provided by adding an activist content to neutrality in the form of attempting to play a variety of intermediary roles in the management and amelioration of great-power conflicts. In so doing this practice of neutrality is designed not only to 'render the rather exceptional status of these countries more attractive in the eyes of other states', but is of course also intended to benefit the neutral countries themselves by reducing international tensions and increasing their own freedom of action.[23] It is for these reasons that I have characterized the neutrality of both of these states in terms of their *parametric* nature: as attempts to ameliorate superpower tensions and thus contribute actively to an international situation more amenable to the interests also of small European states. A policy of neutrality of this kind therefore does not aim to increase the foreign policy *autonomy* of the state concerned, but rather to secure her interest as a sovereign state by means of inviting the superpowers to avail themselves of their good offices in reducing international conflict. In short, rather than trying to influence the superpowers directly (as I will argue is the case with Sweden), the attempt here is to influence the relations between the superpowers by helping to shape the arena for their interaction. As Hakovirta notes, they do this 'for a mixture of reasons, notably to safeguard their own security, to display international solidarity, and to accumulate new resources for their policies of neutrality'.[24] This being the case, these types of neutrals did not – as is the case with both Switzerland and Sweden – invest heavily in military defence, since their foreign policies are not in the first hand based on exerting power in such terms. Their security policies have, on the whole, been based on the international agreements and guarantees regulating their status as permanent neutrals, whereas their foreign policy has been to use their neutral status as a means for playing a constructive role in improving the parameters of international life.

With regard to membership in the European Community, these two neutrals had one important factor in common, namely, their long-standing beholdenness to the Soviet Union's view on this question. However, they differed substantially on how far they were willing to incur the displeasure of this superpower. The Finns, given their geostrategic position as well as much closer economic and political links with the Soviet Union, were far more circumspect than the Austrians, who already in the 1960s strove to obtain an agreement with the EEC. This *Alleingang* was for various reasons not successful (due only in part to Soviet hostility), and it was not until July 1989 that Austria presented her request for membership to the EC. This application made it very clear that she intended to retain her status as a permanent neutral as codified in the Federal Constitutional Law of 1955. The Soviet reaction at this time was surprisingly low-key, however, and was subsequently not a decisive factor in Austria's accession to full membership, primarily because of the former's step-by-step dissolution during this period.

In the agreement between Austria and the EU the former fully accepted all the rights and obligations attaching to the Union and its institutional framework (the *acquis communautaire*) as it applied to the then current members of the EU. This included full acceptance of, and active participation in, the Common Foreign and Security Policy (CFSP) of the Maastricht Treaty. In practice this has meant that Austria, as well as the other new members, did not have to promise more than the 12 original members of the EU were obliged to do with respect to CFSP.

Due to her extreme sensitivity to Soviet reactions, Finland's desire for membership was very slow in germinating, but once the possibility presented itself – in the vacuum created by the Soviet Union's demise – it took only ten months for her to reach a decision. This is in glaring contrast to her earlier remarkably weak record in integrative relations with Europe: formally she became a full member of EFTA only in 1986, and of the Council of Europe as late as 1989. She, too, accepted EU membership in its entirety, and seems to have done so with fewer regrets than either Austria or Sweden, since at this point Finland clearly had the most to lose by remaining outside the Union.

Sweden: the policy of strategic neutrality

Swedish neutrality goes back to the early nineteenth century, but contrary to popular belief (and, at times, the officially purveyed image of Swedish foreign affairs as well), it has led a surprisingly chequered life during this long time-span. I will here not go into this history, however, except to note that the tragic fate of all other neutrals except Switzerland during the early part of World War II shook Sweden to her roots, leading to a radical reconsideration of her own policy once the war was over. As a consequence, the policy of neutrality practised since then is essentially a post-1945 phenomenon, differing in all but name from the preceding forms of Swedish neutrality stretching back to the Congress of Vienna.

The rationale underlying the practice of post-war Swedish neutrality has an ancient and eminent pedigree, expressed most memorably in Ulysses' pre-emptive command to his crew, when faced with the fatal seductiveness of the Sirens' song, that 'you must bind me hard and fast, so that I cannot stir from the spot where you will stand me ... and if I beg you to release me, you must tighten and add to my bonds'.[25] Elster has referred to the type of behaviour exemplified here in terms of the logic of precommitment, which essentially is a strategy of *a priori* excluding the feasibility of certain options (usually attractive) in order to achieve a desired future state of affairs.[26] Binding oneself – or forcing oneself to be bound – in this manner typifies the kind of imperfect but self-enlightened rationality that results from being weak and knowing it, and using this insight to set into motion an exogenous process aimed at limiting the adverse effects on oneself of such a condition. Higher-level preferences are made to override lower-level preferences, thus illustrating (in Elster's view) the innate and unique capacity of human beings to think not only of their immediate gain but also of the longer-term benefits that depend exclusively on the efficacy of indirect strategies.

The main consequences of the Second World War for Swedish foreign policymakers was to accept – indeed, to insist upon – the following two fundamental limitations on the country's freedom of action in the sense discussed here: (1) that 'no commitments ... be made in peacetime that prevent us from fulfilling the obligations of a neutral power under international law in a war between other states'; and (2) that 'in peacetime we must pursue a policy that inspires and sustains the confidence of the rest of the world in our determination and ability to remain a neutral and independent state in wartime'.[27] Closer reflection shows that both of these tenets are based on the logic of precommitment adumbrated above, although in different ways and with different consequences for Swedish foreign policy. The thrust of this claim, as well as the point of distinguishing between the two principles of action posited above, can perhaps best be appreciated if we think of them in terms of, respectively, the concepts of sovereignty and autonomy as previously discussed.

When it is claimed that 'no commitments ... be made in peacetime', this refers to commitments that have the effect of, in Wallace's terms, 'yielding up a portion of [Sweden's] sovereignty to some international authority'. In other words, this refers to that aspect of Swedish neutrality that has involved a strict precommitment not to be swayed by any Siren's song in the form of either international alliances, agreements or guarantees, however appealing they may sound to the ears of a small country left – admittedly by choice – to her own devices on the high seas of world politics. This is not only a very precise and measurable policy but one that also differs from those of the other Euro-neutrals, all of whom – as we have seen above – are in some sense or other signatories to international accords specifying and/or guaranteeing their neutral status in war. However, although Swedish neutrality is not regulated in an international agreement of any kind (and never has been), this self-imposed structural constraint has at the same time contained the explicit implication that this policy – precisely because of this strict interpretation of non-alignment – will lend special force to Sweden's expectation of being treated as a *bona fide* neutral power under international law in the event of warfare beyond her borders.

The second limitation on Swedish freedom of action refers to policy autonomy rather than state sovereignty: the ability of a state to achieve the objectives that it has set for itself within an issue area. In this particular case, this goal is to remain unbeholden to both superpowers during peacetime, with the view of being able to retain her neutral status in the event of a future war in Europe. It is also this latter conception which lies at the very heart of the type of foreign policy discussed here, since the ultimate aim, that is, intended effect, of Swedish foreign policy has been to convince the superpowers not only that Sweden will remain neutral during a conflict between the two, but also that it is in their joint interest that she does so. She has attempted to do this by maintaining that she will allow neither of the superpowers to obtain a Swedish bridgehead against the other, or to violate Swedish sovereignty in some other way that may be construed as detrimental by either. To back up this claim of Swedish neutrality as being a joint strategic good in superpower relations, Sweden built up what she felt was a sufficiently powerful defensive capacity to give not only diplomatic but political credence to such a promise-*cum*-threat.

In contrast to a parametric policy, this is thus a quintessentially *strategic* approach to international relations, as illustrated in Figure 5.1(c) above.[28] In other words, rather than aiming to reduce international tension, this approach focuses exclusively on an actor's pursuit of autonomy. This figure also shows the sense in which one can claim that Swedish neutrality is based on a 'realist' rather than 'idealist' conception of the requirements of autonomy in the international system, namely that neutrality must perforce – if it is to move beyond sovereignty to the exercise of foreign-policy autonomy – be pursued on the basis of one-to-one influence relationships with both of the leading world powers. In other words, the policy of Swedish neutrality has *per se* nothing to do with either remaining 'aloof' or trying to 'improve' the international system by making it more amenable to the interests of neutral (or other) states. Rather, despite the ameliorative aura that is often claimed to emanate from this policy (or, perhaps, from some of its more unctuous representatives), it has essentially been a wilful doctrine aimed at maximizing and sustaining Sweden's foreign-policy autonomy in the present international system by way of exercising direct influence on the superpowers. This is an important part of the legacy of obduracy bestowed upon posterity by Östen Undén, a decidedly unsentimental man who was also Sweden's most important post-war foreign minister as well as prime architect of her Cold War neutrality.[29]

This type of policy does not in itself rule out membership in organizations such as the United Nations, as long as such membership cannot be construed as favouring one of the superpowers over the other. Since it was assumed – given the veto of the members of the Security Council – that the United Nations would be unable to pursue policies not approved by both superpowers, Sweden became a member of the United Nations very soon after it was established. However, joining the EEC proved to be a much stickier issue. The first time this issue was broached – by prime minister Tage Erlander in a famous speech in 1961 – it was made clear that Sweden's policy of neutrality in this regard was no less strict than that of the other European neutrals, despite the absence of any formal international commitments or declarations *à la* Switzerland and Austria. In the latter part of the 1960s a change of attitude occurred (primarily due to the so-called

Luxembourg compromise and its de-emphasis of supranationalism), leading to the submission of an open-ended application to the EEC. However, once serious discussions were under way in 1970–1, it became clear that Sweden was internally strongly split on this issue, and Olof Palme's government came to the conclusion that membership in the EEC was not a realistic option after all in view of her policy of neutrality. Not until 20 years later did this position change as a result of two major factors: the demise of the Cold War and the rejuvenation and consolidation of the European Community. Taken together they made inevitable a fundamental and expeditious reconsideration of Sweden's future relations with Europe.

As it turned out, her response was to deal with the latter challenge first by essentially bracketing or downplaying the issue of future foreign and security policy for the time being and, instead, to face head-on the broader socio-economic challenges posed by post-1992 European developments. To the surprise of many, this was accomplished without much public soul-searching or partisan strife, and in October 1990 Sweden thus made explicit her intention – subsequently formalized – to apply for full membership in the EC. Equally surprising is that this was not done in consultation with her neighbouring states (particularly Finland), despite a long-standing tradition of cooperation on issues of this magnitude. After extensive negotiations in Brussels, and a hard-fought referendum, and only with the barest of a majority vote, she – together with Austria and Finland – became a full member on 1 January 1995.

EU MEMBERSHIP AND CONTINUED NEUTRALITY

In the above discussion of the post-war foreign policies of the Euro-neutrals I have consciously kept my nose very close to the ground; and I will continue to do so as I attempt to sniff my way to some conclusions regarding the compatibility of EU membership with neutrality. Or rather, my focus will be on the compatibility of *continuing* the type of foreign policy which has hitherto characterized these countries while actually or potentially being a member of the EU. This means that I will not engage in painting possible future scenarios for neutrality as a policy option within the framework of the Community; I will simply concentrate on the more specific question whether the three types of neutrality which I have discussed above are viable options within the broader framework of EU membership. This will also mean that I will forego discussing neutrality as a foreign and security policy option for the Community itself; this is an issue which calls for a very different type of analysis from the one presented here.

Before looking more specifically at the three types of neutrality discussed above in the light of this query, something must first be said about the nature of the Common Foreign and Security Policy (CFSP) as codified in the second pillar of the Maastricht Treaty.[30] As is clearly indicated in Article J.1, this is intended to be an intergovernmental form of policy, and is not part of the Community system itself nor subject either to the latter's decision-making procedures nor to judicial review by the European Court of Justice (ECJ).[31] Furthermore, as noted by Nicoll and Salmon,

> Article J.1.4 of Title V gives responsibility for determining that the principles of the CFSP are complied with to the Council. In addition, article J.8.2 makes it clear that 'The Council shall act unanimously, except for procedural questions' ... If there is no agreement, then only peer and Commission disapproval, and a general weakening of confidence prevents a member state from going it alone.[32]

Furthermore, with regard to the aims of the CFSP, it is noted in article J.4 – in what is perhaps the most frequently cited passage in this context – that it 'shall include *all* questions related to the security of the Union, including the eventual framing of a common defence policy, which might in time lead to a common defence'.[33]

As we have seen above, one reason why the three Euro-neutrals who became members could accept the Maastricht Treaty as a whole was that the CFSP does not require them to acquiesce to anything more substantial within the area of foreign and security policy than to accept in the final goals of the Union (the *acquis politique* and the *finalité politique*). This was not impossible for them to do, in view of a lack of clarity as to what these goals in fact are. As noted by Nicoll and Salmon:

> At Maastricht it was not possible to resolve the underlying debates about a European security identity or CFSP. There is no resolution of the alphabet soup of institutions, of the definitive role of EU, WEU and NATO, of 'Atlantic Europe' or 'European Europe', of whether the future is to be inter-governmental or federal, a common defence policy or common defence, incremental drift or real change. Maastricht left as an open question what the role of the European Union was to be.[34]

And, they add significantly: 'A further complication is the impending membership of Sweden, Finland and Austria, the former European neutrals, in the Union and CFSP.'[35] Let us turn to this complication, and look at each of the three types of neutrality in turn and with reference to their compatibility with the above principles.

Defensive neutrality and EU membership

Although the Swiss have decided the question posed here by a resounding if indirect no, this vote in itself does not *ipso facto* mean that her neutrality is incompatible with EU membership. This latter issue is an *analytical* one, and hence one which cannot simply be determined by a democratic vote, as little as referenda in the other Euro-neutrals decided in favour of such compatibility simply by being in favour of membership. The pertinent issue here is thus the following: is defensive neutrality as defined and discussed above possible within the EU as it is constituted today?

The answer is clearly no, and it is negative as a consequence not so much of its foreign policy – which, as I have suggested, is virtually non-existent – as of the very tight socio-political interlinkage between Swiss neutrality and her domestic political structure. Clearly, as noted by Thomas Pedersen, 'Switzerland would have to reshape its political institutions if it became a member of the Community'.[36] The reason for this necessity is, of course, that the very unique political structures governing Swiss politics and defining her self-identity are not compatible with those of the Union. In other words, it is not so much the second pillar of the Maastricht Treaty which is the problem here; it is the first pillar and hence the very nature of the Community itself as political system. This is, of course, ironic, given the roots of Swiss neutrality as *par excellence* a policy and doctrine with roots in the international system of the nineteenth and twentieth centuries rather than in domestic politics.

Parametric neutrality and EU membership

As argued above, the form of neutrality practised by Austria and Finland differs from that of Switzerland not only because of its radically different origins in the Cold War but also due to its decidedly international orientation in the form of active bridge-building between the East and the West. Since their security policies were to a significant degree based on agreements with either or both of the superpowers, they felt able to decouple these from their foreign policies and hence to pursue the latter *qua* Euro-neutrals trying to ameliorate international tensions rather than to protect their own narrower national interests.

This ability to reorient neutrality as a juridically defined doctrine into an activist policy aimed at influencing the structures governing the Cold War international system makes this type of neutrality the most flexible of the three discussed here; and for this reason, I would like to suggest, its compatibility with membership in the EU cannot, *a priori*, be excluded.

More specifically, it is not inconceivable that neutrality as a peace-promotive policy within the European Union can be pursued without, on the one hand, alienating national electorates at home still in favour of neutrality (if only in name), or, on the other, undermining the goals of the Union as presently formulated in the Maastricht Treaty and agreed to by the former Euro-neutrals when they became members. This is politically possible, in my view, because of the increasingly weak linkage between national security issues and foreign policy issues which accompanied the development of this form of neutrality in Austria and Finland during the period discussed above. This ability to decouple the two has made it possible for both of these countries to promise to tie their future defence and security policies closer to those of the Union without necessarily having to give up neutrality in the activist form discussed here. In other words, the relative autonomy of these two policy spheres allows for flexibility *vis-à-vis* both on the part of the governments concerned; and as long as the CFSP remains as future-oriented and tenuous as it is today, it is difficult to see how neutrality in this form cannot – if so desired by a member state – be accommodated within the Community in some form or other.

It can also be argued that although this policy had its heyday during the most bitter period of the Cold War, the fact that it was not exclusively defined in terms of bipolarity adds to its potential functionality in the post-Cold War era, particularly since the pacific hopes initially invested in the latter have by now more or less evaporated. In principle, therefore, the pursuit of neutrality by individual members in the form of providing good offices or bridge-building facilities seems possible; and it is my guess that at least Austria continues to think that this is feasible in practice as well.

Strategic neutrality and EU membership

Clearly, strategic neutrality as discussed here is not compatible with membership in the European Union. This has not been maintained by the Swedes, nor has Brussels given any indications that such a notion would be entertained by the Community. In fact, one of the main reasons why Sweden could apply for membership in the first place was the fact that there was no longer a perceived need for this policy on her part – in short, its *raison d'être* had disappeared. Hence she was more than willing to forego it in order to become a full-fledged member of the 'new' Europe symbolized by the emblematic dates of '1989' and '1992'. In this sense the question posed here is academic and hence in little need of further elaboration.

However, Sweden still continues to speak the language of 'neutrality', even though Carl Bildt, while still prime minister, maintained that this word no longer has an adequate function in the vocabulary of Swedish foreign policy. Since then it seems to have rehabilitated itself, although it is still unclear in what capacity and for what purpose. One thing seems clear to me, however, namely, that even if Sweden would want to pull off a feat of foreign policy adaptation similar to that of the other two former Euro-neutrals, this is not a viable option, given the very close identification of Swedish neutrality with her security and defence policy. In other words, although strategic neutrality may or may not have been a successful policy *vis-à-vis* the superpowers in a bipolar world (it is still difficult to know either way), it was a policy defined, practised and justified explicitly in terms of the special strategic logic of such a relationship. This identification of neutrality with security and defence continues today. Thus, instead of abandoning neutrality altogether, or adopting the current Finno–Austrian variant, there is an urge to remain within the tradition of her post-war policy while taking cognisance of the fundamental changes which have occurred after the demise of the Soviet Union and the resurgence of the European Union. Current discussions thus revolve around attempts at reformulating neutrality into a policy defined not – as in the past – in terms of specific external actors but, rather, of remaining free of all military alliance entanglements. That this new conceptualization of Swedish neutrality continues to retain the strong security and defence connotations of the earlier policy should therefore not surprise us, since this is the only type of neutrality which has had any real political meaning and acceptance in Sweden.

Although the goals of CFSP are opaque, I find it difficult to conceive that strategic neutrality in its current and uncertain form is in any sense more compatible with EU membership than the neutrality practised by Sweden prior to membership. Certainly, if the words 'a common defence policy, which might in time lead to a common defence' are to have any meaning whatsoever, they exclude the possibility of a member state excusing herself from the attempt to achieve either the first or both goals due to a commitment – in the name of neutrality – not to bind herself externally. The whole thrust of the second pillar is, after all, to achieve some form of joint defence and security policy. Sweden will have to make a clear-cut choice here, and if she decides to go her own way, she will have to bear the full brunt of Community disapproval. Of course, it is quite possible that she can postpone this choice once more, given the general uncertainty which continues to characterize not only the foreign, defence and security aims of the Community itself but also the issue of eastward enlargement as well as the broader strategic situation beyond her current borders.

CONCLUSION

In a thought-provoking and very frank appraisal of the possible role of neutrality beyond the Cold War, Perrti Joenniemi raises the question whether neutrality is doomed to fall into oblivion in European politics. The answer he gives is 'a qualified yes'.[37] Although this answer may sound discouraging to some of us, the reasons he offers for it are in fact heartening, since his argument is essentially that neutrality has not been defeated politically but, rather, that it has been successful – indeed, that 'recent events have proved too favourable for neutrality'.[38] He elaborates on this theme as follows:

> For historical reasons, the concept of neutrality has been so deeply identified with modern policies aimed at division and exclusion that it may inevitably be seen as an anomaly in the porous and interdependent environment of contemporary European relations. Even so, neutrality may still serve as a bridge, linking the past with the present and opening up creative solutions to current dilemmas in a fashion that respects societal concerns and democratic principles.[39]

However, this was written in the early part of the present decade, and since then events have tended to make most of us more pessimistic about the demise of both interstate conflict in Europe and of sovereignty as the prime organizing principle among its states. As a consequence we may have more reason today than five years ago for *not* writing off neutrality as a policy with a viable role in contemporary Europe.

Indeed, against the backdrop of the ongoing ethnic and other deep-rooted conflicts close to the borders of the Community an increasingly strong case can be made in favour of the continued *need* for neutrals which can act as bridge-builders and providers of good offices, both within Europe and further afield. Given this need and the claim, as argued above, that this type of innovative neutrality is not incompatible with EU membership, surely it follows that neutrals of this kind should not only be tolerated by other member states but in fact be welcomed by the Community as a whole?

Notes

1. Oppenheim, *Political Concepts: A Reconstruction* (Oxford: Basil Blackwell, 1981), p. 10.
2. A. Baldwin, 'Power Analysis and World Politics: New Trends Versus Old Tendencies', *World Politics* 31:2, 1979, p. 163. See also David A. Baldwin, *Economic Statecraft* (Princeton: Princeton University Press, 1986), pp. 16f, 20.
3. 'Power Analysis and World Politics', pp. 163ff.
4. Wallace, 'What Price Independence: Sovereignty and Interdependence in British Politics', *International Affairs* 62: 3, 1986, p. 368.
5. *ibid.*
6. Richard N. Cooper, *Can Nations Agree? Issues in International Economic Cooperation* (Washington: Brookings Institution, 1989).
7. Russell, *Power* (London: Macmillan, 1975), p. 25.
8. Elster, *Explaining Technical Change* (Cambridge: Cambridge University Press, 1983), p. 75.
9. *ibid.*, pp. 75f.
10. Wildhaber, 'Swiss Neutrality – Legal Base and Historical Background', in *Neutrals in Europe: Switzerland* (Stockholm: Swedish Institute of International Affairs, Conference Papers 10, 1988), p. 5.
11. C. Church, 'The Changing Domestic Dimensions of Swiss Neutrality', paper prepared for a planning session on 'The EFTA Neutrals and the EC: Foreign Policy Implications of Membership', ECPR Joint Sessions of Workshops, Leiden University, April 1993, p. 1.
12. *op. cit.*, pp. 3–7.
13. *op. cit.*, p. 2.
14. Harto Hakovirta, *East–West Conflict and European Neutrality* (Oxford: Clarendon Press, 1988), p. 59.
15. On Austrian neutrality, see Hakovirta *op. cit.* and Ephraim Karsh, *Neutrality and Small States: The European Experience after World War Two* (London: Routledge, 1988).
16. Hanspeter Neuhold, 'The Permanent Neutrality of Austria: A Status Similar to and Different from Sweden's "Non-Alignment"', in Bo Huldt (ed.), *Neutrals in Europe: Austria* (Stockholm: Swedish Institute of International Affairs, Conference Paper 7, 1987), pp. 6–9.
17. *op. cit.*, p. 10.
18. *op. cit.*, p. 119.
19. *op. cit.*, p. 63.
20. *op. cit.*, p. 12.
21. *op. cit.*, p. 214.
22. *ibid.*
23. *op. cit.*, p. 12.
24. *op. cit.*, p. 212.
25. From *The Odyssey* in Jon Elster, *Ulysses and the Sirens: Studies in Rationality and Irrationality* (Cambridge: Cambridge University Press, 1979), p. 36.
26. Elster, *Ulysses and the Sirens*, pp. 36ff.

27.   Åström, *Sweden's Policy of Neutrality* (Stockholm: Swedish Institute, 1983), p. 9.

28.   Elster, *Explaining Technical Change*, pp. 75f.

29.   Specifically, Undén's policy was to make a clear distinction between questions pertaining to, respectively, Swedish national security, international disarmament and the pursuit of human rights and democratic principles in the international arena. Neutrality, in his view, pertained only to the first of these issue areas. One implication of this view – not always fully appreciated abroad, either conceptually and/or normatively – is that Sweden has felt no compunctions about the need to be 'neutral' with respect to the other two areas. Indeed, very often the opposite has been the case.

30.   For an authoritative discussion of the evolution of European Political Cooperation (ECP) – the precursor of CFSP – into the current policy, see William Nicoll and Trevor C. Salmon, *Understanding the New European Community* (New York: Harvester/Wheatsheaf, 1994), pp. 185–212. On the EPC, the most thorough treatment is Simon J. Nuttall, *European Political Co-operation* (Oxford: Clarendon Press, 1992).

31.   Nicoll and Salmon, *op. cit.*, p. 207.

32.   *ibid.*

33.   *op. cit.* p. 208.

34.   *op. cit.* pp. 211–12.

35.   *op. cit.*, p. 212.

36.   Thomas Pedersen, 'The Common Foreign and Security Policy and the Challenge of Enlargement', in Ole Nørgaard, Thomas Pedersen and Nikolaj Petersen (eds), *The European Community in World Politics* (London: Pinter Publishers, 1993), p. 36.

37.   Pertti Joenniemi, 'Neutrality Beyond the Cold War', *Review of International Studies*, Vol. 19, No. 3 (1993), p. 294.

38.   *op. cit.*, p. 295.

39.   *op. cit.*, p. 303.

6 The Indivisible Continent: Russia, NATO and European Security

Michael MccGwire

In May 1995, the US Secretary of State received a letter from a group of retired senior State Department officials, expressing concern about 'the potential consequences of the administration's policy of promising to extend NATO membership to the Czech Republic, Hungary and Poland'.[1]

The 18 signatories included Jack F. Matlock, recently retired as Ambassador in Moscow, six others who had served as Ambassador to one or more East European countries, plus a former Under Secretary of State, and two Directors of Policy Plans. But the most notable member of this prestigious group was Paul H. Nitze.

As Director of Policy Plans in 1949–50, it was Nitze who largely wrote NSC 68, the presidential directive which provided the rationale for the massive build-up of US forces that would allow the US 'to check and to roll back the Kremlin's drive for world domination'. Nitze was both a Deputy Secretary of Defense and the Secretary of the Navy in the Kennedy/Johnson adminstrations. In the 1970s he was a leading member of the hawkish, bipartisan 'Committee on the Present Danger', which worried about 'windows of vulnerability' and attacked Carter's defence policy. In the 1980s, he was Reagan's arms control supremo.

Paul Nitze was closely involved in national security affairs throughout the Cold War and is the last man to be unduly solicitous about Moscow's sensibilities. Yet he and the other 17 senior officials consider that the present policy of extending NATO membership to former members of the Warsaw Pact will 'convince most Russians that the United States and the West are attempting to isolate, encircle, and subordinate them, rather than integrating them into a new European system of collective security'.[2] They also believe that the 'policy risks endangering the long-term viability of NATO, significantly exacerbating the instability that now exists in the zone that lies between Germany and Russia'.

The policy of extending NATO to include former members of the Warsaw Pact was first affirmed in the declaration following the January

1994 NATO summit and confirmed by President Clinton's subsequent statement that 'the question is no longer whether NATO will take on new members, but when and how'. Given the collective experience of the group that signed the letter,[3] one must ask how such a policy came to be adopted?

The first part of this chapter seeks to reconstruct the conjunction of circumstances that led to this shortsighted decision. It then evaluates the official and other reasons that are said to justify the policy in terms of the future security of Europe. As those reasons are seriously wanting, almost half the chapter is devoted to assessing the nature of present and future threats to security in Europe. The final section suggests a set of principles that should underlie any policy intended to enhance security in Europe in the years ahead.

Note that 'security *in* Europe' is conceptually distinct from 'the security *of* Europe'. The latter assumes, albeit implicitly, an external threat to a Europe that does not include Russia. That assumption is explicit in the organizational structure and geographical scope of NATO and the Western European Union (WEU),[4] and in the prominence given to defence as an aspect of security.[5] Security *in* Europe is a more inclusive concept, reaching from the Atlantic to the Urals. It is sensitive to the danger of self-fulfilling prophecies and believes that the security *of* Europe can only be achieved by the cooperative endeavours of all states having interests in the larger region.

ACTORS AND INSTITUTIONS

In 1990, the year that saw the formal end of the Cold War, the reunification of Germany, and the certainty of Soviet withdrawal from the satellites, there was no suggestion that the membership of NATO should be extended. Indeed, Henry Kissinger gave as his opinion that the most realistic security system for Poland, Czechoslovakia and Hungary was neutrality. While the NATO summit in July that year had recognized that the Soviet Union was now a partner, rather than an enemy, and had outlined plans to foster political and military cooperation with the countries of Central and Eastern Europe (CEE), it was widely assumed that the Conference on Security and Cooperation in Europe (CSCE) would provide the most appropriate institutional framework. This presumption seemed to be confirmed at the CSCE Paris summit in November, which reaffirmed the values and prescribed new structures and institutions for the CSCE process.

In the space of three years, this inclusive approach to the problems of post-Cold War Europe had been replaced by the divisive idea of extending

NATO membership to erstwhile members of the Warsaw Pact. To some extent, this reversal could be explained by the perceived capacity of the available institutions to respond to the drumbeat of events, be it the break-up of the Soviet Union and subsequent developments in Russia, or the steadily deteriorating situation in Yugoslavia and then Bosnia. But the real explanation was to be found in Washington, where two quite different forces were at work. The more important was a byproduct of the debate about US national security in the wake of the Cold War. The other was Washington's long-standing insistence that NATO was the primary vehicle for US multilateral involvement in European security matters.

The standing Conference on Security and Cooperation in Europe stemmed from a Soviet initiative in the early 1970s (a time of *détente*) that was taken up by Western Europe, Germany seeing it as part of its Ostpolitik and France as a way of bypassing the sterility of East–West negotiations and the US domination of NATO.[6] For several years, the US resisted this development, but finally agreed to participate in the Conference if there were parallel talks on multiple balanced force reductions. The agreement was formalized at Helsinki in 1975 when 33 European states, plus Canada and the US, signed the Final Act.

For its first ten years, the CSCE was used by the West mainly as a platform for berating the Soviet Union for its record on human rights. However, Gorbachev's accession to power allowed significant progress to be made at the review conference in 1986, when NATO and the Warsaw Pact agreed on substantial Confidence and Security Building Measures (CSBMs), and the CSCE aquired new importance as a political–military forum.

Following the revolutions of 1989, the political relevance of the CSCE grew rapidly, its underlying principles were emphasized repeatedly in NATO and European Community forums (particularly the guaranteeing of human and civil rights and the committment not to change borders by force), and the Conference was finally provided with an appropriate institutional structure, which gradually grew in size and scope.

In 1990, it had seemed that the CSCE was set to assume the leading role in providing for security in Europe, but by the Helsinki summit in July 1992, this optimism had been severely eroded. The reasons were several and included the active scepticism of the US and the UK; the cooling of German support; the preoccupation of Russia with domestic problems; and the explosion of CSCE membership from the original 37 to an even more unwieldy 53.[7] But of critical importance was its impotence when faced by the attempted coup in Moscow in August 1991, and by the ineffectiveness of its principles and procedures in preventing the slide to war in Yugoslavia. That conflict was set to breach the core principles of the CSCE, and the fact that the major powers chose not to use the Conference as a vehicle for discussion or action persuaded CEE leaders such as Václav Havel that, if they were to have a say in the security of Europe, they would need to be members of NATO or the European Union.

At Maastricht in December 1991, the European Economic Community had redefined itself as the European Union (EU), symbolizing a further step in the movement towards greater political and economic integration. As a necessary adjunct to this more clearly defined European identity, it was decided to develop a Common Foreign and Security Policy (CFSP), which would 'include all questions related to the security of the [European] Union, including the eventual framing of a common defence policy, which might in turn lead to a common defence'.

To that end, the Maastricht Treaty requested the Western European Union (WEU) to elaborate and implement decisions and actions of the European Union which have defence implications,[8] and the WEU sub-sequently agreed on the need to develop a genuine European security and defence identity (ESDI), the lack of which had been highlighted by the Kuwait crisis and Gulf War. The driving force behind this idea came from Paris, supported strongly by Bonn; following reunification, the long-established goal of binding Germany into a political confederation had became even more important.

The idea of the WEU emerging as a coequal partner to NATO was strongly opposed by Washington, the Bush administration insisting that there could be no substitute for NATO as the provider of US defence and Europe's security. This opposition was shared by Atlanticists such as the UK and largely accounted for the lack of progress in carrying out the EU's mandate. But US opposition softened with the change of adminis-tration in Washington and the elections in France and, by the end of 1993, there was a new consensus that the WEU should become the vehicle for strengthening the European pillar of the North Atlantic alliance.

It was claimed that this would bind America more closely to Europe, but it is likely that this unexpected consensus owed more to Western concern about revived Russian activism in foreign affairs. Moscow was increasingly involved in the major powers' efforts to limit the war in Bosnia and devise some way of halting it, usually on the other side of the argument to Washington and often in agreement with one or other of the Europeans. Russia was also showing a renewed interest in the CSCE, advocating a greater role and pressing for a more effective organizational structure and an improved decision-making capability, including a mini-European version of the Security Council. This had been suggested by

Czechoslovakia in 1992, at which time the idea had a measure of support among the 'Europeanists' in NATO, but was anathema to the US. By accepting the WEU as the European pillar of NATO, Washington undercut Europeanist support for a strengthened CSCE.

At its summit in June 1993, the EC promised membership to the four Visegrad states (Poland, Hungary, Slovakia and the Czech Republic), but it made no attempt to specify a date. It was at this time that discussion of extending NATO membership became serious, it being simpler to extend the umbrella of a military alliance than the complex structure of an embryonic political union. For obvious reasons, the CEE states favoured this idea, but so too did Germany. It was tired of being in the front line and welcomed the prospect of the Visegrad states taking over the role of frontier zone for Western Europe. Bonn also preferred the early extension of some kind of Western institutional membership to the likely alternative of increasing German hegemony in the region.

However, as previously indicated, the strongest pressure for extending NATO membership came from an unexpected alliance of interests in the US domestic debate on national security. Following the Soviet withdrawal from the Cold War, the traditional political cleavage concerning the scope and nature of US involvement in world affairs had re-emerged. On one side stood the isolationists, who distrusted entangling alliances; on the other stood the internationalists who favoured active global involvement.

In the Washington debate on defence and foreign policy, the isolationists challenged the need for NATO and argued that the wealthy Europeans were rich enough to provide for their own defence. They were supported in this argument by the substantial numbers in Congress who were seeking to cut or rearrange allocations within the Defence Budget. The internationalists generally agreed that Europe should provide for its own defence, but NATO's traditional role was no longer their primary concern. Rather, they saw the US presence in Europe as an essential element of America's global military posture. NATO was important partly as a forward base and staging post, but also as a political–military forum and the organizational template for joint operations with European allies outside the NATO area.[9]

Given the public mood in the wake of Somalia and the growing conflict in Bosnia, the internationalists knew that if they were to prevail in the Washington debate, they would need to espouse an issue that drew support away from the isolationist camp as well as increasing the strength of their own. The only such issue was the extension of NATO membership to the central and east European states. This would enlist the support of a coalition of interests whose roots reached back to the nineteenth century, and which had been consolidated by the history of the past 50 years, including the 'betrayal' of Yalta, and the declaratory policy of 'roll back' in the 1950s.

This coalition, which included the influential Polish–American lobby and other ethnic-based groups, tended to view Russia, whether tsarist, communist or quasi-democratic, as an inherent threat to the region, an opinion that was shared by a large part of the American electorate, which did not distinguish between the new Russian Federation and the former Soviet Union. Freeing the CEE states from Soviet domination was seen as one of the more important outcomes of winning the Cold War. Any failure to ensure that this victory led to successful political and economic reform in those states would represent a failure of US foreign policy.

It was in this context that the continuing US presence in Europe and membership of NATO provided common ground for both parties to the political alliance in Washington. It could be argued that there was a pressing requirement to fill the security vacuum left by the withdrawal of the Soviet Union from CEE and the subsequent dismantling of the Warsaw Pact, and that NATO was the only institution with the credibility and the means to move into that space. In other words, rather than a single-purpose organization whose *raison d'être* had all but vanished, NATO could be an adaptable and cost-effective instrument of US policy throughout the breadth of Europe.

NATO already had institutional links with former members of the Warsaw Pact through the North Atlantic Cooperation Council (NACC), which was set up in December 1991. This intergovernmental organization had formal ties with NATO headquarters and was intended to reach across the former NATO–Warsaw Pact divide and engage the CEE states and republics of the former Soviet Union (FSU) in an ongoing security dialogue. In June 1992, the WEU had set up a comparable Forum of Consultation, although FSU participation was limited to the Baltic republics, thereby avoiding CEE complaints that inclusion of the Asiatic republics in the NACC vitiated its intended purpose.[10] But neither of these institutional arrangements met the security concerns of CEE states, which had been heightened by the political mobilization of nationalists in Russia and Yelstin's confrontation with parliament in October 1993.

That same month, in an attempt to meet those concerns while avoiding isolating Russia or drawing new lines of confrontation in Europe, the US Secretary of Defense floated the idea of a Partnership for Peace (PfP) with NATO. This would be offered to all the CEE states and the republics of the FSU, the aim being to facilitate transparency in defence policy and budgeting, to ensure the democratic control of defence forces, and to develop the capability of individual partners for joint operations with members of NATO, initially in the field of peacekeeping and humanitarian operations.[11] The creative feature of this American initiative was that individual countries would negotiate with NATO a bilateral agreement (the 16 + 1 formula), tailored so that each country could develop and restructure its forces and doctrine to the extent and at the pace it felt desirable.

In terms of the debate in Washington, these customized PfPs were expected to contribute to political stability and civil order through the former Warsaw Pact. They were also intended to increase the number and quality of national contingents available for UN peacekeeping, thereby serving US global interests, while obviating the need for direct US involvement. At the same time, PfP would provide an institutional framework whereby individual states could bring their military establishments up to a standard of probity and proficiency that might ultimately qualify them for NATO membership.

PfP went some way to meeting the wishes of the Visegrad states, but not far enough to satisfy the coalition of interests that made up the other half of the internationalist alliance in Washington. They pressed for a firm commitment that NATO membership would be extended to the Visegrad states (at least), rather than the possibility of such membership in some unspecified future. This commitment was needed to demonstrate that the CEE states would never be allowed to return to the Russian sphere of influence.[12]

The Partnership was to be formally launched at the NATO summit in January 1994, but the advocates of an explicit commitment to the Visegrad states had by then already prevailed in the Washington debate. They criticized PfP as an attempt to head off consideration of NATO expansion and as tacitly accepting a Soviet veto over new members. The Clinton administration was already in trouble for being unduly tolerant of Yeltsin's Russia and for indecision about Bosnia, and the White House chose to buy time by accepting the principle of extending NATO membership,[13] shifting the debate from 'whether' to the equally vexed questions of when, how, and who.

The new policy on expansion 'as part of an evolutionary process' was announced at the January summit, at the same time as formal approval of PfP and the decision to institute planning for a number of Combined/Joint Task Forces (CJTF). The latter involved the creation of mobile multinational and multi-service headquarters. These would obviate the need for the WEU to create its own operational command structure in competition with NATO, and allow both organizations to draw on the common national forces as circumstances might demand.

This conjunction of developments at the end of 1993 – the new consensus that the WEU should become a vehicle for strengthening the European pillar of the Atlantic alliance, the CJTF concept, and the decision in principle to extend NATO membership – had the markings of an intra-alliance deal. The EU had already agreed that the Visegrad four would become full members of the Union, albeit at some unspecified date. The argument that a public commitment to extend NATO to include those same four states[14] would ensure a continued US military presence to Europe was sufficient to ensure European support for the statement of principle at the January summit, particularly since Germany was generally in favour.

THE OFFICIAL RATIONALE FOR EXTENDING NATO

Given the genesis of this policy, it is understandable that it has been difficult to formulate a rationale for extending NATO membership that is persuasive in political–military terms. In an exposition of the Clinton administration's policies, Deputy Secretary of State Strobe Talbot gave three main reasons for NATO's decision,[15] and another four have been advanced by the many advocates of that policy.[16]

The first 'official' reason is an 'ought' statement. While acknowledging that the threat NATO was created to counter has been eliminated, it states that collective defence remains (1) an imperative, and (2) should be extended to new democracies that have regained their independence. There is no explanation of *why* NATO should be extended in this way.[17] Nor is there any mention of which state might need to be deterred or defended against at some future date, but the meaning is inescapable. NATO ought to incorporate former members of the Warsaw Pact so as to increase its collective defence capability against the potential threat of a resurgent Russia.[18]

In an attempt to dilute this interpretation, Strobe Talbot noted that the enlargement of NATO is not a new issue and makes the surprising claim that the reasons for and consequences of the progressive growth of the alliance between 1949–82 strengthen the case for doing so now.[19] The evidence does not support that claim.

The accession of Greece and Turkey in 1952 formalized an evolving situation that reached back to the start of the Cold War in 1947–8, at which time the US took over from the UK in Greece, deployed a newly formed fleet to the eastern Mediterranean, and began building up Turkey's military capability. Their joining NATO formally committed the two countries to active collective defence, clarified the command structure in the eastern Mediterranean, and tightened the ring of containment, but did not substantially change the bilateral relationships.

When West Germany joined NATO in 1955 (via membership of the WEU in 1954 and agreement that it should rearm), American, British and French forces had been stationed on its territory for ten years, initially as armies of occupation and subsequently deployed against the threat of Soviet aggression. Spain did not join NATO until 1982, following Franco's death, before which its membership had been vetoed by European members. However, the US had long before established a significant military presence in the country, including operational air bases, numerous support facilities, and the equipping of Spanish forces.

Not one of these cases provides an argument for eastwards expansion today. What is more, NATO's history actively undermines the most prominent of the 'unofficial' arguments, which claims that NATO extension would 'project stability' to the east, and that a failure to do so will actually import instability. One could imagine that NATO is some kind of all-purpose floor covering that will effortlessly upgrade the uncarpeted rooms of the European home, and without which the termites will take over. But the lesson of the past 50 years is somewhat different.

For a start, the circumstances are not the same. The political liberation of western Europe was a progressive process, begun in 1943 and 1944 and carried out within a framework of tight military or civilian control. Market economies had continued to operate under German occupation and it was not difficult to re-establish pre-war forms of government after a gap of 4–5 years. By contrast, the CEE states were under communist control for 40–45 years, the countries concerned were mainly the creation of the post-World War I settlement, and in the inter-war years, only Czechoslovakia had managed to preserve a semblance of democratic government. If one has to make comparisons, the situation of the CEE states in 1990 was closer to that of Germany in 1945. There, the Allies imposed a military government, attempted political cleansing, and established new structures of democratic governance.

Meanwhile, the most important factor in bringing stability in the wake of World War II to what became NATO Europe was the vast disparity in wealth and resources enjoyed by the US in relation to the countries that had been devastated or impoverished by war, a disparity that provided powerful political and economic leverage in the post-war decade. The Marshall Plan and other assistance programmes were major examples, but it also took the form of direct financial pressure, as when France and Italy were forced to evict communist parties from their parliaments in 1947, or of clandestine payments, as in the 1948 Italian elections.[20] Although some countries were already members of NATO when they received US military assistance, the programmes were all bilateral and the leverage lay with the US.

The political situation (civil war) in Greece was stabilized using US resources, and since the fight was with communism, people weren't too fussy about the means. Only when stability had been restored did Greece join NATO. Similarly, Turkey joined NATO after the bilateral aid programmes had taken effect. But its membership of NATO, along with Britain and Greece, did not prevent Turkey from mounting a military invasion of Cyprus in 1974 and taking over the northern part of the island. Nor did NATO membership deter a military junta from seizing power in Athens (1967–74). Similarly, NATO showed more concern than pleasure when, in 1974, a putsch brought an end to half a century of dictatorship in Portugal.

Given this kind of evidence (and the most recent confrontation between Greece and Turkey over islands in the Aegean in February 1996),[21] the claim that membership of NATO would dampen aggressive nationalism and promote democracy is unpersuasive. So, too, is the claim that membership of NATO would prevent the renationalization of defence policies among former members of the Warsaw Pact. One has only to consider the persistence of strongly individualistic national defence policies among the existing members of NATO, from the days of the Suez crisis to the Yugoslav imbroglio, to see the weakness of this argument. In any case, the PfP programme was specifically designed to achieve many of the military and defence-related benefits that are claimed for NATO expansion.

Moving on to the other main reasons advanced by the Clinton administration, both are aspirational. It is claimed that 'the prospect of membership' provides an incentive for the CEE and FSU states to (1) strengthen democratization and legal institutions, ensure civilian control of their armed forces, liberalize their economies, and respect human rights, including national minorities; and (2) resolve disputes peacefully and contribute to peacekeeping operations.

These criteria apply equally to membership of the EU and WEU, therefore the pertinence of these two reasons depends on the argument that the EU is not yet ready to expand further and that economic harmonization is anyway more difficult, while the WEU, lacking US participation, is not militarily meaningful. For that argument to stand up, the incentive of NATO membership would have to be on offer to all FSU republics west of the Urals, especially those who would otherwise be unlikely to adopt the criteria. That is clearly not the case and, in practical terms, the incentive is only available to the Visegrad states, who are already on track. Are we to suppose that without that incentive, those countries would reverse their present policies? A variant of the official 'incentive' argument is the claim that membership of NATO is needed to 'reassure' states that still have some way to go to meet EU requirements. Again, are we to suppose that without such reassurance they would abandon their efforts? And where would they turn?

Lastly, NATO expansion has been justified for reasons to do with Germany. Some see expansion as a way of binding Germany firmly into Europe, the only alternative being German hegemony over CEE. It is argued that there will only be a real Europe when there has been a deep and wide-ranging reconciliation between Germany and Poland.[22] Others see NATO expansion as less dangerous than a race between Russia and Germany to fill the security vacuum, which they consider as otherwise inevitable. Accepting that reconciliation with Poland is important, it is even more important with Russia, and that could be threatened by NATO expansion. And why does reconciliation require Poland to be a member of NATO? German reconciliation with France was achieved primarily through economic means, binding the two together in the European Coal and Steel Community and then the EEC. And is the necessary alternative to extending NATO, a Russo–German race to fill a so-called security vacuum? Or is that just another assertion to support a favoured policy?

The extent to which the arguments advanced for extending NATO rely on assertion, slogan or sentiment is notable. Writing in *Foreign Affairs*, a key member of the Clinton administration asserts that 'expansion of NATO is an essential consequence of the rising of the Iron Curtain' and, without any further justification, moves to discuss the new security architecture to be built around that central pillar.[23] The metaphor of 'a security vacuum' assumes a physical reality; the catchphrase 'project stability' is taken to resolve the complex questions concerning the very nature of political and social stability and how to ensure it. And there is a sentimental, if some-what selective assumption of common European values, allowing 'the wrongs of Yalta' to be translated into a right to join NATO.[24]

The difficulty in developing a persuasive case for the expansion of NATO is only to be expected, as the policy is not the product of a dis-passionate political–military analysis of the threat to security in Europe. Rather, the policy is a tactical response to the challenge by the isolationist tendency in the US domestic debate to the cost-effectiveness of continued participation in NATO. The promise to expand NATO was needed to craft a coalition of sentiment and interests in Congress that would be strong enough to ensure the continued funding of an American military presence in Europe.[25] But to justify such a policy in terms of security in Europe rather than US global policy, it was necessary to gloss over the costs and magnify the supposed benefits.[26]

For old and new members alike, the economic costs would be substantial,[27] but these will be insignificant compared to the political costs of expansion. The most obvious is the inevitable Russian reaction to the idea of incorporating former members of the Warsaw Pact into NATO. But there are also the divisive effects of drawing new lines across Europe, whereby existing economic and cultural differences are reinforced and exaggerated by Western-determined political–military and geostrategic considerations.[28] The political costs of such stratification are inherent, but they will be greatly magnified by the Russian reaction to NATO enlargement.

In that respect, the denial practised by these advocates of extension is almost total, as evidenced by the internal contradiction in their argument. The stated objective is to enhance security in Europe. It is accepted that there is no Russian threat to the CEE states 'for the next decade or more'.[29] There is general agreement that the security of Europe requires the integration of the republics of the FSU, especially Russia, into a stable security system.[30] Yet it is widely recognized that Moscow will be worried by the hostile implications of NATO expansion and that Russia has 'legitimate concerns' about this development.[31]

Suggestions on how to square this circle by alleviating those concerns have been of three kinds. One addresses the problem directly with ideas as to how Moscow might be propitiated or reassured. For example, by renegotiating the 1990 treaty on Conventional Forces in Europe and by according Russia special status *vis-à-vis* NATO and within PfP; by combining the expansion of NATO with a new transcontinental and transoceanic security architecture in which Russia would have a major place;[32] and by refraining from deploying troops and nuclear weapons from existing member states to the territory of new members.[33] It is also argued that the US should make greater use of the CSCE (which became an Organization in December 1994), and ensure that the OSCE played a more important role in European security,[34] a suggestion that is vitiated by the concurrent insistence that the OSCE can neither replace NATO nor can NATO be in any way beholden to the OSCE.[35]

A second response is that, in the event, Russia's concerns will be allayed by the transparency of the expansion process. Moscow will be fully informed of bilateral negotiations with future new members and of subsequent agreements concerning force structures, deployments and command arrangements.[36] It is not explained *why* this transparency should allay Russia's concern over the adverse effects of enlargement. The third kind of response consists of 'ought' statements. Russia *ought* to recognize that NATO is an explicitly defensive alliance; that expansion is an inevitable evolutionary development; that it is in no way 'anti-Russian'; that it is in Russia's interests to accept the inevitable and to actively seek reconciliation with the CEE states.

Two of these approaches are almost willful in their inability to see Moscow's side of this European dilemma and to admit the consequences of ignoring its legitimate concerns. In particular, they slight the problems that will inevitably be created if NATO extends its eastern perimeter to the Ukrainian border.[37] The Russo–Ukrainian relationship is already fraught with difficulties and potential dangers, and the enlargement of NATO will inject a destabilizing factor into an evolving and delicately balanced situation.

THE THREAT TO SECURITY IN EUROPE

The conflicting agendas underlying the debate on NATO expansion remind us that the concepts of threat and security are highly subjective and that one country's security can be another's insecurity. For that reason it is counter-productive to focus on the security concerns of one or a few countries. Security must be seen in relation to the whole of Europe, which, for the purpose of this analysis, is taken to extend from the Atlantic to the Urals – the general area covered by the Conventional Forces in Europe (CFE) treaty.

It is unlikely that each nation or ethno-community will enjoy the same level of micro-security, if only for reasons of political geography. But they all have a common interest in the macro-security environment, whether in Europe or at the global level, since this will inevitably affect security at the micro level. Security in Europe depends largely on the state of relations between the major powers.

Potential threats to security in Europe fall into three main categories. One is related to Russia's political and territorial aspirations. Another is to do with nuclear weapons and the control of fissile material. And the third is the possible breakdown of political and civil order in the process of transforming socialist societies into market economies and democracies. It is this last threat which is said to require the expansion of NATO membership.

THE BREAKDOWN OF ORDER

From everyone's point of view, security in Europe requires peace in Europe. The Yugoslav conflict illustrates vividly how the breakdown of political and civil order can threaten peace by spreading to neighbouring states, by drawing other countries into the conflict, and by generating refugee flows and an illegal arms trade.

For quite some time, a general war in the Balkans seemed a live possibility, and the danger has not yet passed. The ineffectiveness of the European Community's efforts at conflict resolution following the declaration of independence by the Republics of Slovenia and Croatia in June 1991, the inability of the major European powers to agree even on the question of recognition, and the steady slide to war in the Republic of Bosnia-Herzegovina, raised serious doubts as to whether the conflict could be contained. The population of Kosovo, an autonomous province considered vital to the integrity of the Republic of Serbia, was 90 per cent Albanian Muslim. The Republic of Macedonia, with its ethnically mixed population, was subject to historical claims by neighbouring states, including Greece and Turkey.

Similarly, the disintegration of the Soviet Union in the second half of 1991 allowed long-standing claims between and within the constituent Republics of the USSR to blaze into open conflict, as in the war between Armenia and Azerbajzhan over Nagorno-Karabakh, or secessionist wars in Georgia. The potential for disorder was high in other parts of central and eastern Europe, where pressures 'to right historical wrongs' had been held in check by the Warsaw Pact.

As for ethnic minorities, there were some 3.5 million Hungarians living in some seven European states, including 2 million in the Transylvanian region of Romania, about 600 000 in southern Slovakia, 450 000 in Serbia, and 160 000 in the Ukraine, concentrated mainly in distinct geographical areas. There were Romanian minorities in Moldavia and the Ukraine, Polish minorities in the Ukraine, Byelorussia and Lithuania, and large Russian minorities in Estonia and Latvia. In the Ukraine, there were some 12 million ethnic Russians (out of a total of some 55 million) and in the Crimea they constituted 75 per cent of the population.[38]

While historical animosities may contribute to the savagery of a conflict, to blame them for the breakdown in order is to ignore structural factors. In the case of Yugoslavia these included the economic decline caused by a programme intended to promote economic liberalization and resolve a foreign debt crisis, and by the disintegration of the previously existing international order, where Yugoslavia occupied a unique position tied to the organization of the Cold-War world.[39] Similarly, the socialist societies in central and eastern Europe have had to cope with the domestic problems involved in transforming themselves into market economies and democracies, while being denied the security of Comecon and having to operate as best they can in a continuously changing economic environment.

There are actual or potential crises of political authority and fragmentation throughout the central and eastern parts of Europe, and the appropriate way for outsiders to respond to these competing claims and incipient conflicts is not at all clear. As the West has discovered in Yugoslavia, the difficulty lies as much in conceptualizing the problem correctly as in devising ways of dealing with it.[40] For several years, Yugoslavia has been at the centre of European, NATO and UN attention, yet there is still no consensus on what initiated the process that led to this Balkan tragedy. It is because we have such a poor understanding of the reasons underlying the breakdown of social order that we find it difficult to formulate policies to prevent it from happening, or the appropriate responses when we fail to do so. We are 'seeking solutions to a set of problems that are not (and perhaps can not be) fully understood in any simple causal sense'.[41]

We can, however, be certain that in the event of breakdowns of this kind in central and eastern Europe, the nature of Russian involvement in Western attempts to resolve or contain the situation will be crucial to the outcome. The experience of the past ten years and the history of the past 200, indicate that peace in Europe depends very largely on the extent to which the major powers are able to collaborate effectively on resolving the various problems that arise in the area. We have seen it in Yugoslavia with the Five Nation Contact Group, and we saw it in the first half of the nineteenth century with the Concert of Europe.

This leads to an obvious conclusion. If we are seriously concerned about the breakdown of political and civil order in central and eastern Europe and the danger that it will lead to more serious conflict, any Western policy designed to prevent that happening must provide for the cooperative involvement of Russia. Given our poor understanding of the problem and the absence of any proven solution, a Western policy that does not respect that principle can only increase the threat of political disorder and wider conflict in the rest of Europe.

NUCLEAR WEAPONS AND MATERIALS

There are two very different issues here. The one that has attracted most attention is the danger of unintended nuclear proliferation (the 'loose nukes' problem), which extends from concern about the control of fissile material, through the mechanics of transferring to Russia the nuclear assets deployed in Kazakhstan, Ukraine and Byelorus,[42] to procedures for dismantling nuclear weapon systems and warheads, and the verification of disarmament agreements. Coming within this general category is concern for the continuing safety and effectiveness of command-and-control systems and procedures for the operational strategic missile forces.

In 1991–2, the US approached this problem with imaginative generosity, recognizing that it was in its own interest to enable what would be a difficult, costly and lengthy process. While that process is proceeding more slowly than hoped, significant progress has been made and the process was reaffirmed at the Moscow summit in May 1995.

It is, however, an inescapable fact that the continued success of the process depends absolutely on full and willing Russian cooperation. In January 1996 there was a report that US officials were concerned over Russia's lack of progress in following up various confidence building and information sharing measures that were agreed at the May summit.[43]

The other and, in the longer term, more important nuclear issue is the Russian attitude regarding the utility of such weapons. Towards the end of the 1960s, the evolving military situation prompted a shift in Soviet nuclear requirements from 'strategic superiority' to 'parity at as low a level as could be negotiated'. In January 1986, this was carried to its logical conclusion with a formal arms-control proposal that all nuclear weapons should be eliminated within 15 years.[44] (As the Soviets did not subscribe to Western deterrence theory, they did not believe that nuclear weapons prevented nuclear war; rather they recognized that nuclear weapons made nuclear war possible. Since their overriding concern was to avoid nuclear war, the aim of eliminating nuclear weapons was only logical.) This policy objective was carried over from Soviet to Russian strategic policy and was reaffirmed by Yeltsin in October 1994.[45]

Quite separately, in the wake of the Gulf War, the US national security establishment came to recognize that nuclear weapons in the hands of an unfriendly Third World state could negate the global reach of America's conventional forces. There was general agreement that US nuclear forces should thenceforth be de-emphasized, with an influential body of opinion arguing for their progressive marginalization, leading to the progressive atrophying of the nuclear instrument.[46] A small (but prestigious) group were actually recommending elimination.[47]

In other words, in 1993–4, a conjunction of unrelated circumstances (the post-Cold-War hiatus, the Gulf War, Soviet nuclear doctrine) opened a window of opportunity for the nuclear powers to adopt the firm and serious policy goal of eliminating nuclear weapons and to embark on the process of achieving that goal within 20–30 years. Fortuitous pressure towards the same end was provided by the 1995 review conference on extending the Nuclear non-Proliferation Treaty and by the negotiations on a Comprehensive Test Ban (CTB) treaty, which aimed to reach agreement by October 1996. That same month, the report of the Canberra Commission on the Elimination of Nuclear Weapons would be presented to the UN General Assembly by the Australian government, undercutting the standard excuse that the nuclear powers would love to give up their weapons, if only they knew how it could be achieved.

However, for the objective of a nuclear-weapons-free (NWF) world to be adopted, it is necessary that both the US and Russia should consider the elimination of nuclear weapons to be in their interest. Unfortunately, in the past 2–3 years, Moscow has become increasingly frustrated by its exclusion from the key European decision-making processes and by the failure of the US to deliver on promises of a new strategic partnership that would make Russia a critical player in the creation of a new world order.[48] Not only has Washington excluded Moscow from a meaningful role, but it has gone on to insist on the extension of NATO, a military alliance with an explicitly anti-Soviet (and hence anti-Russian) orientation.

Faced by a stronger NATO to the west and China's mass armies to the east, can Russia really afford to relinquish 'the great equalizer', its nuclear capability? Reflecting the reality of this concern, the Russian military has adopted a policy of 'nuclear first use' – reversing the doctrine that ruled in the 1970s and 1980s. But it is not only relative military capabilities that are shaping Moscow's attitude towards nuclear weapons. The experience of Yugoslavia, where history gives Russia's regional interests a special edge, demonstrated that the only way to get Washington's attention was by obduracy, and this reopened the long-standing debate on how best to handle the US.

In the Soviet era, it was generally believed that Washington's willingness to negotiate (to cooperate, even) on various issues in the first half of the 1970s was a direct result of the Soviets having achieved a measure of strategic (that is, nuclear) parity. In the internal Soviet debate that followed the collapse of detente and the US return to Cold War at the beginning of the 1980s, a strong case was made for an intransigent stance, on the grounds that Washington mistook conciliation and concessions for weakness and, rather than reciprocate, would seek to exploit it.[49] To many Russians, this assessment is seen to have been borne out by the outcome of the conciliatory policies adopted by Gorbachev and Shevardnadze from 1987 onwards.

Even more widespread is the belief that the US only responds to strength, be it economic or military. This implies that it is essential for Russia to retain the nuclear trappings of the former Soviet nuclear power.

This does not necessarily mean that it would refuse to join with the USA in a joint statement embracing the goal of a NWF world, but it does mean that Russia has moved from being the leading advocate to a country that will need persuading.

Meanwhile, there are disturbing indications that all is not well with other aspects of the nuclear relationship. Ratification of SALT II is still held up by the Russian Duma, because of the treaty's relatively unfavourable terms and because the US Congress is once again pushing for anti-ballistic missile (ABM) defences that would breach the ABM treaty.[50] And although Russia would have nothing to gain and much to lose by the failure of the CTB treaty, in the most recent negotiations, it was adopting a newly negative attitude.[51]

RUSSIA'S POLITICAL AND TERRITORIAL ASPIRATIONS

Dispassionate analysis of its aspirations is handicapped by the fact that Russia, whether tsarist or communist, has long served as a bogeyman for the West. One reason has been the ideological divide: conservative absolutism versus liberal constitutionalism in the nineteenth century; and authoritarian socialism versus democratic capitalism in the twentieth. That divide, added to a racist image (Mongol hordes), and the often brutal nature of Russia's domestic regime certainly reinforced the idea of a bogeyman. But the more important reason is the tenacious belief that Russia was inherently expansionist, in a way that other great powers were not. That belief persisted despite the fact that it was France in the nineteenth century and Germany in the twentieth who set out to conquer and control the whole of Europe. And that it was Russia's armies which not only repelled the agressors at immense cost, but were largely responsible for the enemy's defeat on his native soil.

The charge of expansionism was initially promoted by Great Britain in the nineteenth century, concerned about a possible threat to its interests in the eastern Mediterranean and its lines of communication with India and the Far East. The charge was resurrected in 1946, when it was combined with the Marxist vision of a socialist world to justify Washington's claim that Soviet communism was set on military world domination.[52] And one of the features of Western rhetoric during the Cold War was the extent to which Russia and Soviet communism were held equally to blame for the evil in the world.[53] As a consequence, Russia remains a bogeyman today.

If, therefore, we are to assess the threat posed by Russia to security in Europe in the twenty-first century, we must first clarify the historical record, setting Russian behaviour in the context of its times, and clear away the distortions of Cold War propaganda.

Is Russia inherently expansionist?

The European global expansion that would come to dominate the world in the first half of the twentieth century began to gather momentum in the sixteenth. States bordering the Atlantic expanded overseas; Russia, hemmed in to the west and south, expanded over land to the east. Russian policy was no more expansionist than that of other Western (or westernized) powers, and in the latter part of the 400 year period it was less so.

Russian colonial expansion had largely run its course by 1885, when the 'grab for Africa' by the Western Europeans was just getting under way. Russian involvement in China had trailed by more than 40 years that of the Western maritime powers, who had engaged in two punitive wars in 1839–42 and 1858–60 in the attempt to force the failing Manchu empire to open its hinterland to trade and investment. Russian penetration of northern China was halted and reversed in 1905 after war with Japan, while the Western (or westernized) assault on China continued in various forms until 1945.

Russian behaviour towards the inhabitants of the areas it occupied or conquered was well within contemporary norms. There was colonization of the northern Caucasus, Bashkira, the northern Kazakh steppes and parts of Turkestan, but no attempt was made to Russify the local population. Unlike the Portuguese and Spanish, the Russians did not have the mission of spreading Christianity, by force if necessary. Nor did they relocate or effectively eliminate the original inhabitants of the territories they occupied, as happened in Australia and North America. Tsarist imperial expansion was just part of the general pattern of European behaviour, and the objection that the Western Europeans ultimately withdrew from their overseas empires is only partly true. To the indigenous peoples of the Americas,[54] Australia, New Zealand and South Africa, the European colonists are still very much in place.

In Europe, Russia's frontiers had been largely established by the end of the eighteenth century, by when it had finally pushed back the Swedish and Polish–Lithuanian empires to the west and the Ottoman empire to the south. The period of the Napoleonic wars added Bessarabia and the trans-Caucasian territories of the Persian empire, and detached Finland from Sweden to become an autonomous Grand Duchy beholden to the tsar. The war also brought Russia into Europe, with its armies campaigning in northern Italy and finally in France, and at the time of Napoleon's defeat in 1814, Russia was the most powerful continental power.

Once Russia had pushed back the borders of encroaching empires, the possession of European territory ceased being an end in itself, as long as influence and security could be achieved by other means. As a Grand Duchy (1809) Finland was allowed to keep its own laws and institutions and these were respected by Russia for nearly a century. Re-establishing Poland as a separate kingdom under the tsar (1815) was another, if less successful, example of an alternative to full incorporation into the Russian empire.[55]

These limited interests were evident following its victory over Turkey in the war of 1827–8, which achieved the independence of Orthodox Greece.[56] Russia renounced all territorial claims to the conquered lands (Romania and most of Bulgaria) except for the relatively small area between the Russian frontier and the Danube delta, which allowed it to enjoy freedom of navigation on that waterway. On the eastern side of the Black Sea, to the disappointment of the local Armenians, Russia restored all the lands it had won from Turkey, except for two Georgian districts.[57] This was at a time when Russia still largely enjoyed the political prestige and military strength it had acquired in defeating Napoleon.

It is of course true that Russia (like Austria, the other directly adjacent state) hoped to gain influence and its share of territory from the long-delayed break-up of the Ottoman empire,[58] besides which it had a genuine and politically popular concern for the fate of its fellow Slavs and/or Orthodox co-religionists living under the 'Ottoman yoke'.[59] But Russia had no great incentive to territorial aggrandizement. Its objective in the Balkans was not to acquire more possessions, but to facilitate and hasten the emergence from Turkish rule of Christian nation-states that would turn to Russia for protection and would heed its interests.

The Turkish Straits were a partial exception. A large part of Russia's exports passed that way and, prior to the nineteenth century, its primary concern had been to ensure their safe and economic passage.[60] Increasingly thereafter, the concern shifted to preventing the passage of unfriendly warships into the Black Sea, since the maritime powers could (and did) concentrate their fleets at will, while the Russian navy remained divided between its three widely separated fleet areas. In the absence of an effective legal regime excluding warships of non-riparian powers, physical control of the Straits was the only certain way of achieving this.[61]

In other words, Russia in Europe was conforming to contemporary great power norms as it jostled for power, influence and security, using its armed forces to promote and protect its interests. So did other powers, including the United States when, through war in 1845–8, it acquired the half of newly independent Mexico that extended 600–900 miles north of the Rio Grande and Gilla rivers.[62] The US dream of an even larger Union was frustrated by Canadian federation in 1867, but that same year it agreed to buy Alaska from the Russians, they having decided to withdraw from North America.[63] In the Caribbean, the spoils of the war with Spain (1898) were Puerto Rico and a protectorate over Cuba.[64] Thereafter, the United States made it clear that it saw the Caribbean basin as its own fiefdom, and proceeded to act accordingly. In 1903, the Panamian ismuth was detached from Columbia, and the US acquired the territory through which the canal would run.

In sum Russian actions were well within the norms of contemporary great-power behaviour and the evidence does not support the claim that Russian policies in the nineteenth and early twentieth centuries were driven by an urge to expansion. Indeed, by comparison with Great Britain's worldwide gains at the end of World War I or the punitive conditions the Germans imposed on the new Soviet state in the Treaty of Brest-Litovsk (1918), Russian policy in Europe, if not actively benign, was notably non-acquisitive.

Nor does the pattern change under communism. It was World War II – a war they did their best to avoid – that brought the Russians into Europe. At the end of the war they withdrew forces that, in the process of driving back the Germans, had advanced about 250 miles into Norway; they withdrew from Finland, Yugoslavia, Czechoslovakia, and the strategically located island of Bornholm in the Baltic; they agreed to four-power control of Berlin, a city captured by the Soviets at immense cost and well behind their lines; at British request, they made Bulgaria withdraw its army from Thrace and the Aegean coast; and they refused help to the grassroots communist insurgency in Greece. In the 1950s the Soviet Union relinquished military bases in Porkala, Finland and in Port Arthur, China; and it withdrew from Austria.

That is not the behaviour of a country set on military domination of the world, and those who make that claim must also explain why the Russians did not exploit other opportunities for expansion that came their way.[65] For example, why didn't they move into Afghanistan in 1958, in response to the formation of CENTO, which linked Iran and Pakistan in an anti-Soviet alliance?[66] It was at this time that the US and Britain intervened militarily in Lebanon and Jordan. Why didn't they take over Xinjiang in the mid-1960s, while China was embroiled in its cultural revolution? In the late 1960s, with more than half a million Americans tied down in Vietnam, the British committed to withdrawing from east of Suez, but the US tilt to China and the arming of Iran yet to come, why didn't the Soviets use their local military preponderance to achieve gains in Iran? And if the invasion of Afghanistan in 1979 was an example of planned expansion, why did the Soviet Union choose to mount the operation at short notice in midwinter and only use limited force?

But the most persuasive refutation of any urge to military world domination lies in the structure, posture and deployment of Soviet forces during this period. This is not the place for a detailed exposition, but it can be said with certainty that Soviet military requirements between 1948 and 1986 were shaped by the reasonable assumption that war with the West – world war – was at least possible. Throughout the period, the Soviets' overriding concern was the danger of world war – a war they absolutely wanted to avoid, but could not afford to lose. They couldn't afford to lose because US statements and Western capabilities made it clear that in such a war the capitalist objective would be to overthrow the Soviet system.[67]

While the charge of unbridled Russian expansion stemmed from a partisan reading of nineteenth-century history, the image of a Soviet urge to military aggression was reinforced by the tendency to equate Communist Russia after World War II with Nazi Germany in the 1930s. This was wrong on three scores. One (which will not be pursued) was the very different implications of these fundamentally dissimilar ideologies in terms of *national* aspirations.

Another was the failure to realize that the post-World War I analogue for the Soviet Union in 1945–53 was not the defeated and disgruntled German nation of the 1920s, whose damaged pride allowed the rise of Hitler and his policy of courting war in order to harvest the fruits of victory. For the Soviets, who lost more than 20 million dead in defeating Hitler's armies, the appropriate analogue was the British and French, whose victory over the Germans in World War I cost them so dear that they went to extreme lengths in the 1920s and 1930s to avoid precipitating another such war.

The third mistake relates to an even broader canvas and concerns the quite different locations of Russia and Germany on their respective developmental curves. While the global expansion of Europe's quarrelsome nations didn't reach its apogee until the second half of the nineteenth century, in respect to the European region, the long-established powers (including Russia) were mainly 'satisfied' with the provisions of the Congress of Vienna (1815). However, three new 'western' nations emerged in the second half of the century (Italy, Germany and Japan), and they were *not* satisfied. Arriving on the scene towards the end of a highly lucrative period of history, they sought their share of the spoils. It was these ambitions that ultimately led to the Forty Years War that ended in 1945, a year that marked the apogee of European military world domination.

This broader canvas allows us to see interesting parallels between the 1940s and the final stages of the Napoleonic wars; and the breakdown of the anti-Axis alliance is more readily understood if set in its historical context. However, for the purposes of this chapter it must suffice to note that in World War II, America played the role opposite Russia that Britain had played in the final years of the Napoleonic wars. Similarly, Britain (which dominated the Eastern Mediterranean in 1944) assumed the role that Austria had played in the nineteenth century as the other great power (besides Russia) with territories adjoining the failing Ottoman empire: hence the agreement between Stalin and Churchill on spheres of influence in the Balkans, which were part of Hitler's disintegrating empire.

In that respect, if one replaces 'Muslim' by 'Capitalist' and 'Christian' by 'Socialist', it will be seen that Russian interests in the Balkans had remained much the same. Except for some relatively minor geostrategic adjustments, Russia was not interested in acquiring territory beyond its 1917 borders.[68] Rather, it sought the emergence from capitalist domination of socialist states that would turn to the Soviet Union for protection and support its interests in the Balkans.

Eastern Europe

Soviet forces entered Eastern Europe in the course of achieving final victory over the Axis armies, who fought as tenaciously in retreat as they had when advancing one thousand miles into Soviet territory. Germany did not capitulate until its armies went down to defeat on their native soil, and the Soviet advance through Eastern Europe was a prerequisite for that defeat.

Stalin had always made it clear that Russia's immediate aims in World War II were to defeat the Axis powers and to secure the country's western frontiers. The validity of the latter objective was accepted by Roosevelt and Churchill, who acquiesced in the reincorporation of the Baltic states and agreed to Poland's physical displacement westward, aligning its eastern boundary with the 1919 Curzon Line.[69] The longer-range Soviet objective was to keep Russia strong and Germany weak, with German reparations and a Soviet sphere of influence in Eastern Europe as essential means to that end. This, too, was accepted by the other two, who acknowledged, explicitly or implicitly, the primacy of the Soviet Union's political interest in the countries of the region.[70]

This did not, however, imply that Stalin was contemplating the *conquest* of Europe, as Stalin's Russia was not built to the same mould as Hitler's Germany or Napoleon's France. Harking back to the parallel with 1815, what Stalin had in mind was a new *Concert* of Europe. He perceived a congruence of 'vitally important and long-lasting interest' in avoiding war,[71] and saw the collaborative relationship established during World War II as a means to that end.[72] In the circumstances then prevailing, this was not unrealistic.[73]

Except in the most general terms, Stalin did not have clear-cut plans for the countries that came to comprise the Warsaw Pact. The basic requirement was to establish a buffer between the USSR and the resurgent Germany that could be expected to emerge in 15–20 years, and this implied governments that were amicably disposed towards the Soviet Union, or at least not hostile. This would not be easy to achieve, since Romania and (to a much lesser extent) Hungary had fought against Russia in both world wars, and there was a centuries-old enemity with Poland, whose government had been actively hostile in the inter-war years.[74]

However, having been welcomed as liberators in Eastern Europe, the Soviets probably genuinely believed that governments that represented the mass of the people would be positively disposed towards the Soviet Union, a Marxist prediction that seemed to have been validated in Albania and Yugoslavia, and again by the free elections held in Czechoslovakia in 1946. Nor was this assumption unjustified. The Communist parties of the Eastern European states were not alone in wanting the foreign policies of their countries to be based on an alliance with the USSR. Other political groups agreed that the Soviet Union was a surer safeguard against renewed German aggression than were the Anglo-Saxons or the French.

The pattern that finally emerged in Eastern Europe was not preordained, despite the ideological prejudice that the interests of the working class could only be properly represented by the world communist movement led from Moscow. Given the case of Finland and the differentiated Soviet approach to the other countries in 1945–7, it is likely that Stalin was prepared to live with a variety of left-leaning or resolutely neutral regimes. Communist control of the state apparatus was not seen as uniformly mandatory, although it may well have been the inevitable outcome for most countries.

This relatively relaxed approach changed abruptly in 1947–8, following the Truman declaration in March 1947, matched by Zhdanov's 'two camps' doctrine in September. This led to a switch in Soviet threat assessments from 'Germany in 15–20 years' time' to the more immediate danger of a capitalist coalition led by the Anglo-Saxon powers that would be ready for war in 1953. Eastern Europe must now serve as a defensive glacis in both military and ideological terms, and the latter requirement evoked the worst kind of centrally enforced Stalinist orthodoxy.

During the next 25 years Eastern Europe evolved from an ideological glacis to a cross between an ideological empire and an alliance, and it became an important part of the metropolitan core of the growing socialist system and growing world communist movement. At the same time, its importance as a military glacis increased steadily as contingency plans were reshaped to reflect changes in Soviet military doctrine about the probability and likely nature of a world war.

However, by 1985, Soviet interests in the area were badly out of balance. Economically, it was a net burden and in all six countries, large sections of the populace were more or less openly hostile to the government apparatus. There were strong arguments on political, ideological and economic grounds for the Soviet Union to get out of Eastern Europe, the loss of face notwithstanding.

The obstacle to such a move was the area's vital importance in Soviet plans for the contingency of world war. That obstacle was, however, removed in January 1987 by a reformulation of military doctrine that effectively ruled out the possibility of world war and required the military to plan on the assumption that war would be avoided/prevented by political means. This lifted the requirement for Soviet forces to be deployed in Eastern Europe and, by May 1987, discussions were afoot within the Warsaw Pact about unilateral force reductions and the ultimate withdrawal of Soviet forces. East European party chiefs had already been told by Gorbachev that they could not expect Soviet military intervention to keep them in power.[75]

The pattern of events in 1987–8 argue strongly that the Gorbachev leadership deliberately set in motion the process that would lead to the collapse of communist rule throughout Eastern Europe by the end of 1989, and Moscow appears to have actively abetted the process whereby popular forces removed existing Communist party regimes from power, the East German case being the most blatant. This is not to say that the Soviets foresaw the rapidity with which events would move, but it is certain that Moscow addressed the possibility of some kind of unified Germany as far back as mid-1987, and the final outcome is likely to have been less of a surprise in the Soviet Union than in the West.

For ten years after World War II, Moscow had sought a neutral and unified Germany. Following Germany's accession to NATO in 1955, Moscow accepted the division as irreversible – however, East Germany did not join the Warsaw Pact until 1964, and even then the size of its forces was kept proportionally low.[76] With the advent of Gorbachev's 'new political thinking about international relations', of the concept of a common European home, and of the view that the division of Europe should be overcome, new ways of countering the potential threat of a resurgent and revanchist Germany became feasible. German unity and the modalities of Germany's reincorporation in a restructured European political system were once again an open question.[77]

The near abroad

While it is possible to be reasonably definite about Russian attitudes towards the states of central and eastern Europe, its aspirations in relation to the 'near abroad' – a euphemism for the other 14 Republics of the former Soviet Union (FSU) – are less easily defined, if only because they differ so greatly in respect to the different entities.

In the ebb and flow of rival empires, virtually all the European territories of tsarist Russia had been acquired by the end of the eighteenth century. (To put that date in perspective, it was some 50 years before the US incorporated the western third of its continental territory, three-quarters of that area having been yielded by Mexico under various forms of duress, including war.) To the east of the Black Sea and south of the Caucasus, the Russian border with Persia was agreed in 1828 (and with Turkey in 1878), while the Caucasus (including Chechnya) had been occupied by 1859. To the east of the Caspian, the turkic Khanates had been mainly conquered by 1885. (In timing, this compares with the US annexation of Midway, Samoa, the Hawaiian Islands, and Wake in 1867–99, plus the fruits of war with Spain in 1898–9.)

In the wake of World War I, the collapse of Russia's armies, the Bolshevik revolution and the eastward advance of the Central Powers deep into Russia, parts of the tsarist empire took the opportunity to secede, but only the three Baltic states were successful in breaking away for any length of time. Georgia, Armenia and Azerbajzhan had been reincorporated by 1922, as had the eastern parts of Byelorussia and the Ukraine, the western parts being absorbed by Poland. But the latter were recovered in 1939–40 when, for largely strategic reasons, the Soviets colluded with Germany so as to reincorporate the eastern parts of Poland (the population being largely Byelorussian and Ukrainian), plus Bessarabia (Moldavia) and the three Baltic states. The extra depth provided by the latter made the fragile difference between failure and success in the subsequent defence of Leningrad. By the end of World War II, most of tsarist territory had been regained, the legitimacy of the post-war frontiers having been endorsed by Roosevelt and Churchill.

This means that at the time of its disintegration at the end of 1991, the Soviet Union was the contemporary manifestation of a state entity that had, for the most part, existed in its current form for some 200 years, an entity that within the living memory of a quarter of its population had been successfully defended against foreign invasion at a very great cost. Given that historical background, the most striking aspect of the dissolution of the Soviet Union is the peaceable nature of the process, particularly when compared to the examples of the Russian and American civil wars, and the British, French and Portuguese withdrawals from empire.

This may be explained in part by the emphasis on national identity that stemmed from Marxist theory; the Soviet Union comprised 15 'Union' Republics, each dominated by a single ethnic group, with its own government and representation in the Council of Nationalities in Moscow. It was often claimed that the USSR was a union of more than 100 nationalities, and many of the Union Republics contained within their borders 'autonomous' republics, regions and districts with concentrations of other ethnic groups. But most of the nationalities were very small, and in practical terms just over half the Soviet population was Russian, another 20 per cent were also Slavs (Ukrainian and Byelorussian), 20 per cent were traditional Islamic people, 3 per cent were Christian Caucasians (Armenians and Georgians), and 3 per cent Balts.

The Union Republics ranged in size from tiny Estonia (with a population of 1.6 million at the end of the 1980s), to the Russian Federation (population 147 million, roughly half the total of the USSR), stretching from the Baltic to the Pacific. In the main, the Russian Federation (RSFSR) comprised the territories that made up tsarist Russia at the end of the seventeenth century, while the other 14 Union Republics comprised additions to the empire during the eighteenth and nineteenth centuries.

In 1989, the newly elected Supreme Soviet in Moscow was already reworking the law on the federal relationship that linked the 15 Republics in a single union and delimited the division of powers; it was also preparing a new law, which had hitherto not existed (and does not exist in many federal states) on the mechanics of secession. This required that two-thirds of the voters opt for secession and that there be a five-year transition period during which the political, military and economic terms would be negotiated. This measured approach was, however, overtaken by the disintegrating forces of perestroika, glasnost, democratization, and the relaxation of Soviet control in Europe. The process was hastened when Yeltsin exploited the issue in his struggle with Gorbachev, and became irreversible when he withdrew the Russian Federation from the Union, which had the effect of denying Gorbachev a power base, while enhancing his own.

Somewhat in the same way that the Soviet Union chose to walk away from the political, economic and military burden of Eastern Europe, the Russian Federation chose to walk away from the massive economic and political problems of the USSR. The general acceptability of that policy decision was demonstrated by the lack of support for the coup in August 1991 that was intended to prevent it happening, and Yeltsin's subsequent (if short-lived) popularity.

Certain conclusions can be drawn from this brief historical review and from subsequent events in the former Soviet Union. First, while there may be calls to restore Russia's 'greatness', the political drive to reconstitute the Soviet Union or the tsarist empire is absent, as is the military capability to do so.[78] Second, Russia has long-standing and legitimate interests in the former republics; these include geostrategic concerns and the continuing presence of some 25 million Russians who were living outside the borders of the RSFSR. Moscow will, therefore, take a close and direct interest in their affairs, just as the US does in Central America and the Caribbean, although Russia does not enjoy a comparable military and economic predominance in the wider region. And third, there are persuasive indicators that Russia will conform to existing norms of great power behaviour, such as they are.

- By the end of 1988, it was already becoming clear that Moscow saw the Baltic states as a special case and would be willing to negotiate an orderly secession if it didn't jeopardize the larger Union. By virtue of their location, ethnic makeup and existing infrastructure, the Baltic states were ideally suited to serve as the major economic interface between Western Europe and the Soviet Union. Meanwhile the strategic imperatives that had justified their annexation in 1940 and retention after the war had ceased to apply once it was ruled that world war would be averted by political means. It was therefore appropriate for Moscow to view the Baltic republics in terms of the Soviet–Finnish relationship, which had proved to be a satisfactory way of achieving physical security, while opening the Soviet Union to Western technology and trade.
- In 1991, 41 per cent of the population of Kazhakhstan was Russian, compared to only 37 per cent native Kazakhs, and the Russian population was largely concentrated in the northern part of the republic, adjoining the Russian Federation. In the throes of dissolution, it would

have been very simple for Moscow to have annexed that region to the RSFSR.

- There were sizeable Russian minorities in the Baltic states (Estonia – 36 per cent, Latvia – 28 per cent). Albeit under Western pressure, Moscow has nevertheless met its obligations to withdraw all Russian forces and has relied on negotiations to achieve compromises in the Baltic states' restrictive citizenship policies that were designed to disadvantage and often exclude ethnic Russians.
- Despite Russia's relative preponderance, the complicated process of apportioning the Union's assets between the 15 Republics has been achieved with surprisingly little rancour. This is most notable in respect to military resources, where Russia had to consider its external security requirements, as well as the zero-sum implications of the internal apportionment.
- The case of the Black Sea fleet and its base at Sevastopol is particularly relevant. Russia conquered the Khanate of Crimea in the 1780s and in the 1920s it was designated an autonomous republic within the Russian Federation. For domestic political reasons, the Crimea was transferred to the Ukraine in 1954 by Khrushchev. Despite the suspect legality of this transfer, the fact that 75 per cent of its population is Russian, and the absence of a comparable naval base on the Russian Black Sea coast (the Ukraine has Odessa), Moscow has relied on intensive negotiations rather than populist pressure or military force to resolve this contentious issue.

While these examples are reassuring, the vexed question of Russia's long-term relationship with the Ukraine and Byelorus remains uncertain. To some extent Yelstin was playing politics when, four weeks before the formal dissolution of the USSR, he agreed with the other two Slavic republics to join in creating the Commonwealth of Independent States.[79] But the agreement also reflected an assumption that by virtue of their shared ethnicity and common history, there was some affinity of interests between the three.[80]

As Byelorus and the Ukraine have had their seats at the UN since its inception, Russia can hardly argue that their separate identity is an accidental by-product of the tsarist and Soviet administrative systems. Nor have their relations always been amicable. Both countries declared independence at the time of the revolution; most of the Ukraine was 'White' territory, it supported the Polish invasion of Russia, and in the wake of the 'Red' victory, some 650 000 fled the country as refugees. The Ukraine suffered disproportionately from collectivization and significant numbers supported the Germans in 1941, who were able to raise a Ukrainian division. There was no shortage of collaborators to head the puppet regimes established by the Nazis[81] and, after the war, US-supported Ukrainian partisans were active in the Carpathians through 1952.[82]

Nevertheless, there is a significant measure of interdependence between them which, in the case of Byelorus, is close to dependency. The relationship with the Ukraine is more complex, not least because of the difference between the eastern and western parts of the country, particularly in terms of their links to Russia and to Poland, forged by the circumstances of history, which is also reflected in religious orientation. But both states are of crucial geostrategic concern to Russia. Whereas in the past, they provided defence in depth, Moscow is now within 250 miles of its western border, while Russia's southern flank has been exposed to hostile reinforcement by sea.[83]

Overall assessment

The historical record does not support the belief that Russia is inherently expansionist; there is no reason to suppose that it has an urge to add to its existing territories.[84] It does, however, see the former republics of the Soviet Union as coming within its National Security Zone and Moscow would react strongly to any attempt to turn them against Russia or to move them any further away than a position of strict neutrality.[85]

Russia's attitude towards these new states will be conditioned by its assessment of the overall security environment and where it stands in relation to the West in general, and the US in particular, on the continuum that runs between valued partner and potential enemy. As regards Russia's attitude towards the Ukraine, there are appropriate analogies in both ethno-cultural and geopolitical terms. One is Britain's attitude towards the Irish Free State when it was flirting with Germany in 1939–40. Another is how the US views Canada. One can envision the reaction in Washington if it were believed that Ottawa was being weaned away from its traditional stance of a compliant ally.

There is no reason to suppose that Russia has any aspirations in respect to the countries of Eastern Europe, other than the natural interests of a great power in a nearby area, with which it has long-standing historical and cultural links. By the same token, Moscow will react against attempts to draw those countries into a potentially opposing bloc.

Where Russia does have large and largely unfulfilled aspirations is in the level of respect it should be accorded by virtue of its history, its physical and intellectual resources, and its geopolitical situation. Despite having fallen on hard times, Russia continues to insist on great-power status, a claim that has overwhelming domestic support.

The widespread disillusion over the massive disparity between Western promises and deliveries since the dissolution of the Soviet Union and the move towards political democratization and economic liberation is exacerbated by a Western triumphalism that allows Russia no credit for the new political thinking that led to the end of the Cold War and opened the possibility of a new security regime in Europe.

Nor was Moscow given any credit for the unilateral force cuts and subsequent concessions that enabled the treaty on Conventional Forces in Europe (CFE) to be negotiated; Western practice was to pocket concessions and ask for more. And when the dissolution of the Soviet Union and the Warsaw Pact invalidated the treaty's carefully wrought balances, the West insisted that its terms must stand, to Russia's serious disadvantage.[86] Add to this the fact that SALT II focused on US concerns and committed the Russians to new expenditures, and it is unsurprising that the Gorbachev and Yeltsin leaderships are vulnerable to the politically dangerous charge of having pandered to the Americans and selling their own people short.

AN OVERVIEW OF THE THREAT

Having bewailed the absence of democracy in Russia for the past 200 years, it would be ironic if the West were to jeopardize security in Europe by ignoring the strongly held opinions of Russians at all levels of society,[87] on the grounds that they 'didn't oughter' feel like that.

Russia's aspirations are not extravagant. It wants to be treated as a fully paid-up member of the international community and accorded the respect due to its past achievements, current capabilities and future potential. It wants: to have due account taken of its opinions and sensibilities in international affairs, especially in central and eastern Europe; to receive the sustained economic and political assistance needed to transform Russia into a market economy and a democracy; to establish a mutually supportive political and economic relationship with the former republics of the Soviet Union; to enjoy a cooperative relationship with the Western powers, particularly the United States; to promote the OSCE as the primary vehicle for ensuring cooperative security and preventing conflict in Europe. And (of steadily increasing importance), Russia does *not* want to find itself disadvantaged by the political–military realignment of former members of the Warsaw Pact.

In themselves, Russia's aspirations present no threat to security in Europe. A constructive relationship with Russia does, however, depend on the West's capacity to meet those concerns; and the West's ability to avert the real and present dangers to security in Europe depends on the continuing existence of that relationship.

The possible breakdown of political and social order in the new or newly liberated communist states is one such threat. The proximate reasons for such breakdown are poorly understood, but there is a clear link with economic factors, domestic and foreign. Besides the timely involvement of mediation and conflict prevention services by international organizations and others, the most effective means of averting this threat is likely to be the politically sensitive provision of appropriate (that is, non-doctrinaire) forms of economic and financial support and assistance. It has still to be demonstrated that the PfP programme has any relevance to this threat.

One thing is, however, certain. Unless the major powers cooperate in responding to potential and actual breakdowns of order, security in Europe will be undermined. If the major powers (including Russia) do not present a united front in seeking practical solutions that respect the realities of the situation, and in then implementing and enforcing their agreed decision, the virus is likely to spread.

Similarly, to avert both aspects of the nuclear threat requires whole-hearted Russian cooperation. As regards 'loose nukes', it is already difficult to achieve the levels of efficiency and veracity needed to control and verify the ongoing dismantling and destruction process. The problems would be near insurmountable if the Russians followed the letter rather than the spirit of the various agreements, or withdrew their active cooperation. The Russians have the further option of deferring action on the grounds that the US Congress is actively considering programmes that will breach the terms of the 1972 Anti-Ballistic Missile (ABM) treaty.[88]

If Russian cooperation is withdrawn, there is a significant danger of all that has been achieved since 1990 in terms of halting and reversing the build-up of nuclear arsenals being lost, and with it the possibility of eliminating nuclear weapons. Whether or not a nuclear-weapons-free world is politically feasible, the possibility of a new and more dangerous nuclear arms race (this time including space-based systems), is a threat to be avoided at all costs.

Retrospective analysis of the past 40 years has shown how close the world came to accidental and inadvertent nuclear war during that period.[89] Second time round, we are unlikely to be so lucky, as we will be involved in a multi-polar game, where there is even less understanding between players and a greatly increased possibility of systems failures. Meanwhile, the dynamics of a new nuclear arms race and its associated doctrines will kill off the still tender shoots of cooperation and conciliation, and ensure that the international system reverts to the confrontational policies of the Cold War years.

In short, the primary threat to security in Europe is the withdrawal of Russian cooperation. This would be the result of steadily mounting Russian frustration at what they see as Western bad faith and the increasingly uneven nature of their relationship with the West in general and the US in particular.

The source of this threat is to be found in Western attitudes and habits of mind. In our ignorance of the historical realities of the past 200, 100, even 50 years, and our continued readiness to believe the distorted versions provided by Cold War propaganda. In our moralistic triumphalism that places all the blame for the Cold War and its costs on the Soviet Union and justifies a self-righteous approach to Russia today. In our fixation with worst-case analyses that lead to self-fulfilling prophecies, and our zero-sum approach to interstate relations that inhibits sharing and compromise. And in our pandering to single-issue pressure groups whose narrow ethnic interests are incapable of accommodating the broader requirements of macro-security in Europe.

PRINCIPLES FOR PROMOTING SECURITY IN EUROPE

The argument is straightforward. In the collective judgment of most Western specialists on Russia, including a highly respected group of former senior State Department officials, the enlargement of NATO threatens Washington's cooperative relationship with Moscow. This judgment is shared by the Russian elite, who, for that and other cogent reasons, are strongly opposed to the policy.[90]

If Russian cooperation is withdrawn, macro-security in Europe (and in the wider world) will be undermined. So, too, will the micro-security of individual countries in the region, because the very nature of Russia's political and strategic interests in the former republics will change adversely. At the same time, the international and domestic constraints on pursuing those interests through political, economic and military means will be weakened or removed completely, as the security of the Russian homeland assumes its traditional place at the head of Moscow's concerns.

In seeking the psychological comfort of NATO membership, the Visegrad four and their Western sponsors are ignoring the harsh realities of international politics, where one country's security is another's insecurity. Will Poland really feel more secure in the front line of a redivided and rearmed Europe? And can the claims of cultural affinity justify jeopardizing the security of the newly independent states of the FSU? What will happen to tiny Estonia, strategically located across the south-western approaches to St Petersburg? And what kind of political and economic pressures will Moscow bring to bear on the Ukraine?

In short, the enlargment of NATO will have serious repercussions for the security of non-member states, both directly and through adverse political developments in Russia. The latter are of vital concern to Russia's neighbours and to its own citizens, and the situation is still in flux. There continues to be the danger that a sense of unfairness, when added to the existing feeling of national humiliation, the high unemployment, and low and falling living standards, will generate a fully-fledged Weimar syndrome. At the very least it will weaken the movement for democratic reform and strengthen those who wish to reincorporate the other Slav republics.[91]

Clearly, it is nonsense to claim that the future composition of NATO is solely a matter for its present members. The prevalence of this attitude underlines the need for rethinking our approach to security in Europe.

THINKING ABOUT SECURITY IN EUROPE

It was Gorbachev's 'new political thinking about international relations' that underlaid the fundamental changes in the second half of the 1980s and brought about the Soviet withdrawal from Eastern Europe and the Cold War.[92] The West was happy to garner the fruits of those changes, but dismissed the 'new thinking', with its emphasis on cooperation rather than competition, as utopian propaganda. And while the NATO summit in July 1990 recognized the Soviet Union as a partner in building security in Europe and the concept of 'cooperative security' assumed a new prominence in Western discourse, cooperation as-between-equals was only on offer when vital interests were at stake, as in the redeployment and disposal of the FSU's nuclear assets. This implies that before we can develop a new way of thinking about security in Europe, we must rid ourselves of Cold War habits of thought.

The concept of 'war' lay at the heart of Cold War thinking. World War II practice ensured that threat assessments focused on worst-case rather than most likely Soviet behaviour, assessments that were then made concrete by the assumptions justifying nuclear deterrence. As a result of Munich, compromise was seen as appeasement and the emphasis was on military rather than diplomatic solutions. As in war, strategy and tactics were zero-sum, while the negative objective of containment (exclusion and blockade) ruled out positive inducements to cooperative Soviet behaviour.

Many of these attitudes persist today and we have yet to admit the reality of self-fulfilling prophecies.[93] We emphasize military responses to worst-case contingencies, brushing aside the adverse long-term consequences, and neglect opportunities to structure the future through political means. We have still to accept that by unilaterally seeking to improve our own security we automatically reduce the security of others, meanwhile diminishing overall security by increasing the danger of conflict.

These age-old principles remind us that in rethinking security in Europe, we should not overlook the political arrangements that served us well in earlier times, such as neutral states and buffer zones. The Concert of Europe has already been mentioned, but we need to eschew its corollary – balance of power politics. These are inherently adversarial and divisive. Rather than a balance of power, we should think of balancing interests.

BALANCING INTERESTS

There are four entities whose security interests need to be weighed and reconciled: Russia, America, Western Europe, and newly independent Central and Eastern Europe (including the FSU republics). All four have a vital interest in peace-in-Europe, but that peace depends absolutely on constructive cooperation between the major powers.

All three European entities strongly favour a continued US military presence. The American interest is less clear and 'the NATO enlargement debate is really a debate ... over whether, when, and how to anchor the United States in Europe ...'.[94] It was because the isolationists and budget-cutters in Congress put the answer to those questions in doubt that the internationalist wing of the US defence debate sought additional support. They found it in a coalition of interests that viewed Russia, whether tsarist, communist or quasi-democratic, as an inherent threat to the region. The price of that support was the enlargement of NATO.

Such enlargement will, however, violate Russia's legitimate interests and already threatens cooperation between the major powers. Having voluntarily withdrawn from Eastern Europe and joined in the dismantling of its former empire, Russia had to accept NATO as a historical fact. But it was not alone in believing there was agreement that former members of the Warsaw Pact would remain militarily non-aligned.[95] With justification, Russia sees the proposed enlargement as not only a threat to its interests but as a serious breach of trust.

It thus falls to Western Europe to be the 'balancer' between the interests of Washington and Moscow. While they face no territorial threat in the forseeable future, the countries of Western Europe consider a continued US presence to be essential to the long-term security of the greater European region. It is also clear that constructive cooperation by Moscow is essential to that security. This means taking active steps to avert the danger of Russia being driven to adopt an assertively defensive stance that would lead to renewed confrontation and new divisions in Europe.

These differing interests could be reconciled if the West Europeans were to provide a justification, other than enlarging NATO, for Congressional funding of US forces in Europe. US internationalists agree with the isolationists that the continuing defence of Europe is the primary responsibility of the European members of the alliance, but they also see the US presence there as an essential element of America's global military posture.[96] As demonstrated in the Gulf War, NATO has a new importance for the United States as a forward base and staging post, but that war also showed European powers joining with America in defending common interests outside the NATO area.[97]

If the major European members were willing to spin off from the WEU a semi-formal alliance structure that would commit those powers to joint operations with the United States outside the NATO area, that direct military contribution combined with the indirect contribution of basing rights could be considered to balance out the financial cost of the US military presence in Europe.[98] This would likely enlist the support of conservative isolationists in Congress, removing the need for support by the coalition pressing NATO enlargment.[99] From the European viewpoint, a contribution of this kind would compensate for US limitations in the field of peacekeeping, while providing more direct access to the US policy process.

This leaves the interests of the Central and East European states to be considered. Since the micro-security of individual countries depends ultimately on the macro-security of the region, the security interests of each and all the CEE states would be best served by a binding declaration of neutrality, guaranteed by the major powers in a multilateral treaty.[100]

Europe is still in transition, feeling its way from Cold War confrontation to some kind of cooperative security structure. Competitive alliance-building would be fatal and, for the time being at least, the role of the CEE should be that of a neutral buffer zone, preferably girded by a lattice of non-aggression and arms-limitation treaties.[101] Military neutrality need not, however, exclude membership of other groupings.[102]

COOPERATIVE SECURITY

It is foolish to pretend that NATO would respond in kind, should Russia take military action against directly adjacent states, such as Estonia or the Ukraine. The independence of those states depends on the effectiveness of the encompassing cooperative security regime, and the latter's viability requires that Russia feels secure. Cooperative security is based on the principles of partnership and reassurance.[103] It is clearly the opposite to reassuring if one of the nominal partners (NATO) sets out to increase what is already a preponderence of effective military power in Europe.[104]

At this time, Russia's need is more for psychological than physical security, and that can only be provided through constructive partnership, primarily with NATO and the United States. This is widely acknowledged and there is a range of relatively simple institutional adjustments that would 'recognize Russia as a great European power with which NATO should engage extensively' by providing the necessary consultative mechanisms.[105] Preferably codified in treaty form, this would be a two-way street, giving NATO the routine opportunity to discuss with Moscow security developments in the Atlantic-to-the-Urals region (including the CIS).

However, despite the rhetoric of partnership, the trend since 1991 has been away from recognizing Russia's need for symbolic equality as a great power. This was exemplified by the PfP programme, which provided an obvious opportunity for according Russia the special treatment warranted by its existing military capability, its latent power, and the record of consultation between Washington and Moscow, established over some 25 years. Instead, as if deliberately to humiliate, NATO insisted that Russia should observe exactly the same arrangements as tiny Estonia and Tajikstan.[106] Another example was US reluctance to recognize Russia as a major player in dealing with the Bosnian conflict. Similarly, Washington continues to resist Moscow's proposals for providing the OSCE with a management structure that would allow the organization an effective role in crisis prevention, while recognizing Russia as a great European power.[107]

The responsibility for remedying this deteriorating situation lies squarely with Britain, France and Germany. Russia is in no position to take remedial action; moreover, democratization has made it harder for Moscow to meekly acquiesce in what is widely seen as unfair treatment and a breach of trust. America *is* in a position to take action, but lacks the capacity to do so; as so often, this foreign policy issue is enmeshed in US domestic politics.

By virtue of their agreement to the policy of enlargement, Britain, France and Germany are as much to blame for the present situation as America.[108] They also have the greater stake in security in Europe, and they possess the capacity to reverse this dangerous trend. If the Europeans work together, they can ensure Russian participation in security decision-making on Europe and, by making firm commitments, they can reshape the Washington debate about Europe's place in US global strategy.

The most immediate requirement is to challenge the complacent acceptance of past policy decisions, a complacency that is manifest in the assertions by the protagonists of NATO expansion that Russia will just have to like it or lump it. It is equally evident in the cynics' claim that once the financial implications are understood, Congress will never authorize it; by then, of course, the damage will be done.

History may not repeat itself exactly, but parallels have already been drawn between current developments in Russia and those in Germany during the Weimar period. There are also parallels between the situation in Washington in 1993–4 and that in 1945–6. Both were times of public debate about America's global role in the wake of a war from which the United States had emerged supreme; times when decisions were taken that shaped future relations with Moscow.[109] In both cases, those decisions identified Russia as a potential enemy – implicitly in 1994 and explicitly in 1946.[110]

By 1948, both sides were amply fulfilling the other's prophecies, and Korea just served to confirm the West's prognosis.[111] As we move towards the year 2000, Russia's relations with Iran could provide the same kind of confirmation (albeit in a lower key), while US space-based missile defences would echo the US atomic monopoly. We might even find Russia and China once more lined up together against the West, only this time bound by an identity of interests, rather than the brittle ties of ideology.

That is speculation. But the actual and opportunity costs of the Cold War in terms of human suffering were too high and the threat to human survival was too real to risk repeating that experience. That, however, is the direction in which we are now heading. The adverse effect on Russia's legitmate interests of enlarging NATO and our implicit designation of Russia as a potential enemy are a certain recipe for acrimony and dissent, rather than the cooperative engagement on which security in Europe must perforce depend. As to the Weimar syndrome, it is early days yet. It was 15 years after the Great War before Hitler came to power.

Notes

1. A copy of the letter, dated 3 May 1955, was republished in *New York Review of Books*, 21 September 1995, p. 75. The original letter enclosed a draft of the article by Ambassador Jonathon Dean 'Losing Russia or Keeping NATO: Must We Choose?' that was due to appear in *Arms Control Today* (Washington), June 1995.

2. At this same period, Senator Richard G. Lugar gave as his informed opinion that 'Russians ... see United States policy on NATO enlargement as part of a larger shift in US policy designed to squeeze Russia out of Europe. In their minds, enlargement is linked to the US support for Bosnian Muslims, as well as the Ukraine. These moves have been seen as part of a larger strategic design to consolidate the geostrategic gains of the Cold War at Russia's expense.' *NATO's Future: Problems, Threats, and US Interests* (Washington: US GPO, 1995) Senate Committee on Foreign Relations: Hearings before the S/Cttee on European Affairs, 27 April, 3 May; p. 47.

3. In a review of opinion in NATO members, Philip Gordon observed that students of Russian politics (former Sovietologists) generally oppose the enlargement, while those who originate from or interact with Central Europe have more sympathy for the proposal. 'NATO's Grey Zone', *Prospect* (London: April, 1996), p. 68. A significant aspect of the debate is the number of former Cold War warriors and anti-Soviet hawks who now oppose NATO extension, in addition to those who signed the letter to the Secretary of State. See, for example, the testimony of Arnold Horelick and Fred C. Ickle at the Lugar hearings, *NATO's Future*, pp. 11–25.

4. At their meeting in Madrid on 14 November 1955, the WEU Council of Ministers was presented with a report by the Permanent Council on *The WEU Contribution to the European Union Intergovernmental Conference of 1996* and with a 40-page 'White Paper' entitled *European Security: a common concept of the 27 WEU Countries*. The latter comprised ten full members (who are also members of NATO and the EU), three associate members (also members of NATO), and nine associate partners, comprising six East European states and the three Baltic Republics.

5. For example para. 84 of the *WEU Contribution* (under the section headed 'European defence within the Common Foreign and Security Policy') refers to the WEU's 'collective defence commitment' while para. 3 refers to 'the eventual framing of a common defence policy' as one of the objectives set out in Article B of the Maastricht Treaty. In the *Common Concept*, under the section headed 'The European Security Environment' (which excludes

the territories of the 27 WEU countries), the sub-section on Russia and the newly independent states of the former Soviet Union is the longest, and heads the list of six 'constitutive other' areas of the world, where there are military or other risks.

6. This summary history of the various Organizations, Unions, Conferences and Programmes draws primarily on Catherine M. Kelleher, *The Future of European Security: an interim assessment* (The Brookings Institution, 1995); also on Centre for Defence Studies, *A Common Foreign and Security Policy for Europe: the Inter-Governmental Conference of 1996 [CDS-IGC]* (London: Kings College, July 1995); House of Commons Defence Committee, *The Future of NATO: the 1994 Summit and its Consequences* (London: July 1995) Tenth Report; Lawrence Martin and John Roper, *Towards a Common Defence Policy* (Paris: Institute for Security Studies, WEU, 1995). Those writings have also informed other parts of this chapter.

7. Following the break-up of the Soviet Union, Czechoslovakia and Yugoslavia.

8. Although they both originated in the late 1940s and had overlapping memberships, the WEU and EU were quite separate in purpose and function. The distinction is captured by their original designation as a 'Treaty Organization' and a 'Community' respectively.

9. For an important discussion of these issues see Paul R.S. Gerhard, *The United States and European Security* (London: IISS, Feb. 1994) Adelphi Paper No. 286. See particularly pp. 37, 67–8.

10. The WEU accorded these nine states associate membership in May 1994.

11. There was also the promise that NATO would 'consult' with a Partner who perceived a threat to its territorial integrity, political independence, or security. For details of the 'Invitation' and 'Framework Document' see Kelleher, *Future of European Security*, App. B.

12. By April 1995, all members of the NACC except Tadzhikistan had signed the Framework Document. However, Russia insisted on public acknowledgment of a form of 'special relationship' with NATO, by virtue of its particular capabilities.

13. Some observers consider that another factor in the White House decision was the need to distract attention from the failure to pass the Clinton Health Care Bill.

14. Congress had already approved (in the Fall of 1993) the so-called Brown amendment, which stipulated that the four Visegrad states would henceforth benefit from the special cooperative priviliges in logistics and weapons acquisition otherwise reserved to NATO members. Zbigniew Brzezinski, 'A Plan for Europe', *Foreign Affairs*, (Jan/Feb 1995), p. 40.

15. Strobe Talbot, 'Why NATO Should Grow', *New York Review of Books*, 10 August 1995, p. 27. This article reminds one of those in the Communist Party house organ *Kommunist*, where the losers in an internal Soviet debate were required to publicly recant by expounding the official party line.

16. See Michael E. Brown, 'The Flawed Logic of NATO Expansion', *Survival* (IISS, Spring 1995) 37:1, pp. 36–40. Brown discusses six main strategic and political arguments for expansion, the last (not considered here) being the need for WEU and NATO membership to be coextensive.

17. At the Lugar Senate Hearings, Fred C. Ikle observed that NATO was 'not a free-trade area or a club for democracies'. *NATO's Future*, p. 21.

18. Jonathon Dean notes that 'NATO leaders do not speak much in public about … insuring against a resurgent Russia, but it is much in their thoughts'. He goes on to give chapter and verse. ('Losing Russia', pp. 3–4).

19. Talbot p. 28, col. 1.

20. November 1956 provided a telling example of US financial clout, when Britain was forced to break off the Suez operation.

21. It is relevant that Assistant Secretary of State Richard Holbrooke, having berated the Europeans for their inactivity, gave Washington (*not* NATO) credit for defusing this potential conflict.

22. Brzezinski, 'A Plan for Europe', *Foreign Affairs* (Jan/Feb 1995) p. 30.

23. Richard Holbrooke, 'America: A European Power', *Foreign Affairs* (March/April 1995), p. 42. At the time of writing, Holbrooke was Assistant Secretary of State for European Affairs, before which he was US Ambassador in Bonn.

24. Jane M.O. Sharp, 'Reassuring Central Europe', in Sharp (ed.), *About Turn, Forward March with Europe* (London: Institute for Public Policy Research/Rivers Oram Press, 1996) p. 2. Her writing assumes that the West has an unquestioned obligation 'to right the wrongs of Yalta'. Understandably, the advocacy of the ethnic lobbies is motivated more by sentiment than by dispassionate political analysis.

25. For the background see Gerhard, *The United States and European Security*, particularly pp. 37, 67–68.

26. This is not surprising, as the debate on extending NATO had 'not focused on what it was going to cost'. Testimony by Ambassador Matlock, Lugar Senate Hearings, p. 87.

27. See *Study on NATO Enlargement* (London: BASIC) Research Report 95.2, October 1995. It cites 'The Defence Program Question: the Military and Budgetary Dimensions of NATO Expansion', a paper by Richard L. Kugler, RAND, presented at a Symposium on NATO, Fort McNair, Washington DC, 24–5 April, 1995.

28. Zbigniew Brzezinski refers to the need for 'strategic differentiation' quoting Senator Richard Lugar. 'A Plan for Europe', p. 29.

29. This is the administration's line. See also General William Odom (Lugar Senate Hearings p. 27), Brzezinski pp. 34–36, Holbrooke p. 45.

30. Holbrooke, 'America: a European Power', p. 50.

31. Brzezinski, p. 34.

32. Brzezinski pp. 35–6; Jane M.O. Sharp, 'Tasks for NATO: move east and revise the CFE', *The World Today* (London: RIIA, April 1995), pp. 67–70.

33. Henry Kissinger, cited by R.T. Davis, letter to *New York Review of Books*, 21 Sept 1995, p. 74.

34. Brzezinski, p. 35; Holbrooke, p. 48.

35. Holbrooke, p. 48.

36. Holbrooke, p. 45.

37. See, for example, Brzezinski pp. 38–9, and Holbrooke pp. 50–1.

38. These figures are derived, in the main, from *CDS-IGC* p. 6 (see note 6 above).

39. Susan L. Woodward, *Balkan Tragedy: Chaos and Dissolution after the Cold War* (The Brookings Institution, 1995), pp. 15–17. This 500+ page book provides a disturbing analysis of the unintended consequences of well-intentioned political and economic restructuring, prompted by the West.

40. Abram and Antonia Chayes discuss this problem in the introduction to their *Preventing Conflict in the Post-Communist World: Mobilizing International and Regional Organizations* (The Brookings Institution, 1996), pp. 1–6. See also the chapters by Keitha S. Fine, Jean E. Manas, and Wolfgang Reinicke.

41. *ibid.* p. 2.

42. On 1 June 1996, it was announced that the last nuclear warheads had been transferred from Ukrainian territory. *Disarmament Diplomacy* (Bradford: DFAX, June 1996), no. 6, pp. 40–1. The transfer of warheads from Kazakhstan was completed in Spring 1995, and from Byelorus some time before that.

43. *Disarmament Diplomacy* (Bradford: DFAX, February 1996), no. 3, p. 42, citing *Washington Post* 28 January 1996.

44. Michael MccGwire, *Perestroika and Soviet National Security* (The Brookings Institution, 1991), pp. 60, 194–204.

45. Through 1992, Russia continued to advocate complete nuclear disarmament. In September 1994 at the United Nations, Yeltsin advocated further cuts in strategic weapons beyond SALT II, in order to provide for the eventual possibility of a NWF world.

46. See Stephen A. Cambone and Patrick G. Garrity, 'The Future of US Nuclear Policy', *Survival* (London: IISS, Winter 1994–5), 36:4, pp. 74–7.

47. General Andrew J. Goodpaster, *An Evolving US Nuclear Posture*, (Washington DC: Henry L. Stimson Center, December 1995), Second Report of the Steering Committee, Project on Eliminating Weapons of Mass Destruction.

48. For an excellent summary of the West's failure to deliver on exaggerated promises and Russia's disenchantment with how it has been excluded from the policy formulation process, see Robert D. Blackwill in Blackwill, Roderick Braithwaite and Akhito Tanaka, *Engaging Russia* (New York: The Trilateral Commission), 1995, pp. 15–17.

49. MccGwire, *Perestroika*, p. 122.

50. The US only ratified START II in January 1996. For a review of the Congressional politics underlying these issues see John Steinbruner, 'Unrealized Promise, Avoidable Trouble: the unwitting drift of international security', *The Brookings Review* (Washington, Fall 1995), pp. 10–13.

51. Rebecca Johnson, *Comprehensive Test Ban Treaty; the end game* (London: Disarmament Intelligence Review, April 1996), Acronym No. 9, p. 31.

52. Marxist–Leninism was always explicit that the capitalist system was destined to fail and would be replaced by world socialism. But it spoke in terms of historical inevitability, of inexorable social forces, not of military conquest. Indeed, once the civil war was behind them, the Soviets consistently refuted the idea that war by itself caused revolution, or that revolution could be exported. Military forces were needed to defend socialist gains against attempts to reverse them. This requirement was vividly demonstrated by the intervention of counter-revolutionary capitalist forces during

1918–21 and was revalidated many times thereafter. But the idea of communist world domination was a capitalist bogey and not a Marxist–Leninist concept.

53. A particular feature of Western rhetoric during the Cold War was the underlying and often explicit assumption that the communist Soviet Union and tsarist Russia were all of a piece. For an example, see Vice President Bush's speech in Vienna on 21 September 1983, summarized in MccGwire, *Perestroika* p. 113. See also Winston Churchill's statement in 1942, when proposing a Council of Europe, that 'it would be a measureless disaster if Russian barbarism overlaid the culture of the ancient states of Europe', quoted by Jean E. Manas in 'The Council of Europe's Democracy Ideal and the Challenge of Ethno-National Strife' in Chayes and Chayes, *Preventing Conflict*, p. 103. Most recently, the debate on the 'National Reconstruction Act' passed in February 1995 by the Republican-dominated House of Representatives made it clear that the expansion of NATO was motivated by traditional fears of Russia. Jonathon Dean, 'Losing Russia or Keeping NATO: Must We Choose?' *Arms Control Today*, June 1995, p. 6.

54. It is estimated that before the year 1600, something like one million native Americans lived north of the Rio Grande. In 1783, the newly independent US had a settler population of a little more than three million. Geoffrey Barraclough (ed.), *The Times Atlas of World History* (London: Times Books, 1978), pp. 220, 236.

55. The persistent problem of Poland, a traditional enemy for hundreds of years, is reminiscent of England's 'Irish problem'. But, unlike the Irish, the Poles were a military threat in their own right, as was demonstrated anew in 1918–20. They were also the spearhead and the avenue of the more general political, military and social threat that lay beyond.

56. In going to war against Turkey, Russia was fulfilling its treaty commitments to Great Britain and France.

57. Armenia and the remaining bit of Georgia were acquired in 1878 after war with Turkey, at which date Russia formally annexed the Caucasus. The interaction of the Ottoman, Persian and Russian empires in this area was complex, but it is fair to say that at this period the Georgian and Armenian people welcomed the protection afforded by Russia. Hugh Seton-Watson, *The Russian Empire 1801–1917* (Oxford University Press, 1967), pp. 57–61, 290, 416–17.

58. It was, of course, the British and French who profited from the collapse of the Ottoman empire.

59. In the war of 1827–8, Russia made the greatest military contribution to the liberation of Orthodox Greece. The terms of the subsequent peace also confirmed the autonomy (under Ottoman suzerainty) of Serbia and the two Romanian principalities.

60. This is the source of 'the historic drive for warm water ports' a British distortion during the imperial competition in the nineteenth and early twentieth centuries.

61. Russia had achieved such a regime by agreement with Turkey in 1833, but that was overridden by a five-power agreement in 1841, which only constrained the passage of warships in time of peace. When at war,

Turkey could grant passage to whom it chose, as it did to Russia's opponents in 1853–6, 1877–8 and 1914. In 1918–21 the Straits were a primary route for British and French intervention forces and for supplies to the White army.

62. What is now California, Nevada, Utah, Colorado, Arizona, New Mexico and Texas.

63. The Russians had crossed over into Alaska in the eighteenth century, moving south along the coast, where they met the Spaniards coming north from California. Claim to the area that is now Oregon, Washington (state) and British Columbia was for a time in dispute.

64. In the Pacific, the war yielded the Phillipines and Guam as spoils. It also justified the formal annexation of Hawaii and Wake, thus completing the 'life line' to China.

65. That claim was still being made by senior government officials in 1983–4, despite its obvious absurdity. This view was widely held in the first Reagan administration and it seems to have been believed that the Soviets had embarked on the necessary military build-up in the wake of the Cuban missile crisis. See, for example, statements by Secretary of Defense Caspar Weinberger in 'Face the Nation', CBS television 13 March 1983; interview with *USA Today*, 11 August 1983; Fred Hiatt, 'Pentagon Sees Space Buildup by Soviets', *Washington Post*, 11 April 1984.

66. This could be seen as breaching the Soviet–Iranian treaty of 1921.

67. MccGwire, *Military Objectives in Soviet Foreign Policy* (The Brookings Institution, 1987), pp. 15–20.

68. However, as in the case of the failing Ottoman empire, if Axis possessions were to be divided among the victors, then Russia wanted its share; hence its bid for the Italian colony of Libya.

69. The British had already given *de facto* recognition of Russia's claims to the Baltic states in 1942. Roy Douglas, *From War to Cold War 1942–48* (St. Martin's Press, 1981), pp. 7–9, 188.

70. Isaac Deutscher, *Stalin* (Pelican Books, 1970), pp. 522–4; John Lewis Gaddis, *The United States and the Origins of the Cold War* (New York: Columbia University Press, 1972), pp. 90, 139, 143, 157, 168, 202, 354–5; Lynn Davis, *The Cold War Begins: Soviet–American Conflict over Eastern Europe* (Princeton University Press, 1974), pp. 143, 165, 171, 390; Voytech Mastny, *Russia's Road to the Cold War* (Columbia University Press, 1979), pp. 121, 147, 158; William Taubman, *Stalin's American Policy From Entente to Detente to Cold War* (W.W. Norton, 1982), pp. 68, 121, 147, 158.

71. Taubman, *Stalin's Policy*, p. 73 quoting Stalin in *Sochineniya*, vol. 2, pp. 164–70. Stalin was hopeful that the permanent members of the UN Security Council, which formalized the wartime entente, would provide the means of 'preventing new aggression or a new war, if not for ever, then at least for an extended time'.

72. Stalin wanted to preserve the best possible relations with Washington and shifted from 'entente' to 'detente' to 'cold war' reluctantly, and each time under pressure from the West. Taubman, *Stalin's Policy*, p. 8. See also William H. McNeill, *Survey of International Affairs, 1939–46* (Oxford University Press, 1953), p. 609.

73. The role played by the Council of Foreign Ministers in the 1944–7 period was distinctly reminiscent of their predecessors' role in the 1815–22 period. In 1815, Russia, Prussia, Austria and Britain were determined to prevent the resurgence of a Bonapartist France. At Potsdam in July 1945, America, Britain, France and Russia were determined to prevent the resurgence of Germany.

74. Romania served as the southern springboard for Hitler's invasion and provided some 30 divisions and incurred nearly half a million casualties, as it sought to extend its frontier to the River Bugg. Hungary had joined the Axis in November 1940, and its troops fought against Yugoslavia as well as the Soviets, while its transportation system was essential to the supply of both the Balkan and the Russian fronts.

75. In late 1986. MccGwire, *Perestroika*, 355–63.

76. MccGwire, *Military Objectives*, p. 129.

77. Karen Dawisha, *Eastern Europe, Gorbachev and Reform: the Great Challenge*, 2nd edn (Cambridge University Press, 1988), Ch. 7.

78. Roger Braithwaite points out that the collapse of the Soviet Union was a failure not only of the Communist system, but of something much older: the Russian political and economic tradition evolved over many centuries. *Engaging Russia*, p. 75.

79. The agreement was signed on 3 December. As the result of pressure from the non-Slavic republics, membership of the CIS was extended to eight of them on the 23rd, the three Baltic states and Georgia declining to join. Georgia joined (under pressure from Russia) in 1993.

80. Russia had its origins in the ninth-century state centred on Kiev (now capital of the Ukraine) and subsequently re-emerged centred on Moscovy, which shook off the Mongol yoke in 1480. The eastern parts of the original state (including Kiev) were recovered from the Polish–Lithuanian empire in the sixteenth and seventeenth centuries, the western parts (including Byelorussia and the rest of the Ukraine) towards the end of the eighteenth century.

81. Most of the collaborators, both Ukrainian and Byelorussian, had withdrawn with the Germans and ended up in refugee camps, where they were recruited by British and US intelligence. By 1946, the Western allies were working closely with General Gehlen, former chief of German intelligence on the Eastern Front, as they sought to build up their knowledge of the Soviet Union. John Loftus, *The Belarus Secret* (Alfred Knopf, 1982), pp. 11–12, 54–7, 61–6.

82. Western intelligence had started infiltrating refugees back into their home countries in 1946. The Carpathian operation was part of an attempt to establish partisan capabilities in nine East European countries and Soviet republics, none of which were successful. The Soviets eliminated the last of the Ukrainian partisans in late 1952. Thomas Powers, *The Man who Kept the Secrets* (Alfred Knopf, 1979), pp. 39–43; Loftus, *Belarus*, p. 79.

83. The Black Sea provided the main route for Western intervention forces and supplies in 1918–21.

84. In this context it is relevant that the demarcation of the former Soviet–Chinese border (that is, including China's border with Kazakhstan, Tadzhikistan and Kyrgystan), which was initiated by Gorbachev in 1985, was formally agreed in April 1996.

85. For a succinct survey of Russia's dealings with the other republics, see Blackwill, *Engaging Russia*, pp. 9–15.

86. The West persisted in this stance for four years, but at the First Review Conference on the CFE Treaty (held in May 1996), it finally agreed to some adjustment to Soviet force levels on 'the flanks'.

87. See Senator Lugar's informed opinion in *NATO's Future* (n. 2 above) and the overview by Blackwill in *Engaging Russia*, pp. 16–20. See also the reports of the Office of Research and Media Reaction, US Information Agency: *The New European Security Architecture* (Sept 1995), p. 24, and *Four Russian Regions view the United States* (May 1996, R-2-96), pp. 21–7.

88. See Steinbruner, *Brookings Review*, above. The US Strategic Defense Initiative (Star Wars) announced by President Reagan in March 1983 would have breached both the letter and the spirit of the ABM Treaty, as understood by the Americans who negotiated it. The Reagan administration sought to reinterpret it.

89. See, for example, Bruce G. Blair, *The Logic of Accidental Nuclear War* (Washington: Brookings Institution, 1993), pp. 22–6, 186–94; Scott D. Sagan, *The Limits of Safety: Organisations, Accidents, And Nuclear Weapons* (Princeton NJ: Princeton University Press, 1993).

90. Blackwill, *Engaging Russia*, pp. 18–19.

91. The possibility of a Weimar syndrome was raised by Sergei Karaganov in 'Where is Russia Going?' in *Foreign and Defence Policies in a New Era*, PRIF Report 34 (Frankfurt: Peace Research Institute Frankfurt, April 1994), p. 7, quoted by Kelleher. See also Blackwill, *Engaging Russia*, p. 19.

92. The 'new thinking' was prompted by the new possibility of human extinction, the most immediate threat being the increasing danger of nuclear war. This led to the conclusion that a radically different approach to international relations was essential, particularly as regards the question of security. For a synopsis of the new thinking about international relations see MccGwire, *Perestroika*, pp. 179–86. For the effects of that thinking on Soviet military and foreign policy behaviour, see Chapters 6–9.

93. Pro-Western Soviet elites insist that enlarging NATO to include former members of the Warsaw Pact would produce a self-fulfilling prophecy – a hostile and revisionist Russia intent on overturning an emerging European security system that it regarded as profoundly inimical to its vital national interests. Blackwill, *Engaging Russia*, p. 19.

94. Senator Richard G. Lugar, *NATO's Future*, p. 47.

95. This belief is shared by various American officials, including Jack Matlock, then ambassador in Moscow, who has spoken of a 'geopolitical deal' that NATO would not move eastwards. Quoted by Philip Zelokow (who thinks otherwise) in 'NATO Expansion Wasn't Ruled Out', *International Herald Tribune*, 28 July 1995.

96. This draws on the argument by Paul Gerhard, *The United States and European Security*, p. 37.

97. NATO was also important as a political–military forum and the organizational template for joint operations with European allies outside the NATO area.

98. At $Bn 98, the combined defence expenditure of France, Germany and Britain constitutes two-thirds of the estimated total expenditure by EU members in 1996. It compares to the US expenditure of $Bn 279 (both in 1994 dollars). See 'Table of Defence Expenditure Estimates for 1996', Martin and Roper (eds), *Common Defence Policy*, pp. 48–9. The commitment need not be limited to those three countries and could be extended to other members 'ready and willing' to contribute to such operations, particularly peacekeeping. Recent organizational innovations in NATO and the WEU, including the Combined Joint Task Force concept, will make it easier to move in this direction.

99. Janne E. Nolan identifies three disparate sets of principles in the American security debate, which she labels Pax Americana, isolationism and multilateralism. She notes that only the liberal theory of isolationism advocates true disengagement, while the conservative isolationists accept intervention as necessary to impose American values. In practical military terms, there is convergence between Pax Americana and conservative isolationism. 'Cooperative Security in the United States', in *Global Engagement: Cooperation and Security in the 21st Century*, ed. J.E. Nolan (Washington, DC: The Brookings Institution, 1994), pp. 508–11.

100. This would be comparable in some ways to the 1955 treaty between Austria and the four occupying powers, although that only forbade union with Germany. However, a condition of Soviet withdrawal was the Austrian 'Constitutional Law on Neutrality', which committed Austria to permanent neutrality. House of Commons, *The Future of NATO*, p. 72.

101. Sweden and Finland would provide the anchor for a neutral and nuclear-free zone, extending from the Arctic in the north to the Black Sea in the south. Both Byelorus and the Ukraine are pressing for this zone, neutral or not, to be be declared nuclear-free.

102. The argument that Moscow would find Visegrad membership of the EU even more objectionable than membership of NATO is based on the silent assumption that Russia has an urge to invade those countries.

103. See Janne E. Nolan 'The Concept of Cooperative Security' in *Global Engagement*, pp. 1–8.

104. For example, in the Fall 1993, the US Congress approved the so-called Brown amendment, which stipulated that the four Visegrad states would thenceforth benefit from the special cooperative privileges in logistics and weapons acquisition otherwise reserved to NATO members. Noted by Brzezinski, *Plan for Europe*, p. 40.

105. Blackwill, *Engaging Russia*, pp. 40–3. He suggests weekly meetings with the North Atlantic Council, represented by a troika comprising the United States, Britain/France/Germany, on a rotating basis, and one other member. There would also be regular gatherings with NATO's Defence Planning Committee, the Nuclear Planning Group, and corresponding frequent meetings among Defence and Foreign Ministers. Catherine Kelleher suggests Russian membership of the informal but legitimated core NATO groupings, the Quad (US, UK, Fr, Ger) and Quint (plus Italy), which allow for special consultation in crisis and action as appropriate. See 'Cooperative Security in Europe' in *Global Engagement*, Janne Nolan (ed.), pp. 332–4.

She also stresses the value of architectural redundancy and the importance of a multiplicity of relationships (pp. 299–300).

106. For the terms of Partnership for Peace, see Kelleher, *The Future of European Security*, Appendix B.

107. Blackwill suggests a managing body of seven permanent members (Br, Fr, Ger, US, plus Poland, Russia and the Ukraine) with four or five rotating members. *Engaging Russia*, p. 50.

108. For a pungent comment on how the three European powers were pre-occupied with domestic concerns, rather than the problems of security in Europe, see *ibid.* pp. 32–4, 41. See also Kelleher, *European Security*, Chapters 4 and 5 for an extended discussion of the institutional and national politics that shaped the outcome.

109. Both in 1945–6 and in 1993–4, a relatively weak Democrat President was coming up to a mid-term election, in which control of both the House and the Senate would pass to the Republicans. In both cases, there was strong Republican pressure to reduce government spending, combined with criticism of the administration's policy and stance *vis-à-vis* Moscow.

110. Early in 1946, the Truman administration embarked on a new policy that had the effect of moving the Soviet Union from the category of an estranged ally to a potential enemy. Gaddis, *Origins of the Cold War*, pp. 313–23, 356; Yergin, *Shattered Peace*, pp. 11, 241–5; William Taubman, *Stalin's Policy*, p. 8.

111. How this came about is explained in Leffler 'US Foreign Policy' and MccGwire 'Soviet Foreign Policy', in *Origins of the Cold War: an International History*, eds Melvyn P. Lefler and David S. Painter (New York: Routledge, 1994), pp. 18–76.

7 European Integration and the Arms Trade: Creating a New Moral Imperative?
Ian Davis

INTRODUCTION[1]

In what relation, if in any, does the arms trade[2] stand to ethical and moral issues? More precisely, how far should moral laws govern the organization of industry or control the mechanisms of trade? The simplest moral attitude to the arms trade – and so to all military preparations, killing and warfare (which is organized killing) – is that in any circumstances it is wrong, irrespective of its profitableness or political expediency. This pacifist view is entirely rational (that is, a blanket ban on arms sales should be matched by a parallel ban on the possession of arms, thereby ensuring a level playing field) but far from commonly sanctioned, particularly by states. Only Costa Rica and Iceland come close to the purely pacifist position, although even here there are some doubts concerning the 'arming' of the national guard in Costa Rica and fishing protection in Iceland. Instead, the majority of states (and individuals) appear to take a more pragmatic position by arguing that the arms trade and military preparations are *prima facie* right but not always so.[3] This diluted moral attitude clearly implies a qualified acceptance of the arms trade, which in turn transfers debate to the question: in what circumstances are arms transfers not justified? Moral absolutes and moral certainties then become dissolved in political and economic discussions which produce compromises around individual transactions and particular weapon systems. In one form or another, therefore, the idea that some arms transfers are good and others bad has been the orthodoxy that has underlined government efforts to regulate the arms trade in the twentieth century.

However, the arms trade is also deeply embedded in the economic, political and military structures of the larger international system of a given period, and I contend that these structures and their major organizing principles also include different and competing moral components.

The international economy, for example, is not simply governed by economic laws: problems such as transnational debt, regional industrialization and trade agreements include among their essential factors moral as well as economic considerations. The fact is that orthodox economists do, as an essential part of their paradigm, unconsciously pass a judgment of moral value – the judgment, for example, that the 'right' end of economic activity is maximum wealth and that any measure incompatible with maximum production of wealth is 'wrong'. In other words, changes in the international system can be linked to changes in the behaviour of key actors (states and firms) in the international arms trade system (Laurance 1992, p. 49).[4] The end of the Cold War, for example, has clearly affected the way arms are traded. What is not so clear, however, is whether the underlying values and principles of the broader international system – and hence those that also underpin the international arms transfer system – are changing.

In this chapter I address this question and present the argument that these values and principles are not changing, at least not sufficiently for a qualitative or systemic change in the nature of the arms trade to take place. In other words, I am suggesting that although changes in the international system are significantly altering the way in which military equipment is produced and traded, the dominant values and principles upon which this trade is based remain largely unchanged in the post-Cold War period. Hence, there may be fewer arms in the system, but it remains essentially right to engage in transfers, unless specific circumstances direct otherwise. I also argue, however, that the process of European integration offers the possibility for creating an environment more conducive to control of the arms trade. But for this to happen, new thinking will need to be demonstrated, particularly with regard to our understanding of security.

The chapter begins with a discussion of the rationale behind the arms trade, including the motives of both supplier and recipient states. This is followed by an explanation of why attempts to control the arms trade by regime creation have failed thus far. I then explore how certain trends since the end of the Cold War are providing the opportunity for change – and why most supplier states and arms manufacturers are failing to seize it. I then offer some reasons why the chance to repudiate the arms trade ought to be taken by member states in the European Union (EU), followed by some suggestions as to how this might be achieved. The chapter concludes with some observations about the prospects for creating a new moral imperative for shaping the arms trade.

STATES, MARKETS AND THE ARMS TRADE

The international arms trade can only be understood within the context of the wider international political economy, and the state–market dichotomy. For about the past 500 years the nation-state has been the primary organizing principle of the international political order and the market has been the primary means for organizing economic relations.[5] Most of the literature on the highly controversial issue of the interaction between state and market usually divides the subject into three broad theoretical perspectives or 'ideologies' of political economy: the nationalist (or neomercantilist) perspective; the liberal (or orthodox) perspective; and the Marxist (or radical) perspective.[6] What then, are the dominant economic ideologies that have shaped the international economy in recent years?

Since the early 1980s the framework in which economic development has occurred in most countries in all parts of the world has been 'globalization'.[7] Although the driving force of globalization is often treated as an economic event rather than a political act, the key economic processes – the internationalization of production, trade, distribution and finance – were triggered by political decisions resulting from a neoliberal model of political economy – a model which seeks to leave almost everything to the market.[8] Thus, trade-driven free-market economic reforms, and particularly the emphasis on privatization, fierce competition and deregulation, have severely weakened the autonomy of national policymakers to control or influence key economic processes.

While this dominant paradigm in the international political economy suggests that national and international economic interests are largely compatible – that is, an expanding international economy is good for everyone[9] – the key exception to this understanding has traditionally been the military sector. In this sector, the belief that national security could potentially be undermined by international commerce in advanced weapons and military technology had widespread support, and meant that military industrial aspects of international security could not be left to market forces (particularly during the Cold War). Privatization of defence industries in the UK and elsewhere during the 1980s represents a partial break with that tradition (although a substantial part of the European defence industry remains in public or quasi-public control, most notably in France, Italy and Spain), but most international defence transactions continue to fall outside of the GATT remit and other mechanisms affecting international commerce. Why is this the case?

The answer can be found in international relations theory. While neoliberalism has dominated the international economy throughout the 1980s and 1990s, the 'neorealist' rationale (its ideological roommate[10]) has dominated thinking in the international political system for much longer. According to realist theory, states are the most important actors in international politics, and they act in a 'rational' way in attempting to preserve and improve their power relative to that of other states. The classic text on realism is by Hans Morgenthau, *Politics Among Nations*, published in 1948 and republished several times since. Neorealism, while mitigating the assumption that power is the only (or primary) objective of state behaviour, asserts that states continue to act in a self-interested manner, but within a structured system of states (Waltz 1979). The system is said to be defined by specific principles, such as decentralization and anarchy, and the relative position of states within it is increasingly a function of their technological and economic development. In many respects this approach not only continues to dominate the study of international relations, but also informs the actions of political leaders in policymaking towards the arms trade and prevents the implementation of alternatives. Indeed, theoretical expositions of the realist doctrine in international relations often profess the rational and quasi-scientific nature of the behaviour of states with all the fervour of a moral creed. Thus, while member states in the EU are increasingly adopting the logic of economic liberalism and the global division of labour in their pursuit of economic prosperity, they remain largely preoccupied with retaining national autonomy in foreign and military affairs. There is, therefore, an underlying tension between nationalistic (state-centred) conceptions of security and the Europeanization (and globalization) of economic activity, which the member states in the EU have yet to resolve. Britain, France and Germany, for example, have all combined some measure of liberalization and economic nationalism to their defence policies.

In most of the arms trade literature, therefore, it no surprise to find the state at the heart of the analysis, with the company as a secondary actor. Supplier (and recipient) states are invariably treated as 'rational, unitary actors' pursuing national interests and, in turn, this provides the framework for a set of 'transfer rationales' or 'motives' to be developed.[11] Most analysts usually break down supplier (state) motives into economic, foreign policy and national strategic concerns (Taylor 1994):[12]

- *Economic motives*. Like all other exports, arms exports generate employment, company profits and foreign exchange. The share of total defence employment in the EU member states provided by exports is difficult to estimate and changes from year to year. In the early 1990s the number of jobs directly and indirectly dependent on arms spending in the seven largest supplier states in the EU was in the region of 1.3 million (Huffschmid and Voss 1991, p. 14).[13] Given that EU countries export about 40 per cent of their production (Taylor 1994, p. 100), it can be estimated that about 520 000 jobs in those countries were reliant on arms exports in 1990. It is also generally recognized that arms exports enable the state to pay a lower price for the equipment purchased for its own forces. Reductions in the cost of domestic weapons procurement can be achieved through economies of scale in production and/or by recouping research and development expenditures.

- *Strategic considerations.* Arms exports help provide the means for a state to sustain a national defence industrial capability. This has both a political and an economic dimension (although there is much blurring around the edges). The predominantly economic rationale is that arms exports help to sustain production (after satisfying initial domestic demand) until a successor system is either ready or affordable. However, this economic argument is contingent on a strategic (political) factor: that domestic weapons production (and national procurement) remain desirable policy objectives.

- *Foreign policy motives.* It is evident that a great deal of political symbolism continues to be attached to major defence contracts. In the past, such contracts were regarded as the 'currency of foreign policy' (Kapstein 1992, p. 141) and although the currency may have been somewhat devalued by the end of the Cold War, arms exports continue to exercise a foreign policy dimension within many states. Foreign policy goals arising from arms transfers are said to include the deterrence of aggression, the enhancement of regional stability and the maintenance of friendships with strategically crucial allies. Export restraint is also an important policy instrument, often linked with securing human rights goals in recipient states. In addition, the broad trend towards removing barriers to free trade in an effort to stimulate economic growth, and the linking of arms sales with bilateral trade promotion, have been important foreign policy goals for several states.

While most, if not all, arms-producing states are subject to the interplay of these motive forces, the 'pursuit of power' or hegemonic behaviour patterns were almost exclusively a US–Soviet prerogative during the Cold War. Secondary suppliers, like Britain, France, Italy and Germany, were *primarily* thought to be concerned with economic motives, due to their lower levels of domestic procurement and reliance on exports and state subsidies. Some of the ideological motives are clearly no longer relevant given the end of the Cold War, and the rationale behind others, particularly some of the perceived economic benefits from arms transfers, are often never as certain as exponents of the arms trade would like us to believe (and some of these are re-examined below). It is also clear that the significance of any single consideration differs from state to state.

The international arms transfer system is also shaped by recipients whose motivations to import are equally as complex and diverse as supplier rationales. As Krause (1994, p. 85) suggests in the context of Middle Eastern acquisition patterns, reasons for importing arms can be driven by regional interstate conflicts, systemic imperatives, internal sources of instability, or some combination of these three motives.[14] Table 7.1 shows that the largest regional market is still the Middle East, closely followed by Europe and the East Asia–Pacific Rim region, and finally, the much smaller markets in Africa and Latin America. Although all of these regional markets show downward trends (with the exception of North America), many analysts have argued that the greatest demand for weapons is now coming from the East Asia–Pacific Rim region, due mainly to expanding economies and rolling modernization programmes.[15] Major supplier states, such as the UK and France, are also now major importers of high technology systems – such as the E-3 Airborne Early Warning and Control System (AWACS) aircraft from the US – because they can no longer afford to produce these from national means. While this post-war trend affects all the states in the international system (and is a major reason for the drive towards collaborative procurement at the European level), the 'big players' in the system are more directly affected because of their perceived need to retain the most advanced military capabilities. It seems likely, therefore, that the future demand side of the market will be dominated by two broad categories or recipients: those looking to import low- to mid-level technology armaments (for example, mainly less-developed countries (LDCs) involved in internal or regional conflicts); and those looking to acquire modern, high-tech systems (for example, mainly the advanced industrial states, including those within the EU, and also a few LDCs – the former to keep their armed forces at the technological frontier, the latter either for reasons of prestige or to pursue regional hegemonic ambitions).

Table 7.1: Arms transfer deliveries, 1983–93: by Euro 4 suppliers and recipient region. Figures in columns 1–6 are in billions of Current Dollars

Recipient		1 UK	2 Germany	3 France	4 Italy	5 Euro 4 total (columns 1–4)	6 World total	7 Col. 5 as % of col. 6
World	1983	1.9	2.1	4.1	1.3	9.4	49.3	19.1
	1993	4.3	1.1	0.7	0.4	6.5	22	29.5
Developing countries	1983	1.3	1.8	4	1.2	8.3	38.9	21.3
	1993	3.6	0.9	0.4	..	4.9	17.2	28.5
Africa	1983	0.1	0.1	0.4	0.3	0.9	7	12.9
	1993	..	..	0.1	0	0.1	0.3	33.3
North America (NAFTA)	1983	0.3	0.1	..	..	0.4	1.4	28.6
	1993	0.5	0.1	0.1	0.1	0.8	1.6	50
Central/South America and Caribbean	1983	..	0.9	0.1	0.2	1.2	3.5	34.3
	1993	..	..	..	0	..	0.3	..
	1993	0.3	0.3	0.1	..	0.7	2.7	25.9
Middle East	1983	1	0.2	3.3	0.6	5.1	19.9	25.6
	1993	3.3	0.2	0.1	0	3.6	9.4	38.3
Europe (East & West)	1983	0.2	0.7	0.2	..	1.1	9.9	11.1
	1993	0.2	0.5	0.2	0.2	1.1	4.5	24.4

Source: ACDA (1994), Table IV

Notes: .. $3 to 50 million

0 Nil or negligible (less than $3 million)

ARMS CONTROL REGIMES

What do these supplier motives and the continuing demand for weapons imply for attempts to control the arms trade by regime creation? First, the problem of how and where to draw the line between goods and services that should be controlled and those that can be traded freely has a long historical pedigree. Forland (1991, 1993) shows that the strategy of *economic warfare* (defined as a continuum of policies aimed at weakening the economic base of an adversary's military power) can result in export controls on a wide range of *strategic goods*. The 'strategic goods' concept has two different interpretations, however. Some analysts use it to describe items solely or predominantly useful for military purposes, while others apply it to all items which are too expensive for an adversary to produce domestically and therefore bring the most rewards from trade. During the Cold War, the restrictions applied to the Soviet bloc by the Coordinating Committee of Multilateral Export Controls (CoCom) were effectively a compromise between these two interpretations, with the US pulling towards the latter and Western Europe generally favouring a much less restrictive regime.

Second, although the problem of dual-use goods continues to tax policymakers, particularly in the Wassenaar Arrangement (the successor forum to CoCom),[16] the debate about 'economic warfare' and 'strategic goods' has lost much of its resonance in the post-Cold War era. Although arms embargoes and wider trade embargoes continue to be applied in specific conflict situations, the rationale for export controls has shifted to the non-proliferation of specific weapons (such as ballistic missiles) and dual-use items to certain 'pariah' states, mainly located in the South. Of course, regulatory structures continue to differ, not only between end-users but between different types of equipment.[17] The transfer of weapons of mass destruction, for example, is heavily restricted: nuclear weapons are covered by the Non Proliferation Treaty (NPT) and the London Suppliers Group; chemical weapons by the Chemical Weapons Convention and the Australia Group of Suppliers; biological weapons by the Biological Warfare Convention; and long-range missiles by the Missile Technology Control Regime (MTCR). However, major conventional weapon systems, dual-use equipment and small arms carry fewer restrictions. Multilateral supply-side regulation of the conventional arms trade in the post-Cold War era is increasingly difficult due to the competition for market share and the almost complete absence of any universally agreed norms or principles governing such transfers.[18] This is because the right of states to possess conventional weapons for the purpose of national defence is seldom disputed, and most governments therefore see no need to forego arms transfers. Indeed, without an internationally agreed standard against which to measure behaviour and regulate the system, the prospect of an economic 'free trade' in conventional arms grows ever more likely.

Within the EU all 15 member states are currently members of all the above multilateral weapon-related export control regimes and conventional arms transfer policy is currently being discussed as part of the process of political union (discussed below). The increasing integration of the European arms industry, coupled with an intensely competitive arms export market, is thought to be reducing the effectiveness of national arms export controls and intensifying the pressure for an integrated European response. At present, however, the EU has no legal mechanism for controlling arms exports, which under Article 223 of the 1958 Treaty of Rome are reserved as a matter for national governments. Moreover, national arms controls differ greatly from one member state to another and arms manufacturers are able to shop around to countries with the least stringent controls. In the absence of common EU controls there is a danger of national export policies being bypassed. In essence, companies are being granted an opportunity to circumvent the more restrictive controls operated by some member states (for example, in Germany, Sweden and The Netherlands) by exporting their goods through partner companies established in member states with weaker export controls. The Swedish company Saab-Scania, for example, is producing its Gripen JAS-39 fighter aircraft in a joint project with British Aerospace, thereby giving the Swedish company access to BAe's large international sales network.

AFTER THE COLD WAR – AN OPPORTUNITY FOR CHANGE?

It might be expected that the recent changes in the international system would have led to significant reductions in the volume of weapons traded and afforded the opportunity for greater international control over the arms trade. The end of the Cold War, in particular, has meant that much of the impetus which drove arms demand in the Third World at that time has now gone. During the height of the Cold War, for example, demand for arms in LDCs was heavily influenced by military aid and grant assistance, and the end of the Cold War has seen a significant decline in such transfers.[19] Thus, the aggregation of the end of the Cold War, the implosion of the former Soviet Union, the unification of Germany within a changing NATO, and the (re)creation of sovereign states in Central and Eastern Europe have allowed the opportunity for security to be obtained by most states in the international system at lower levels of armaments. The present global economic recession has also worked to reduce the demand for military equipment.[20]

These tendencies are reflected in the main data sources[21] which show a downward trend in the volume and value of global arms transfers since the mid-1980s. According to the US-based Arms Control and Disarmament Agency (ACDA 1994), for example, global arms transfers declined from a peak of $74 350 million in 1987 to $21 960 million in 1993 (at constant 1993 prices). Similarly, the Stockholm International Peace Research Institute's (SIPRI 1996) more limited trend-indicator of transfers of major conventional weapons shows a decline from $46 535 million in 1987 to $22 797 million in 1995 (at constant 1990 prices). Not surprisingly, this trend is reflected in the EU with both data sources showing downward movement: total arms exports from member states are down from $14 548 million in 1987 to $6940 million in 1993 (ACDA 1994), and exports of major conventional weapons are down from $7529 million in 1987 to $5778 million in 1995 (SIPRI 1996). Figure 7.1 compares the value of transfers by EU member states as recorded by SIPRI and ACDA. The

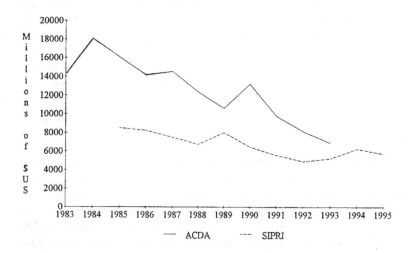

Figure 7.1: EU arms exports: a comparison of ACDA and SIPRI data
Sources: ACDA (1994), Table II; and SIPRI (1996), Table 11A.2
Notes: 1. Portugal and Spain joined the EU in 1986, and German reunification added further capacity from 1991.
2. ACDA data are expressed in constant 1993 prices; SIPRI data in constant 1990 prices.

match between the trends reported appears to be disintegrating in the most recent years, however, with the SIPRI data showing the beginning of an upward trend in transfers of major conventional weapons since 1992. A second feature of the data is that EU member states have increased their share of the declining global arms market. ACDA figures reveal an increase from 19.6 per cent of the total in 1987 to 31.6 per cent in 1993, while SIPRI show an increase from 16.2 per cent in 1987 to 25.3 per cent of the market in 1995. This increase is largely due to the collapse in Russian arms exports during this period.[22]

Although there are clearly fewer arms being traded between states in the international system, I wish to argue that for a variety of reasons there has been relatively little *qualitative* change in the nature of the arms trade – and that an opportunity for rethinking the morality of arms transfers is being lost. There are five main issues which require exploration. The first is that overproduction of arms is continuing, partly as a result of the 'survival' strategies of the major arms companies and partly due to the lack of government support for diversification and conversion. The ongoing decline of the arms market is forcing arms companies everywhere to reduce productive capacity and explore a variety of options, including mergers and alliances, rationalization, diversification, conversion, increased government subsidies and exports. But for those companies that are looking to remain in the defence sector the priority has been to become larger actors and to build up pan-European and overseas links. Integration in arms production on a West European scale, which had been going on throughout the post-war period, intensified in the late 1980s. This trend towards fewer and larger defence corporations in the EU through merger and acquisition nationally (mainly in the military aerospace sector) and multinationally (mainly in the electronics, missile and ordnance sectors), is the industries' principal response to the shrinking arms market and the intense capital requirements for next generation weapon systems. In pursuit of widening markets, many of the large companies are involved in a complicated network of alliances or take-overs with each other and with companies in their own or other fields of interest.[23] Joint ventures, sub-contracting, licensing and inter-firm agreements are the most common examples of these networks.

Despite the ongoing concentration and rationalization of European arms production, huge overcapacities still exist, particularly in respect of military vehicles and aerospace. In the production of advanced combat aircraft, for example, five member states (UK, France, Germany, Italy and Sweden) continue to be primary producers. It can be argued, therefore, that there has been no attempt in the EU to use the peace dividend[24] to address the problem of overcapacity, or to address the adjustment problems being encountered by defence contractors, defence workers and defence-dependent communities. Generally, leading companies have consolidated around defence work and focused their efforts on expanding arms exports. There are no national conversion or diversification policies within the EU, and instead most member states have adopted a free-market approach to defence restructuring, arguing that the arms industries themselves are best placed to make their own decisions on responding to the defence downturn.

Second, defence budgets and export markets show continued signs of vitality. While world military spending has declined from its peak of $1260.01 billion in 1987 to $868.4 billion in 1993 (at constant 1993 prices), spending levels remain unjustifiably high in many countries and regions – see George et al. (1995). In regions of tension, such as the Middle East and South Asia, military spending appears to be increasing, while budget cuts in some of the relatively peaceful regions have been far less than one might have expected. Spending by the former Warsaw Pact countries, for example, declined from $441.4 billion in 1987 to $133.1 billion in 1993, compared with NATO's rather modest decline from $552.6 billion to $480.2 billion over the same period. Indeed, NATO has increased its share of world military expenditure from 44 per cent in 1987 to 56 per cent in 1993 (ACDA 1994).

Third, military research and development is continuing largely unchecked. In the wake of the Gulf War, the idea that technological advantage translates directly into success on the battlefield has become a powerful perception. This in turn has been translated into a seemingly dual-track strategy among the US and major European arms producers, of making quantitative reductions in armaments while continuing the qualitative development of new and sophisticated weapons. Even today, more than a quarter of total European public investment in science and technology goes into developing military systems. The relationship between the arms trade and technology is difficult to disentangle because the process of military technology diffusion is itself subject to intense debate and there is no single explanation for it. Krause (1992), however, convincingly suggests that since the mid-fifteenth century, there have been three discernible 'waves' in arms production and trade, each inaugurated by a burst of revolutionary technological innovation. Each wave contains a period of rapid arms production, transfers and technology diffusion and, finally, a period of stability, arms control and incremental innovation. Some analysts argue that we are at the beginning of a new wave of weapons innovation: the 'information revolution', or the Military

Technology Revolution (MTR) as it is often called in the US. Among the significant new technologies identified are information systems, including advanced sensors, communications, data processing, long-range precision guided weapons and advanced simulation techniques. If these views are correct, the international arms trade will undergo a fundamental transform-ation over the next few decades, with dual-use equipment becoming central to the performance of advanced military forces. Major weapons platforms, which were formerly at the centre of the arms trade, will become less important. As a result it will become more difficult to track proliferation trends simply by monitoring transfers of major weapon systems. According to Trevor Taylor (1992, p. 96), it may also allow some defence manufacturers to distance themselves from their principal lines of business:

> Already some British firms, including BAe, are promoting an internal culture that seeks to remove the 'defence' label. Instead, they are 'elec-tronics', 'engineering' or 'aerospace' manufacturers, serving customers and seeking maximum profit on capital invested. The MoD is on its way to become one customer out of many, important but rather unreliable, and less intimate than others.

This growing emphasis on dual-use production suggests that military capacity is becoming more closely interwoven into 'generic capitalist production' and therefore 'less visible' (Lovering 1994). Not only does this cast doubt on the adequacy of quantitative measures of identifiable arms exports, but may also mean that we are missing an upward trend in unidentifiable transfers of dual-use goods and technologies.

Fourth, a significant second-hand market in major conventional weapon platforms has arisen from the demilitarization of Germany and the imple-mentation of the 1990 Treaty on Conventional Armed Forces in Europe (CFE). Thus, the second-hand market, traditionally the bastion of covert deals in small arms between private arms traders and countries subject to embargo, is now witnessing an upsurge of disposal activity by NATO and former Warsaw Pact governments arising from reductions in their front-line equipment and stockholdings. In the period 1990–4, in particular, Spain and Greece (and Turkey) were recipients of large volumes of surplus weapons from the US, France, Germany and The Netherlands.[25] Another associated trend is the increase in upgrades and refits which are more cost-effective than purchasing new weapon platforms.

Finally, and arguably most significant of all (for it underpins all the above post-Cold War trends), is the persistence of realpolitik in the arms trade. Changes in the international system are causing far-reaching changes in the way military equipment is produced and traded, but it still remains essentially right to engage in transfers, unless specific circumstances dictate otherwise. Indeed, were the international political system to deteriorate again, an upward surge in arms transfers would follow very quickly. Essentially the underlying 'realist' values and principles remain the same: the major arms-producing states continue to be wedded to the notion that they must be able to maintain a *national* high technology base capable of producing both complex civilian and military products, in order to equip sophisticated multi-purpose *national* armed forces. In short, this necessitates an arms trade – and arms control continues to take precedence over disarmament; and the scientific, industrial and bureaucratic institutions with vested interests in the military economy remain largely undiminished. Throughout the 1980s, for example, the free market revolution was sweeping away government subsidies and intervention as inefficient ways of competing in export markets. Quite against this tide of *laissez-faire* economic policy, the arms trade continues to receive more, not less government backing.[26] Without the creation of a new mind-set on these matters, there is unlikely to be any qualitative change in the arms trade.

NEED FOR A 'NEW SECURITY ORDER'

There are several reasons why the chance to repudiate the arms trade *ought* to be taken, however. The first concerns the need to provide real security. There are broadly three post-Cold War models of strategic thought: hard realism; soft neorealism; and common security (Chilton 1995, p. 82). Each carries a range of possibilities concerning the future shape of European (and global) security. The first adheres to a Cold War containment paradigm and portrays an ideological attachment to its alleged irrefutable categories. Hence, in this model, defence should remain a matter for states and alliances, with the core problem of how to organize the security of the European continent being met by the 'collective security' arrangement in NATO. The renationalization of security policy also remains an option within this perspective.

The second and dominant model, subscribed to by both neorealist and liberal traditions, recognizes that member states of the EU are no longer part of a tight bipolar political and ideological international system, but urges caution and a step-wise approach to change. Thus, although there may be a growing awareness of an extended concept of security, preference continues to be given to the military 'collective security' option, either through NATO or the Western European Union (WEU), which comprises the European member states of NATO, rather than reliance on multilateral institutions. The third model, critical of realist and neorealist world views, urges proactive change based around wider conceptions of security, with efforts to strengthen multilateral institutions (the UN, OSCE), given preference over defence. The growing awareness of socio-economic and environmental problems as important causal factors in conflict is slowly transforming the international security system. For some critical theorists, common or cooperative security – as opposed to military security – has become the most desirable and adequate concept for the challenges ahead (Adam Rotfield 1994, p. 4):

> The important thing is that a new global system is being formed not as a result of war, in the wake of which victors impose on the vanquished a new order and rules of conduct, but through negotiations and agreement on common goals, norms, institutions and procedures.

The process of shaping a cooperative security system is still in its infancy, however. The process is not automatic and the outcome is by no means certain. The continued emphasis on military security and power projection within NATO, and the fact that much of the Alliance's Cold War military–industrial structure remains in place, is certainly not conducive to the new realities. Indeed, the failure of NATO to respond in kind to the changes in the East (either with equivalent defence cuts of their own or with economic aid for the reform process in Russia) has encouraged a steady retreat by Russian military leaders away from the Gorbachev-era principles of military sufficiency, and linking disarmament and common security to defence conversion.

Linked to the need for new thinking about security is the need for greater restraint in the arms trade. To show why restraint is in the best interest of supplier states in the EU it is necessary to return to the 'supplier motives' discussed earlier. First, while the arms trade does provide certain economic benefits, these are often outweighed by *economic costs*. Defence industrial employment, for example, has been declining for many years. In the UK, for example, it fell from around 625 000 in 1987 to 350 000 in 1995 (a decline of 44 per cent); and in Germany it declined from 300 000 in 1987 to 210 000 in 1995 (a decrease of 30 per cent) (IISS 1996, Table 10, p. 283). This trend, which can be seen throughout Western Europe, preceded the end of the Cold War and reflects cuts in defence expenditure as well as the major trends of national corporate restructuring, greater commercialization through competitive tendering and the globalization of the defence industry, all of which have led to plant rationalization and redundancies. The importance of arms exports to the balance of payments is also overstated. Arms exports are only a small percentage of total exports in the EU. Even for a major exporter like the UK, arms exports represent less than 3 per cent of total exports, and for most other member states the figure is less than 1 per cent. They are also heavily subsidized by governments (that is, taxpayers) in a number of ways, including the finance of R&D for the development of new systems, and the provision of marketing services and export credits. Moreover, many states cannot afford the weapons they buy and supplier governments are often left with large unpaid debts. France, for example, has been left with debts of around $6 billion for arms supplied to Iraq during the Iran–Iraq war. Although difficult to quantify, it is also clear that military spending by EU governments is driven in part by new threat scenarios arising from arms proliferation (which, in part, is created by exports from the EU member states). In addition, several influential reports have suggested that arms exports have a negative effect on the global economy, and particularly the importing economies in the South (Palme 1982, Thorsson 1982, and Brandt 1991). Thomas Ohlson (1988, p. 9) suggests that two economic consequences would result from reduced arms transfers (particularly from North to South): a redistribution of trade earnings from those countries that supply arms to those that sell mainly civilian goods, and an increase in world trade, which would benefit everyone. In particular, he argues that the higher multiplier effects in civil trade as compared to military trade would enhance the longer-term potential for growth and development, and thus for trade in general.

The limited foreign exchange and employment benefits are being further reduced by the nature of the current market, which is now predominantly a buyer's market. This is enabling purchasers to demand generous credit arrangements (cash deals are now rare), and to locate employment within their own state through a variety of mechanisms, such as licensed production and offset packages. According to Ron Smith (1994, p. 49):

> The final deal is likely to be under a Government to Government Memorandum of Understanding which will cover a complicated package. This package often involves the selling firm committing itself to: technology transfer, counter trade (barter elements), export credits, offsets (purchases from the recipient) and the selling government committing itself to tied aid, subsidized credit and political concessions. In many cases the 'off balance sheet' liabilities, which are part of the package, are as expensive as the equipment itself.

The savings in the cost of domestic weapons procurement are also only marginal. A 1976 study of the US experience by the US Congressional Budget Office suggested that package deals and price cuts offered in contracts reduced the possible savings in R&D and unit costs to an average of $70 million for every $1000 million in exports (Krause 1992, p. 107). The savings also vary depending on the mix of weapons, construction and support services within the sales programme: for high-technology production sectors such as aircraft, aircraft engines, electronics, helicopters or missiles (without support services) the savings may be higher, but for a mix of ships, ammunition, construction and services, the savings are negligible or non-existent.[27]

On balance, therefore, exports (both military and civil) are only a benefit to the economy if they bring returns. If the exporting country has to provide the money to pay for the exports – which is increasingly the case in respect of military exports – then as Samuel Brittan (1992) argues (in the context of UK arms sales to Iraq):

> it is a ludicrous form of employment support. It would be much better for governments to use the money to make direct cash payments to people who would otherwise be working in the arms industry.

Moreover, when foreign countries use EU government loans, credits and money to buy weapons, the result is a transfer of pounds from EU taxpayers to EU weapon manufacturers – and not necessarily a net gain to the EU economy.

Second, the core strategic motivation for arms exports – the need for the state to sustain a defence industrial capability – is also questionable. In 1992, for example, the UK government's decision not to buy further Tornado aircraft for the RAF meant that the BAe assembly line for the Tornado was faced with closure. This prompted the British Prime Minister, John Major, to ask Saudi Arabia to move ahead with the contracts agreed previously under the Al Yamamah programme in order to keep production lines working. Retention of this productivity capacity was deemed essential for future production of the Eurofighter 2000. What this implies, of course, is that by the end of the decade the UK government will be seeking export markets for Eurofighter 2000, in order to retain productive capacity for its successor. This raises the question of whether it is in Europe's economic and security interest to break this cycle.

Indeed, for most states in the EU the maintenance of a defence industrial base is no longer (or has never been) desirable for a combination of economic and security reasons. Moreover, a high level of arms exports is not the only way of resolving this predicament. Several other solutions (or a combination of them) may be possible:

- the development of computer-integrated manufacturing and other industrial advances to make possible effective and flexible low-rate production;
- the development of information-based systems based on civil and dual-use technologies which are cheap to produce in large numbers;
- the development of the 'Japanese model' based on technologically dynamic companies which undertake defence production only as a small part of their overall market strategy; and
- greater collaborative development and production of advanced weapons among the EU (or NATO) member states.

In the context of European integration, the question also arises as to whether the EU's defence industrial base can be restructured so that its future maintenance does not rely on arms exports. In the US, this issue is already on the political agenda,[28] but there are few signs that European political leaders are prepared to consider such a solution.

Finally, the alleged foreign policy goals are also disputable on a number of grounds. First, exporting arms to regions of tension tends to exacerbate existing instabilities. Highly militarized states are more likely to settle their differences by military means, as in the Iran–Iraq War (1981–9), fought almost entirely with imported weaponry, and the subsequent Iraqi invasion of Kuwait. These two examples also show the fallacy of arming perceived allies, who may later turn out to be adversaries. Second, arms exports to military and other regimes which violate human rights run contrary to Western commitments to democracy. Third, the degree of regional influence from arms exports is increasingly marginal (particularly in a predominantly buyer's market) and could, in any case, be achieved through civil exports. Thus, the EU's foreign policy would be better served by establishing more restrictive arms export controls.

Beyond these pragmatic reasons – the need for real security, the economic and foreign policy benefits from a diminished arms trade – there are also moral reasons for grasping the opportunity for change. The arms trade provides a lens through which the values and norms of a given society can be judged. Together the EU and US supplied 80 per cent of arms deliveries to the developing world in 1993. In recent years, EU member states have sold arms to countries in regions of tension (Saudi Arabia), to countries suffering internal instability (Nigeria) and to governments with poor human rights records (Indonesia). What does this tell us about European values? Also consider, for a moment, how these values determine our world-view, our scientific enterprise and technology, and our political and economic arrangements. As we approach the millennium, therefore, the question, 'Does the EU really need to export weapons?' needs to be elevated to the rank of a moral imperative. While it is inconceivable that the member states of the EU will adopt the complete pacifist position in the short to medium term, the potential exists for creating a new moral attitude, in which the arms trade is considered *prima facie* wrong but not always so. This would still entail compromise around specific transactions, but such a qualified repudiation of the arms trade transfers debate to the question: in what circumstances are arms transfers justified? The emphasis shifts to the supplier (and recipient state) to show good cause as to why an arms transfer is necessary. Supplies of defensive equipment (under the auspices of the UN or a future EU procurement agency) might be considered acceptable, for example, in the case of a state threatened with external aggression.

Of course, if stretched (and according to realist ideology it would be), this rationale could be used to justify most of the existing arms trade, as most countries can make a (more or less plausible) case for defence against the possibility of future external aggression. Such scepticism may be unfounded, however. Assuming that it is possible to shift the moral imperative closer to the pacifist position *and* to change the existing export-oriented structural imperatives, these new norms and values would then be pushing in the opposite direction: towards international restraint rather than towards export promotion, as is the case at present. In other words, the conditions will have been created whereby states, particularly the major supplier states, have a vested and common interest in moving away from the accumulation of arms. It would be imprudent to deny that there are major difficulties in turning this aspiration into the 'new realism'. The problem of equitable treatment is particularly severe. For example, would all intra-EU transfers also operate under the auspices of the UN? And under what criteria would the UN judge whether a transfer is necessary? But these are questions to be addressed in future papers. I now wish to make a few suggestions as to how this new security order (and moral imperative) might be constructed within the EU.

SOME PROPOSALS FOR CHANGE

While the current direction of defence restructuring at the end of the Cold War appears to be industry-led, the ultimate structure of the EU arms sector is still evolving. Within the framework of the ongoing Inter-Governmental Conference (IGC)[29] strong political leadership is now needed to shift the EU defence industrial base away from export-dependency. First, Article 223 (which excludes most issues relating to the arms trade from supranational EU competence) should be deleted or amended. This would allow cross-border mergers and acquisitions to be subject to EU competition policy and national subsidies such as export credit guarantees to be challenged. Allowing firms to compete freely in a Single European Defence Market (SEDM) is one solution to the over-capacity in the EU. The emergence of a genuinely European-wide open defence market, operating within a clearly defined political framework, might well eliminate some of the economic imperatives to export arms and provide significant savings for taxpayers.[30] On the other hand, how-ever, it should be recognized that common R&D and procurement are unlikely, in themselves, to prevent extra-EU exports from being sought. As Krause (1992, p. 149) argues, collaborative arms development and coordinated procurement are merely extensions of existing arms export strategies: technology, production and R&D costs are simply divided on a more formal and explicit basis in return for a larger and more stable market. Indeed, the very nature of private companies means that they are unlikely to give up on arms exports simply because production runs are longer and R&D costs are shared. The more likely outcome is that European arms companies would become even more efficient and prosper in the international arms market. The high level of domestic demand in the US, for example, did not prevent US companies from exporting arms worth \$8.7 billion to developing countries in 1993 (ACDA 1994). As one official from the French firm Thomson-CSF explained:

> the day we stop exporting ... that's it. We close up shop.[31]

Rather paradoxically, therefore, if the open European defence market is to reduce or prevent extra-EU arms exports, a second requirement is called for – the creation of a strong regulatory framework at the European level. Just as the Single European Market (SEM) requires organization, regula-tion and a legal framework, then the SEDM would seem to require a similar institutional framework. Some progress has been made in develop-ing a common arms export control policy with the establishment of eight criteria governing arms exports (adopted by EU member states in 1992, and in a slightly different format by the Organization for Security and Co-operation in Europe (OSCE) in November 1993). These criteria – which include such factors as the internal and regional situation of the proposed recipient, their attitude towards terrorism and their level of military spending – have also been included in a new EU Regulation governing the export of dual-use goods that entered into force in July 1995.[32] The main problem, however, is that *there is no common interpretation* of the criteria, and a third requirement, therefore, is for the adoption of an enforceable 'Code of Conduct' to coordinate EU export controls at the highest level.[33] Other potential measures include the harmonization of export credit guidelines for defence products and the introduction of another code of practice for defence trade financing.

A fourth requirement is to maximize the potential from the expansion of 'neutral' states in the EU. Clearly, the post-war environment for the 'function' of the Irish, Austrian, Finnish and Swedish variants of neutrality has vanished and has been superseded by a different, multipolar environment. Commentators, such as Lysen (1992), are also suggesting that the legal 'status' of neutrality is unlikely to survive membership of the EU, and especially membership of the WEU.[34] Moreover, the concept of *armed* neutrality[35] appears to be fully compatible with the right of states to posses conventional weapons for the purpose of national defence – and hence, would seem to add very little to existing norms and principles concerning the transfer of arms. Indeed, the positive image of neutrality has already been challenged by past arms export scandals[36] in three of the neutral states, and the possible abandonment or redefinition of neutrality in the context of EU membership may well provide the green light for expansion of defence production and trade in these states.

Nonetheless, given the impact of neutrality on their history and culture, the potential exists for these member states to make a positive and creative contribution to the development of European security policy. In the past, for example, the neutrals have concentrated their foreign policy efforts on confidence-building measures, peaceful settlement of conflicts and human rights. The vigorous pursuit of these concerns within the emerging Common Foreign and Security Policy (CFSP) may well help to counterbalance some of the more alarming policy declarations from other member states that appear to have as their goal a nuclear-armed Fortress Europe. Clearly, the neutrals cannot remain indifferent to the major changes that are also taking place in the arms trade, and the question arises as to how the neutrality concept can be redefined and applied in operational terms within the EU. Given their continued reliance on arms imports and, in particular, Sweden's role as a significant supplier, it seems unlikely that the neutral states will repudiate the arms trade altogether. But if they were at least to conclude that the EU's foreign, economic and security interests would be better served by a more restrictive arms export control policy –

that the arms trade is *prima facie* wrong, but not always so – then some progress might be possible. In fact, there are some difficult but not impossible routes for the neutrals to pursue. In the EU, only the Swedish government publishes any useful information about national arms exports, and one possible function for the neutral states, therefore, is to lobby for a realistic EU arms production and transfer database. This could be developed in tandem with efforts to enhance the scope and coverage of the UN Register of Conventional Arms.

At a more fundamental level, however, part of the answer lies in recognizing the fundamental changes that have taken place in the security environment and transferring resources to building a new security order based on cooperation and conflict prevention. Another part of the answer lies in crafting industrial readjustment policies in coordination with more restrained export-promotion programmes. This would make longer-term agreement on arms transfer control easier to achieve. The basic argument is that less export-oriented industries, alongside more restrained arms transfer policies by governments, will lay the groundwork for a more serious attempt at harmonization of EU export controls. The existence of production capacities within the EU in excess of domestic demand will continue to create pressures to export. Thus, the peace dividend needs to be used to address the problem of overcapacity and to address the adjustment problems being encountered by defence-dependent communities.

The degree of defence specialism varies between companies and between sectors. But with the exception of certain sectors (such as shipbuilding) and certain key companies (such as Thomson-CSF and Dassault in France) most of the leading defence companies in the EU earn large parts of their income from the civil sector – as shown in Table 7.2. In particular, the German arms industry, despite experiencing the deepest post-Cold War cuts in domestic arms procurement among EU member states, has avoided resorting to an expansion of arms exports due to the high degree of diversification among its companies. The arms sales of the eight leading German companies accounted for 14 per cent of their total sales in 1993, whereas the average across the other 26 EU-based companies listed in SIPRI's 'Top 100' was 46.4 per cent. The potential exists, therefore, to expand the civil side of many of these businesses at the expense of their military side. In many cases, this is made more difficult because the military production is self-contained within fairly autonomous subdivisions within the company. Of those companies that have sought to reduce their defence dependency, most have attempted to do so by selling-off their defence sections or by mergers and acquisitions, rather than by factory-based conversion to civil production. A few companies, however, mainly in the electronics sector, are encouraging their divisions to look for spin-offs to the civil sector. GEC Underwater Systems, for example, is looking for civil applications for its technology, such as underwater exploration of the sea bed for natural resources. Without further disincentives (much deeper cuts in military spending) and incentives (increased funding in other categories of government expenditure) most prime defence contractors are unlikely to diversify.

A key policy objective, therefore, is the promotion of industrial restructuring through a requirement-driven macroeconomic conversion framework.[37] Put simply, what is needed is for national governments, the EU, or preferably both, to develop an alternative research and capital investment agenda to shift industrial, scientific and technological resources away from military objectives and towards broader social and economic objectives. Instead of targeting technologies or simply expanding the supply of consumer goods, such a policy would be driven by specific requirements or 'needs', like environmental restoration, renewable energy, public transport, housing and modernization of Europe's infrastructure. A massive R&D effort to tackle the growing environmental crisis, for example, would not only yield new environmental clean-up and pollution control technologies and products, but would also stimulate technological developments in other industrial sectors.

CONCLUSION

The national character of the European arms industry is being eroded and multinationalism in various forms is becoming ever more prominent. In particular, in attempting to head off the threat of American domination of NATO procurement, monopolistic pan-European producers are beginning to emerge. The institutional and political framework for integration, however, is lagging behind. This means there is a real danger that the institutional framework will be shaped by industrial and supplier state interests. In essence, this is the *realpolitik* of European integration and the arms trade. It is wrong to suggest that there are no alternatives, however.

The defence sector in Europe is being shaped by the ongoing process of European integration, and the enlargement of the EU by the recent accession of three neutral states – Austria, Finland and Sweden – is one of the most important developments since the Maastricht Treaty entered into force in November 1993. This presents an opportunity for 'neutrals' everywhere (including citizens and NGOs in non-neutral states) to challenge the current direction of European integration, the privileged,

Table 7.2: The largest arms-producing companies in the EU, 1993. Figures in columns 5, 6 and 8 are in US $ million

1 Company (parent)	2 Country	3 WR 1993	4 Industry	5 Arms sales 1993	6 Total sales 1993	7 Col. 5 as % of col. 6	8 Profit 1993	9 Employment 1993
British Aerospace	UK	5	Ac A El Mi SA/O	5950	16 161	37	-347	87 400
Thomson S.A.	France	8	El Mi	4240	11 920	36	-705	99 895
Thomson-CSF (Thomson S.A.)	France	S	El Mi	4240	6 055	70	-405	48 858
Daimler Benz	Germany	12	Ac El Eng Mi MV	3540	59 116	6	372	366 736
DCN	France	13	Sh	3440	3 543	97	..	26 892
DASA (Daimler Benz)	Germany	S	Ac El Eng Mi	3250	11 266	29	-420	86 086
GEC	UK	15	El	3210	14 570	22	811	86 121
Aerospatiale Groupe	France	18	Ac Mi	2860	8 979	32	-251	43 913
IRI	Italy	24	Ac El Eng Mi Sh	2090	46 551	4	-6487	327 226
Finmeccanica (IRI)	Italy	S	Ac El Eng Mi	1930	6 971	28	9	52 587
Alenia (Finmeccanica)	Italy	S	Ac El Eng Mi	1930	3 053	63	..	24 650
Dassault Aviation	France	29	Ac	1590	1 998	80	41	9 758
Aerospatiale (Aerospatiale Groupe)	France	S	Ac Mi	1590	5 401	29	-161	25 637
Rolls Royce	UK	30	Eng	1580	5 284	30	87	49 200
CEA	France	31	Oth	1540	3 226	48	..	5 980
GIAT Industries	France	35	A MV SA/O	1300	1 627	80	-204	17 250
INI	Spain	39	Ac A El MV Sh	1110	18 715	6	-982	129 380
SNECMA Groupe	France	41	Eng Oth	1060	3 455	31	-142	23 993
Siemens	Germany	42	El	990	49 385	2	1199	391 000
Matra Hachette	France	44	El Mi Oth	970	9 532	10	27	41 904

Table 7.2: (Continued)

1 Company (parent)	2 Country	3 WR 1993	4 Industry	5 Arms sales 1993	6 Total sales 1993	7 Col. 5 as % of col. 6	8 Profit 1993	9 Employment 1993
Celsius	Sweden	46	A El MV SA/O Sh	920	1 490	62	80	15 217
Eurocopter Group (Aerospatiale/DASA)	France/Germany	S	Ac	920	1 775	52	-82	10 513
Bremer Vulkan	Germany	47	El Sh	860	3 714	23	-116	28 141
Matra Defense (Matra Hachette)	France	S	Mi Oth	860	864	100	..	..
SNECMA (SNECMA Groupe)	France	S	Eng	840	1 916	44	-122	13 084

Source: SIPRI (1995), Table 13A.

Notes: .. data not available

Companies with the designation S in the column for World Rank (WR) are subsidiaries

Key to abbreviations in column 4. A = artillery, Ac = aircraft, El = electronics, Eng = engines, Mi = missiles, MV = military vehicles, SA/O = small arms, Sh = ships and Oth = other.

segregated culture of defence manufacturing, and the distortion of European foreign policy by a minority of vested interests that coalesce around the arms trade. And if, on the threshold of the twenty-first century, we can summon the collective will to repudiate the arms trade (as the slave trade was once repudiated), we could do no better than turn to Schumacher (1974), the visionary who pioneered the 'Small is Beautiful' approach to economics, for a set of norms and values with which to make the transition:

> Any intelligent fool can make things bigger, more complex and more violent. It takes a touch of genius – and a lot of courage – to move in the opposite direction.

Notes

1.   I am grateful to Stacey Burlet, Malcolm Chalmers, Kevin Warnes and an anonymous referee for valuable comments on earlier drafts of this chapter.
2.   There are considerable problems in defining what we mean by the 'arms trade' or 'arms transfers'. Definitions of the arms trade either tend to be too narrow and miss out much of what is of interest, or alternatively, are so broad as to cover items that are not really 'arms'. Although the 'arms trade' is sometimes used to refer to arms transfers conducted on essentially commercial terms, and 'arms transfers' often denotes all transfers of conventional arms irrespective of the contractual conditions in which they occur, in this chapter I use the two terms synonymously. I am also only concerned with conventional weapons and dual-use goods. Conventional weapons include 'major' conventional weapon systems (ships, aircraft, missiles, tanks and so on) and small arms (guns, ammunition, grenades and so on), including spare parts, weapon training and maintenance. The dual-use category includes both equipment (electronic communications equipment, computers, transport vehicles, and so on) and technology, chemicals and other raw materials and components used to manufacture weapons. This means that military equipment covered by weapons of mass destruction regimes (nuclear, chemical, biological weapons and long-range missiles – even though such a division is arbitrary in the case of missiles) and equipment for police forces (torture and other such security, interrogation and anti-insurrection equipment) are excluded from this analysis.
3.   Sometimes this view is cloaked in the argument that the arms trade *per se* is ethically neutral – in other words, there is no presumption that it is either right or wrong. This invariably means that ethical questions concerning the arms trade, and in particular, whether we should repudiate it on moral grounds alone, are largely ignored by academics (on the grounds that the research may become 'politicized'). I take the view, however, that to a greater or lesser extent all research on the arms trade bears the imprint of the researcher and is therefore value-laden and political. My own research is no

exception. Despite aspiring to the highest degree of objectivity, my personal allegiance to the pacifist position is certain to colour my research findings. It will be for the reader to decide on the extent of any discolouring – itself a reflection of the increasing uncertainty about what constitutes knowledge and how knowledge is gathered in the social sciences.

4. A system is a set of interacting units, where a change in one unit or one relation can have effects throughout the system. Typically, some properties of a system are characteristics of a system as a whole. Applied to international relations, the systems approach has tended to concentrate on 'grand systems' that seek to explain the international system as a whole, as opposed to more 'issue-specific' systems like the international arms trade. Harkavy (1975) was the first to assess the impact of broad systematic factors on the arms trade, and this 'international systems analysis' approach has recently been extended by the work of Krause (1992) and Laurance (1992). Laurance, in particular, provides an 'issue-specific system' which examines the changing role of arms transfers, and the economic, political and strategic implications of these changes on the system itself.

5. The terms 'nation-state' and 'market' are not single concepts and are used here as 'ideal types'. Barry Buzan (1991, pp. 57–96), for example, shows that the link between nation and state can take many forms, whereas Robert Gilpin (1987, pp. 16–18), argues that markets differ according to the degree of freedom of participants to enter the market and also the extent to which particular buyers or sellers can determine the terms of the exchange.

6. See, for example, Robert Gilpin (1987) and Kapstein (1992). There is also a more recent body of literature which (despite being largely rooted in neo-Marxist analysis) is as yet insufficiently advanced and coherent to form a fourth general perspective of political economy. That is not to say that such a perspective will not evolve in the future. Indeed, given that economic liberalism emerged from the failings and limitations of mercantilism, and that Marxist explanations arose from similar failings of liberalism, it seems unlikely that we have reached the 'end of history'. This literature encompasses a range of 'new' economic thinking which has emerged over recent years, from theories of 'disorganized capitalism' to feminist and green critiques of the existing paradigms of political economy. Michael Barratt Brown (1995), for example, describes ten different models of capitalist economies, five different models of attempted socialist economies, and four potential future models for building a new social order.

7. The literature on economic globalization is vast and there are various interpretations. Hirst and Thompson (1995, pp. 408–42) challenge extreme versions of the globalization thesis and argue that major nation-states remain central to governance of the international economy. I share their view that 'a world economy with a high and growing degree of international trade and investment is not necessarily a globalized economy'. Instead, what we seem to have is a 'highly internationalized economy in which most companies trade from their bases in distinct national economies' and thereby still allow a fundamental role for 'nation states, and forms of international regulation created and sustained by nation states' (Hirst and Thompson p. 424). This interpretation contrasts with some of the more extreme globalization theorists who see (or aspire to) the

existence of a strictly global economy determined wholly or largely by world market forces and by the decisions of transnational companies. See, for example, Bergsten (1996).

8. Liberalism, a mixture of liberal economic theory (ergo the 'free market' and minimal state intervention) and liberal political theory (ergo individual equality and liberty), can take several forms: with classical, neoclassical, Keynesian and monetarist approaches being the most dominant. All forms of economic liberalism share a commitment to the market and the price mechanism as the most efficient means of organizing domestic and international economic relations. But while some approaches favour social democracy and state intervention, neoliberalism stresses liberty and non-intervention at the expense of social equality (Gilpin 1987, pp. 26–31).

9. Free trade and economic exchange are regarded by liberals as a source of peaceful relations among nations because, first, all nations are said to gain in 'absolute' terms (although it is recognized that the 'relative' gains will differ), and second, such mutual benefits are thought to foster cooperative relations and economic interdependence.

10. For a review of the current debate between neoliberalism and neorealism, see David Baldwin (1993), especially Chapter 1.

11. This state-centric or realist framework is problematic, and can be criticized on at least three counts. First, it is only one of several explanations for behaviour at the international level, albeit the most dominant. Dependency theorists, for example, regard states as stratified (rather than unitary) actors which represent class rather than national interests. Second, the increasing commercial orientation of arms transfers means that the company is of equal (if not more) importance as an actor than the state. Third, the demand and supply sides of the arms market are shaped by a peculiar and intimate mixture of (domestic and international) politics and economics, and are influenced by a large number of actors – such as various state governments, industrial interest groups and unions, armed forces and a large number of commercial enterprises. These represent a range of interests in a number of competing areas of concern, including foreign and alliance policy, military affairs, disarmament, technology, regional politics, employment and profits (Brzoska and Lock 1992, p. 197). Analysts know very little about which actors influence the decision-making process the most, what sort of understanding of wider systemic imperatives they possess, and what role these imperatives play in shaping choices.

12. Also see SIPRI (1971) and Krause (1992). SIPRI identified three types of behavioural patterns, 'hegemonic', 'economic' and 'restrictive'; Krause's more recent study identifies three so-called *motive forces*: the 'pursuit of power' (that is, political motives, such as political leverage or influence over leaders in recipient states, and the maintenance of regional balances of power); the 'pursuit of wealth' (that is, economic motives, such as the maintenance of employment and infrastructure, technology leadership and spin-off, balance of payments, business profits, economies of scale in production and reduction of R&D costs); and the 'pursuit of victory' in war (that is, military motives, such as reciprocation for military bases or intelligence gathering facilities, the cementing of alliances, and substitution for direct military involvement.).

13. The 'EU-7' are: France, UK, Germany, Italy, Netherlands, Spain and Belgium.

14. 'Regional' imperatives include the need to fight wars or guarantee security against external threats; 'systemic' imperatives include supplier–client relationships, technological factors, or the pursuit of status and hegemony; and 'internal' imperatives include the need to secure the regime against internal threats, or the pursuit of 'state-building' through military–industrial development.

15. Indeed, the more recent SIPRI (1996) data show the Asia–Pacific region overtaking the Middle East as the largest regional market for arms imports.

16. Although CoCom was dissolved in 1994, its members agreed to maintain the control lists and apply them on a global basis through their national regulations pending the formation of a successor regime. Often referred to as the 'New Forum' these discussions sought to establish a mechanism for regular exchanges of information and consultation regarding conventional arms and certain high technologies. In April 1996, the Wassenaar Arrangement was finally agreed as a successor to the CoCom regime.

17. Anthony (1991) provides a comprehensive description of national regulations and multilateral export controls, and Anthony et al. (1995) summarizes the recent debate on the latter.

18. One important exception where limits and norms have been agreed in respect of conventional arms exports is mandatory UN arms embargoes. An arms embargo is one form of sanction which can be adopted either in conjunction with broader economic sanctions or independently. Since 1990 the UN Security Council has imposed mandatory arms embargoes on eight UN member states: Angola, Iraq, Haiti, Liberia, Libya, Rwanda, Somalia and the former Yugoslavia.

19. Worldwide military assistance is thought to have reduced from $20.8 (billions of 1993 US$) in 1987 to $4.6bn in 1993. Of the three largest suppliers of military assistance, the former Soviet Union has reduced its commitment from $13.5bn to zero; the US from $5.4bn to $3.4bn; and Western Europe from $1.3bn to $0.9bn (UNDP 1994, Table 3.3, p. 53).

20. A recent IMF study (Hewitt 1993) suggests that economic decline among developing countries in the 1980s and among industrial countries in the latter part of the decade exerted a strong downward effect on military spending. Two other factors are also advanced to explain the decline in military spending: the move towards more democratic regimes in developing countries and the former socialist countries; and the improved world security situation.

21. The problems arising from the lack of any internationally agreed definition of what types of equipment constitute conventional arms are exacerbated by the absence of reliable official data on arms exports in national foreign trade statistics. The trade classifications used by most countries do not clearly identify military-related trade, and Happe and Wakeman-Linn (1994a, p. 7) conclude that 'for most countries, customs data in their present form cannot be used as a source for information on military trade'. We are left to work with four major data sources: the US Arms Control and Disarmament Agency (ACDA) – *World Military Expenditures and Arms Transfers (WMEAT)*; the Stockholm International Peace Research Institute

(SIPRI) – *Yearbook on Armaments and Disarmament*; the US Congressional Research Service (CRS) – *Trends in Conventional Arms Transfers to the Third World*; and the United Nations (UN) – *UN Register of Conventional Arms*. Significant differences exist in the methods used by these organizations to gather and estimate information on arms transfers – see Happe and Wakeman-Linn (1994 a b); Laurance (1992, pp. 16–45); and Chalmers et al. (1994). In this article, SIPRI and ACDA are the main data sources used.

22. Although the most recent evidence (SIPRI 1996) suggests that Russia may now be recapturing part of its former market share – accounting for 17 per cent of total deliveries in 1995 compared to 4 per cent in 1994 – it seems unlikely that it will ever be able to recapture the 43 per cent share recorded by the former Soviet Union in 1986.

23. See Skons and Gonchar (1995) for an up-to-date sectoral analysis of the EU defence industrial base.

24. See, for example, Davis (1996) for a discussion on what happened to the UK peace dividend.

25. Despite the long history of antagonism between Turkey and Greece – and the latest conflict over the disputed islands of the Dodecanese took place as recently as January 1996 – NATO has transferred huge stocks of weapons to both states, many free of charge, under its 'Cascade' programme. Turkey, for example, received 1017 main battle tanks, 600 armoured vehicles and 70 artillery pieces in 1993 according to the UN arms register.

26. There is growing evidence, for example, that the decline in grant assistance is being replaced by a rise in the use of credits and offsets. Wealthy recipients may still be expected to pay cash, but in a predominantly buyer's market both wealthy and not-so-wealthy recipients are demanding that suppliers come up with either generous credit, extended payment schedules or offsets in the form of technology transfers, coproduction and countertrade. Some recipients are even insisting on defence treaties with supplier countries. These trends have meant that arms trade deals have become much bigger and more complicated, and they often require close government involvement in the negotiation and financing of the contract. Indeed, the increased competition between governments in the EU in providing taxpayer-subsidized concessions, loans and credits for arms production is likely to play an increasing role in determining which European companies survive and which do not.

27. The picture is further clouded by the length of the production run. For short production runs – now the norm in second-tier suppliers – arms exports generate relatively greater economies of scale by spreading R&D costs and moving down the learning curve at its steepest point. All estimates for unit cost savings depend on the precise slope of the learning curve, but one estimate for aircraft argues that a doubling of production from 400 to 800 units lowers costs by 15 per cent, with an increase to 1200 units lowering costs by a further 13 per cent. This suggests that the savings from exports of high technology items could be considerably higher than $70 million per $1000 million sales. Based on this second calculation, an aircraft valued at $15 million for 400 domestically procured units would decrease in cost to $12.75 million if 400 units were exported, a saving of

$900 million (or a saving of $176 million per $1000 million sales, assuming no sales costs or discounts) (Krause 1992, p. 141). The savings would further increase if, as is often the case with some EU governments, the price charged for export is higher than for domestic procurement.

28. The US Secretary of Defense, Les Aspin, has advanced a four-point plan for the maintenance of the US defence industrial base so that it does not involve exports: (a) periodic upgrading of major systems and low-rate production of selected new items; (b) continued R&D and extensive use of prototypes without normally building up the new technology into produced systems; (c) keeping technology on the shelf for use when needed; and (d) pressing ahead with 'silver-bullet' advanced systems in such areas as ballistic missile defence where the US would gain a decisive military advantage. However, the practicalities of such a programme have yet to be established (Taylor 1994, p. 108).

29. The IGC commenced its review of the Maastricht Treaty in March 1996 and is expected to deliver a verdict and some fresh proposals in 1997.

30. According to a study carried out in 1992 for the European Commission, the introduction of EU competition mechanisms to defence procurement would allow efficiency savings of between 5 to 11 billion ECUs per annum. In 1990 defence procurement in the EU amounted to about 65 to 70 billion ECU per year, within which expenditure on Article 223 items was estimated at ECU 40 billion. The study suggests savings of around 25 per cent per annum, therefore. Quoted in European Commission (1996, p. 18).

31. Quoted by Keith Krause (1992, p. 141).

32. Developed by the Directorate General of the European Commission responsible for the Internal Market and Industrial Affairs (in consultation with national export authorities), the Regulation on the Control of Exports of Dual-Use Goods will take three years from July 1995 to implement. During this implementation phase EU states will modify national regulations and procedures to effectively eliminate intra-EU controls on dual-use goods formerly covered by the CoCom arrangements. This single internal market will be complemented by harmonized 'equipment and destination lists', which it is hoped will create a strong extra-EU export control regime for dual-use goods. Early indications suggest, however, that those states with a more restrictive approach to exports, such as Germany, are relaxing their rules in order to fall in line with the emerging European standards. See, for example, *Defense News*, 12 December 1994 and Cornish (1995, pp. 40–3).

33. Three UK-based NGOs – Saferworld, British American Security Information Council (BASIC) and the World Development Movement – have been developing such a Code of Conduct which, by January 1995, had been endorsed by the European Parliament and over 600 individual organizations across Europe.

34. Vetschera (1990) draws a distinction between neutrality as a legal status and as a function of power politics. The traditional function of neutrality was to avoid being involved in the frequent wars arising in the European system of 'balance of power'. This abstention from all alliances kept the states concerned out of the bloc division during the Cold War. The four neutral states presently have observer status in the WEU.

35.   It is apparent, however, that some neutrals arm themselves very heavily (Sweden), while others get by with relatively much smaller military capabilities (Austria, Finland and Ireland). See Viotti (1990, p. 4).
36.   These include, for example, Bofors in Sweden, Noricum in Austria and Chemira in Finland.
37.   For a compelling vision, in the context of the US economy, of how public investment can be redirected to rebuild cities, clean up the environment and improve economic performance, see Markusen and Yudken (1992).

References

ACDA (1994) *World Military Expenditures and Arms Transfers* 1991–2, US Arms Control and Disarmament Agency, Washington DC.

Anthony, Ian, Anna De Greer, Richard Kokoski and Thomas Stock (1995), 'Multilateral weapon-related export control measures', in *SIPRI Yearbook 1995*, pp. 597–633.

Anthony, Ian (ed.) (1991) *Arms Export Regulations*, SIPRI (Oxford: Oxford University Press).

Baldwin, David (ed.) (1993) *Neorealism and Neoliberalism: The Contemporary Debate* (New York: Columbia University Press).

Barratt Brown, Michael (1995) *Models in Political Economy*, Second Edition (London: Penguin).

Bergsten, C. Fred (1996) 'Globalizing Free Trade', *Foreign Affairs*, Vol. 75 No. 3, May/June 1996, pp. 105–20.

Brandt, Willy (1991) *Common Responsibility in the 1990s* (Bonn: Foundation for Development and Peace).

Brittan, Samuel (1992) 'Lessons of Iraqgate', *Financial Times*, 23 November 1992.

Brzoska, Michael and Peter Lock (eds) (1992) *Restructuring of Arms Production in Western Europe*, SIPRI.

Buzan, Barry (1991) *People, States & Fear*, Second Edition (Hemel Hempstead: Harvester Wheatsheaf).

Chalmers, Malcolm, Owen Greene, Edward Laurance and Herbert Wulf (eds) (1994) *Developing the UN Register of Conventional Arms*, Bradford Arms Register Studies No 4 (University of Bradford: Westview Press).

Chilton, Patricia (1995) 'Common, Collective, or Combined? Theories of Defense Integration in the European Union' in Carolyn Rhodes & Sonia Mazey (eds), *The State of the European, Vol. 3, Building A European Polity?* (Harlow: Longman).

Cornish, Paul (1995) *The Arms Trade and Europe*, Chatham House Papers, The Royal Institute of International Affairs (London: Pinter).

Davis, Ian (1996) 'The UK Peace Dividend: Whence It Came, Where it Went', *Peace Studies Papers*, Third Series, Department of Peace Studies, University of Bradford, September 1996.

European Commission (1996) Communication from the Commission to The Council, The European Parliament, The Economic and Social Committee and The Committee of the Regions, *The Challenges Facing the European Defence-*

Related Industry, A Contribution for Action at European Level, The European Commission, January 1996.

Forland, Tor Egil (1991) '"Economic Warfare" and "Strategic Goods". A Conceptual Framework for Analyzing CoCom', *Journal of Peace Research*, Vol. 28, No. 2, pp. 191–204.

Forland, Tor Egil (1993) 'The History of Economic Warfare: International Law, Effectiveness, Strategies', *Journal of Peace Research*, Vol. 30, No. 2, pp. 151–62.

George P., Bedeski R., Bergstrand B.G., Cooper J., and Loose-Weintraub, E. (1995) 'World military expenditure', in *SIPRI Yearbook 1995*, pp. 389–433.

Gilpin, Robert (1987) *The Political Economy of International Relations* (Princeton, NJ: Princeton University Press).

Happe, Nancy and John Wakeham-Linn (1994a) 'Military Expenditure and Arms Trade: Alternative Data Sources – Part I', *Peace Economics, Peace Science and Public Policy*, Vol. 1, No. 4, pp. 3–38.

Happe, Nancy and John Wakeham-Linn (1994b) 'Military Expenditure and Arms Trade: Alternative Data Sources – Part II', *Peace Economics, Peace Science and Public Policy*, Vol. 2, No. 1, pp. 10–23.

Harkavy, Robert (1975) *The Arms Trade and International Systems* (Cambridge, MA: Ballinger).

Hewitt, Daniel (1993) 'Military Expenditures 1972–1990: The Reasons Behind the Post-1985 Fall in World Military Spending', *IMF Working Paper* WP/93/18, International Monetary Fund, March 1993.

Hirst, Paul and Grahame Thompson (1995) 'Globalization and the future of the nation state', *Economy and Society*, Vol. 24 No. 3, August 1995, pp. 408–42.

Huffschmid, Jorg and Werner Voss (1991) *Military Procurement – the arms trade – arms conversion in the European Community*, A study commissioned by the European Parliament, Political Affairs Committee, PE 151.454, Brussels: Directorate General for Committees and Delegations, 24 October 1991.

IISS (1996) *The Military Balance 1996/97*, Oxford University Press/The International Institute for Strategic Studies (IISS).

Kapstein, Ethan (1992) *The Political Economy of National Security – A Global Perspective* (New York: McGraw-Hill).

Krause, Keith (1992) *Arms and the State: Patterns of Military Production and Trade* (New York: Cambridge University Press).

Krause, Keith (1994) 'Middle Eastern Arms Recipients in the Post-Cold War World', in Robert Harkavy and Stephanie Neuman (eds), *The Arms Trade: Problems and Prospects* (London: Sage), pp. 73–90.

Laurance, Edward (1992) *The International Arms Trade* (New York: Lexington Books).

Lovering, John (1994) 'After the Cold War: the defence industry and the new Europe' in Brown and Crompton (eds), *Economic Restructuring and Social Exclusion* (London: UCL Press), pp. 175–95.

Lysen, Goran (1992) 'Some Views on Neutrality and Membership of the European Communities: The Case of Sweden', *Common Market Law Review*, Vol. 29, pp. 229–55.

Markusen, Ann and Joel Yudken (1992) *Dismantling the Cold War Economy* (US: Basic Books).

Morgenthau, Hans J. (1963) *Politics Among Nations*, Third Edition (New York: Alfred Knopf).

Ohlson, Thomas (ed.) (1988) *Arms Transfer Limitations and Third World Security*, SIPRI.

Palme, Olof (1982) *Common Security – Report of the Independent Commission on Disarmament and Security Issues* (London: Pan Books).

Rotfield, Adam (1994) 'Introduction: the search for a new security system', in *SIPRI Yearbook 1994* (Oxford: Oxford University Press), pp. 1–10.

Schumacher, Fritz (1974) *Small is Beautiful: A Study of Economics as if People Mattered* (London: Abacus).

SIPRI (1971) *The Arms Trade with the Third World* (Stockholm: Almqvist & Wicksell).

SIPRI (1996) (and various years) *SIPRI Yearbook: World Armaments and Disarmament*, Stockholm International Peace Research Institute (New York: Oxford University Press).

Skons, Elisabeth and Ksenia Gonchar (1995) 'Arms production', in *SIPRI Yearbook 1995*, pp. 455–70.

Smith, Ron (1994) 'Is Europe Pricing Itself Out of the Market?', *RUSI Journal* February 1994.

Taylor, Trevor (1992) 'The British Restructuring Experience', in Brzoska and Lock (eds), *Restructuring of Arms Production in Western Europe*, SIPRI.

Taylor, Trevor (1994) 'Conventional Arms: The Drives to Export' in Trevor Taylor and Ryukichi Imai (eds), Security Challenges for Japan and Europe in a Post-Cold War World, Volume III, *The Defence Trade: Demand, Supply and Control* (London: Royal Institute of International Affairs and Institute for International Policy Studies), pp. 95–123.

Thorsson, Inga (1982) Chairwoman, UN Group of Government Experts, *The Relationship Between Disarmament and Development* (New York: United Nations).

UNDP (1994) *Human Development Report 1994*, United Nations Development Programme (Oxford University Press).

Vetschera, Heinz (1990) 'Comment on Paul R Viotti's and George J. Stein's Comparative Articles on the European Neutrals', *Defense Analysis*, Vol. 6 No. 4, pp. 413–17.

Viotti, Paul R. (1990) 'Comparative Neutrality in Europe' *Defense Analysis*, Vol. 6 No. 1, pp. 3–15.

Waltz, Kenneth (1979) *Theory of International Politics* (Reading, Mass.: Addison-Wesley).

8 Leading by Virtuous Example: European Policy for Overseas Development

David Coombes[1]

INTRODUCTION

Students and practitioners of European integration have often been accused of being 'Eurocentric', especially in relation to the Third World. It is not always clear whether or why such a charge of political incorrectness may be deserved. Certainly, some scholars and politicians do seem obsessed with the European Union for its own sake. It may well be self-righteous and optimistic to vaunt the European Union's contribution to the relief of violence, injustice and deprivation in less materially advantaged parts of the world. It would be a pity, however, if an understandable resentment of post-colonial arrogance and complacency, or even mere disappointment with shortcomings of the European contribution to overseas development, allowed those dealing with the acute material problems of other continents to misapprehend the very considerable significance of European integration for themselves.

Maybe the problem of overseas development cannot be effectively tackled, unless and until the problem of Europe is more satisfactorily resolved, at least heuristically. Indeed, we could begin by asking why and whether the wider, global issue of development should be characterized, 'Eurocentrically', as one of *overseas* development at all. Perhaps the crucial issue is less that so much of the rest of the world is underdeveloped than that Europe is overdeveloped or at least expects to be. In this sense it could be right after all to concentrate on Europe, as the real source of the problem, and on European integration as a possible way of resolving, or at least reducing, it.

Moreover, if European integration does turn out to have some special value indirectly in such a global perspective, by helping to resolve Europe's historically problematic relationship with the rest of the world, then it might also provide a useful comparative example for other regions. Indeed, the recent European experience must be given careful attention by those who recommend 'regionalism', rather than nationalism or globalism, as a political framework for security and development, wherever clusters of highly interdependent, geographically contiguous, but still autonomous states seek to survive as such without excessive dependence on a hegemonic superpower.[2]

The question remains whether what is being done in the name of European integration should be represented as a kind of comparative regionalism, exemplifying a general remedy for major shortcomings of international relations. To call the Europe of the European Union a region is to beg a number of difficult questions, both as to the 'region's' external boundaries (not least the degree of independence these confer) and as to its internal structure (particularly regarding state sovereignty). In both these respects the Union's increasing ambitions for external involvement may confuse, and may be intended to hide, the urgent task of mending its own shortcomings, and may delude itself and others as to the true capacity and disposition of such an ambivalent entity to play a constructive role in the world. Such conceptual weaknesses of regionalism as applied to Europe might well affect its wider application.

The main purpose of what follows is to suggest, nevertheless, that a solution of the problem of Europe is still a priority for peace and development. The question is in what form and by what methods such a solution might be found, and the answer offered here is that 'regional integration' might yet point the way, if it can be defined more rigorously and substantially than has tended to be the case up to now (and appropriately re-conceptualized). In view of the capacity of Europeans, historically, to dominate the rest of the planet in political and economic terms, and no less in view of their continuing claims to military, industrial and cultural prowess, any indigenous movement designed to make Europeans more self-reliant, more generally content and at peace with themselves, and less insecure within their own territorial boundaries would also make life correspondingly easier and less precarious for others. The construction of Europe would be of genuine value, however, only if integration were understood in a more literal sense of genuine wholeness, which in political application must mean a community governed by consensus, and thus so confident of itself as to be fearlessly open to external competition and influence, as well as magnanimous with regard to its own strengths, humble with regard to its own weaknesses.

EUROPE AS A WORLD POWER

Despite internal difficulties, the European Union (EU) is increasingly regarded, from within and without, as an emerging world power. For example, the chief executives and foreign ministers of the governments of the EU, acting as the latter's sovereign authority in external affairs in conference at Madrid in December 1995, presented a statement of policy for more or less every politically significant region of the globe, prescribing cultural, economic and broader political objectives in the short and long term. Indeed, the EU now either already has, or is in the process of negotiating, comprehensive formal international agreements in each of these formally recognized 'regions'.[3]

The *common foreign and security policy* (CFSP), established by the Treaty on European Union (TEU), signed at Maastricht on 7 February 1992, defines objectives that are both *passive* (to defend the security of the Union and its member states and that of the international system as a whole) and *active* (to preserve peace and to promote international cooperation along with other, more fundamental universal values). These aims simply reiterate statements made jointly by the European Community's member states at frequent intervals over the previous 20 years through the procedure of European Political Cooperation (EPC). As the latest in a series of attempts to implement these objectives,[4] the Madrid European Council revealed, in particular, the increased confidence with which the EU now assumes political, and not just economic, responsibilities towards the formerly Third World after the Cold War. However, it also implied that Europeans' perception of their own economic needs and priorities may be changing, and betrayed a growing sense of insecurity with regard to the willingness and ability of less developed, or more especially late developed, societies on other continents to manage their own affairs suitably.

Above all, the elaboration of the CFSP since Maastricht demonstrates the EU's growing inclination to espouse regionalism, as a foundation for peace and development in the 'new world order', in which others increasingly seem to regard it as an alternative pole of attraction and possible attachment to that offered by the USA, if not also that offered previously by the USSR. Not only has the EU been redefining its long-standing priority relationships on a more precise and inclusive territorial basis, particularly in the Mediterranean and Africa, but it has been consolidating and upgrading less stable and familiar, mostly bilateral connections farther afield, also on a regional basis.

Two such sets of embryonic regional partnerships of special importance are those, respectively, with Latin America and with Asia. Each includes an intensification of previous 'political dialogue' and active economic cooperation between the European Community and its member states, on the one hand, and, on the other, individual states and regional or sub-regional organizations. Formal agreements, already signed or still in negotiation, affecting both regions refer explicitly to the encouragement of regional association or integration.[5]

Meanwhile, the special relationship based on the Lomé Conventions between the EC and its 'Afro-Caribbean and Pacific' partners (ACP) continues, Lomé IV having been duly reviewed and confirmed in 1995 for the remainder of its ten-year term (1990–9). This long-established client-relationship has, nevertheless, lost its formerly privileged position within the increasingly global view now emerging from the EU's attempts to fashion its own foreign policy. The ACP formula could itself hardly be more dispersed geographically and variegated in terms of economic and political conditions. However, the EU's interests in overseas development have now become even less selective and reliable, though at the same time more concentrated geographically, so that the ACP partnership might well turn out to be redundant. The Europeans' priority has shifted from the protection of former colonial dependencies, to the protection of their own economic interests and security wherever and whenever these might be at stake. Moreover, the Lomé Convention's contributions in terms of financial aid have not kept step with the inflation either of money or population in the recipient states, suggesting that Europeans may be losing the will and the capacity to pursue overseas development collectively by means of economic patronage alone.[6] The EU's growing aspirations to a military role overseas are illustrated by a special agreement recently made with the Organization for African Unity (OAU), providing, among other direct political links, for the possibility of 'peacekeeping' assistance, including military deployment, to OAU's own *Mechanism for conflict prevention and resolution.*[7]

A general shift of priorities and means is not the only reason why the least developed countries might view the EU's aspirations to a new world role anxiously, or at least sceptically. So far the CFSP does not seem to have changed the Europeans' most constraining preoccupations and prejudices, nor to have improved their capacity to match their ambitions with means.

Transatlantic relations are still an overriding priority for the EU's member states. The 'New Transatlantic Agenda', adopted at an earlier conference of EU governments held at Madrid, with US participation, on 3 December 1995, comprises the same general objectives as the European CFSP itself. The chief reason why the Europeans wanted to reformulate the Transatlantic relationship in this declaratory form seems to be their own insecurity. Despite the end of the Cold War and continued French preference for an independent European military capacity, most European states, whether currently inside or outside the EU, now strain at maintaining a

US military commitment to the defence of Europe. There can be little substance yet, therefore, to any hopes that might be entertained in, or on behalf of, those on other continents that the new Europe might offer an alternative to American hegemony, either ideally or realistically.

The first textual reference on external affairs in the report of the Madrid European Council was to the situation in former Yugoslavia, which also highlights the Transatlantic relationship. The EU's pathetic efforts to resolve the crisis in the Balkans since 1991 expose its ultimate dependence on the USA, and in the resort to military force, the supremacy of NATO. Whatever ambitions the CFSP may express on a wider, even global scale, this unexpected first test of a major breakdown of political order within Europe's own region found the EU tragically incoherent and incapable. Other events since 1992 have confirmed that a common European defence is no more than a vague, long-term prospect, even for Western Europe, and one still fundamentally disputed within. They have also demonstrated that combined military action by European states, for 'peacekeeping' or other objectives, cannot be effective in any foreseeable circumstances without at least the support of technology that is exclusively available to the USA (specifically that of satellite telecommunications), if not also without American political initiative and direction.[8]

The crisis in former Yugoslavia has been the most distressing aspect of the EU's general preoccupation with its immediate neighbours. Most of these, to the east and south of the present EU, have grown (in some cases abruptly) more dependent and demanding, demonstrating that the economic and political problems of peripherality and lesser development arise acutely on the EU's own boundaries and providing a further reason why the expectations of those in regions more remote and even less advantaged might be disappointed.

Nine of the 11 states currently negotiating membership are former allies or dependencies of the USSR in Central and Eastern Europe. These already draw substantial sums directly from the EU's budget. Any global ambitions the EU might have are bound to be clipped for a decade at least as it adapts to the cost of absorbing these prodigals, not to speak of the impact on politics and administration, if only in terms of new diversity and numbers. The two other states currently promised relatively early accession (Cyprus and Malta) are both small, ex-colonial Mediterranean islands, already economically dependent on the EU for trade and aid, but also strategically important, especially with respect to Western interests in the Middle East.

These two states also appear under another heading, along with 13 other Middle-Eastern or North African states, as signatories to a new

Euro-Mediterranean partnership, a project much vaunted by the Spanish presidency and based on the Barcelona Declaration of 27 and 28 November 1995. Security also seems to be at least as important a consideration as commerce in this important new example of the EU's sponsorship of regionalism. The causes of European insecurity here are not only the fragile Middle-Eastern 'peace process' but also the domestic implications of Islamic fundamentalism and political instability, especially in Algeria. Domestic concerns are also apparent in the noticeable emphasis the new partnership places on demographic issues, enjoining the non-European partners, if not in so many words, to check indigenous population growth and take their own measures to stop the existing population emigrating to the EU.[9]

On its neighbourhood problem generally, the EU has so far adopted the politic attitude, doubtless prudent for a relatively prosperous and secure condominium surrounded by those less privileged and reputed to be more unruly, that it is probably both kinder and safer in the long run to open the doors selectively and gradually, while making a careful distinction between those who might eventually prove tolerable on a permanent live-in basis and those who qualify at best as regular visitors (though mainly for commercial or, if necessary, charitable relations, and perhaps the occasional domestic entertainment or public festivity). Even so, there is a difference between those whom one might allow in the bedrooms (and want to admit the fact afterwards) and those it would be wiser to confine normally to the kitchens, or at least the servants' quarters.

The EU's new status as a world power, therefore, conceals both an inner anxiety and indecision regarding its own lack of independent means (or of the will to use those avaliable) and an exacerbated but necessary absorption with local affairs. The relevant issues for Europe's contribution to development and peace on other continents, however, are less those of whether the EU can after all achieve adequate means of providing its own common defence and how it might assert more effective control in its immediate vicinity, or even beyond, but rather the changes in economic and political purpose, as well as those in method, that are indicated by the Union's intensifying search for influence and security on a global scale.

EUROPE'S CONTRIBUTION TO ECONOMIC DEVELOPMENT

Economic development, in the sense of a deliberately ordered and reproductive process of social improvement, was always a primary concern of the European Economic Community (EEC). The original EEC treaty of 1957 actually imposed a legal obligation on the Community to that effect, especially by including in its opening prescription of general functions: '... to promote throughout the Community a harmonious development of economic activities'.[10] The Maastricht treaty (or TEU, which incorporates the EEC within the European Union but as a self-contained entity) confuses this issue somewhat by requiring the member states and the Community to adopt an economic policy '... conducted in accordance with the principle of an open market economy with free competition'.[11] Nevertheless, it would be incorrect to regard the Community Method, at least up to the end of the 1980s, simply as economic liberalism, designed only to exploit comparative advantage and the division of labour and maximize the profit, or even the profitability, of economic activity.

The Community is also committed to promote development externally. One legally binding aim of its commercial policy still is '... to contribute, in the common interest, to the harmonious development of world trade'.[12] The original EEC treaty recognized, and explicitly refrained fom pre-judicing, the member states' existing international obligations, including those to formerly dependent territories overseas, for whose 'economic and social development' it provided a special kind of association, subsequently implemented in the form of the Lomé Conventions.[13] Following revision at Maastricht, the treaty now includes a new *Title XVII: Development Cooperation*, which requires Community policy in this sphere, but without specific territorial limitation, 'to foster ... the sustainable economic and social development of the developing countries, and more particularly the most disadvantaged among them'.[14]

At the same time the Community is to a significant degree *protectionist*. This seeming paradox can be explained by the historical connection between economic development and nationalism. Without the initial and conditional protection afforded by the Community's common external tariff (CET), some of the original member states would have been even less willing to relinquish or modify long-standing mercantilist policies. The EEC's common agricultural policy (CAP) and common commercial policy (CCP) have enabled participants in the common market to moderate the harsher social consequences of international economic liberalization for their own less developed regions and disadvantaged groups.[15]

More difficult to justify is the Community's practice of *exclusion*, in that the existing members determine the price of accession, and of *discrimination*, in so far as non-members are granted selective access only in return for reciprocal favours. Nevertheless, the costs of membership for the new member states in the northern Mediterranean and for Ireland have been compensated by financial transfers from the

Community's expanding budget. Moreover, the Community was able to negotiate progressive, though usually selective, reductions in the CET, either by entering of its own accord into specific agreements for trade and cooperation with non-members or by assisting the implementation of the General Agreement on Tariffs and Trade (GATT). The special association with the ACP partners, though preferential and selective, has not demanded formal reciprocity, while partly corresponding benefits in commercial access have been more widely spread as a consequence of the general scheme of preferences (GSP), adopted under GATT rules in 1972 at the Community's initiative.[16]

To what extent the Community's residual trade protection has unduly inhibited the efforts of others to promote their own economic development is, of course, disputable. The periphery's structural disadvantages with respect to investment and technology have been partly compensated by concerted programmes of financial and technical assistance, of which multilateral European aid has been an important component, mainly through the European Development Fund (EDF), which is confined to the ACP partners, and also lending on preferential terms by the European Investment Bank (EIB).[17]

The special relationship between the EEC and its ACP partners has been criticized as 'neo-imperialist'.[18] This criticism has not been assuaged by the facts that the conventions are negotiated at regular five-yearly intervals by all the parties on at least formally equal terms, and that they are implemented under the supervision of common institutions, in which the overseas partners enjoy equal representation. Indeed, this unique aspect of the association may be seen as reinforcing the involvement of ACP states in what has become in effect a permanent relationship of economic dependency. Certainly, the Europeans depend far less on their earnings from trade with these countries than the latter do on access to the European market. It is often suggested that the special arrangements for trade and aid made by the European Community are designed, in effect, to guarantee an adequate supply of primary products to Europe, often at depressed prices, while discouraging the less-developed countries concerned from seeking other markets for their own exports or adequately diversifying their own economies. In fact, the ACP states face a number of significant legal impediments to their access to the common market, above all: quantitative limitations on the import of some agricultural products, especially those affected by the CAP; the EC's rules of origin', which restrict the importation of goods only partly manufactured in an ACP state; and the right of EC member states to invoke a safeguard clause to restrict the importation of products that compete in a sensitive sector of their own economies.[19]

In fact, European generosity through neither Lomé nor the GSP has been sufficient to prevent an alarming growth in general disparity on a global scale between rich and poor, core and periphery. Despite a steady increase in their number, the ACP states have actually accounted for a no less steadily declining share of the Community's total imports. The massive growth in external trade experienced by most of the Community's member states since the 1950s has been caused mostly by increased trade within Europe or with the USA and Japan.[20] Even though this increased prosperity in the core of the world economy may not have diverted trade from less-developed regions as much as some originally feared, its influence on the movement of capital cannot have been so favourable for those experiencing much slower growth or none at all.

However, even if it were successful in its own terms, the conventional European policy for overseas development, relying on preferential trade and aid, seems to assume that the poor can hope to become less poor only in so far as the rich become more rich. If, indeed, those on other continents, who happen to comprise a majority of the world's population, suffer from *structural underdevelopment* on a global scale, then a dependence on external trade and inward investment, by, respectively, reducing the incentive for indigenous industrialization and incurring heavy burdens of debt-repayment, may even impede the necessary transformation of economic structures. Such a policy is crucially flawed, in theory, in that the continued and inevitable dependency of the periphery on the core leads to a misallocation and an abuse of resources, in other words to unnecessary waste and harmful but avoidable side-effects both for immediate consumers and others. Its main practical shortcoming, of course, is that many of the poor have in fact become poorer.[21]

The 'globalization' of market forces has led to growing disparities between classes within developing countries and between richer and poorer states within the 'Third World'. This very conceptualization is now thoroughly redundant. Not only has the transformation within the past decade of the USSR and its own dependencies rendered the 'Second World' otiose, but it has also become necessary to differentiate the 'newly industrialized countries' (NICs, including the four highly successful East Asian states – Hong Kong, Singapore, South Korea and Taiwan) from the rest of the former 'Third World' (a remainder itself demanding further differentiation). The emergence, mainly in Latin America, the Middle East and Asia, of a category of wealthier, 'semi-peripheral', late-developed rather than less-developed, states of the capitalist world-economy, and within them of new elites formed out of wealth accrued in hard currency, clearly owes much to the Western core's seemingly irreversible and progressive compulsion to consume.[22] However, the astonishingly rapid economic growth in South-east Asia, for example, has been derived increasingly from highly competitive trading in manufactures (automobiles, electronics, textiles and clothing) and even services (finance, air transport), once regarded foundations of Europe's own economic superiority. It has been achieved despite restricted access to the European market, especially with respect to agriculture, textiles and clothing, and electronics.[23]

The NICs' capacity to export to other markets and attract foreign investment (including a substantial proportion from Europe) provides a major reason for the European Community's growing obsession since the beginning of the 1980s with its own decline in 'competitiveness'. The celebrated 1992 programme of measures to complete the internal market was itself a reaction to the EC's poor overall performance in those sectors of manufacture and services that have grown most rapidly on a global scale, partly on account of increased production in the NICs. This new commercial and industrial policy ostensibly relied on internal reforms, and by application of the same economic theories that inspired the initial pro-posal for a common market in the 1950s. Broadly speaking, increased competitiveness would be earned through making economies of scale, by saving costs of frontier restrictions, and by intensifying competition, especially in intra-industry trade and financial services. Nevertheless, in so far as the ultimate object was to give EC producers and suppliers a competitive advantage in world markets, if they are to be successful in their own terms, these measures must increase the competitive *disadvant-ages* for non-members. Less-developed countries are likely to suffer particularly with respect to technical standards.

The EEC's 1992 programme thus drew attention to the limitations of the GATT, provided a major incentive for the Uruguay Round, and con-sequently contributed to the subsequent international agreements to reduce non-tariff barriers worldwide as well as the transformation of GATT into a World Trade Organization (WTO). In other words, the West imposed a conventional treatment for unequal trading conditions between core and periphery by transposing legislative and police powers to an international level.[24] The Europeans of the European Union consequently find them-selves in an all too familiar dilemma in their economic relations with less-or late-developed peoples.

If, on the one hand, they are to treat their problem of 'competitiveness' as one essentially of inadequate *competition*, then a simple solution seems to be at hand: extend to others the liberalization accomplished internally.

In theory, such an open-market approach should benefit non-members in the former Third World, in so far as the predicted economic growth in Europe should lead in the long run to increased imports, including those of goods and services from less-developed countries.[25]

On the other hand, this solution is not as simple as it seems. Current trends suggest that the EU's internal liberalization may not, in fact, deliver the expected growth in domestic investment, employment and income, at least without more 'integration', by means not only of legal harmonization and monetary union, but also of much more coordinated and positive fiscal and industrial policies. Meanwhile, Western Europe now has the additional handicap arising from the dependency of states that belonged to the obsolete 'Second World', which cannot indefinitely be excluded from some kind of membership and with it the privileges of economic and social cohesion. If Europe's own problem of economic underdevelopment, or 'uncompetitiveness', is not likely to improve, despite efforts to increase competition internally, then it will be correspondingly more difficult for the EU to extend its free market policy externally, without incurring a decline in material standards of living. Relative to the past and present experience of those living in less-developed regions, such a sacrifice might not seem unjust or even excessively painful, while it might even have a salutary effect on those addicted to pathological over-consumption. Nevertheless, to the extent that they depend on exporting to Europe for their own economic development, the less-developed countries are unlikely to benefit from any general reduction in Europeans' propensity to consume.

Moreover, any reduction in material standards within Europe, consequent on increased liberalization of trade and capital, would have inequitable effects. Above all, the owners and managers of capital are likely to suffer far less than others.[26] For the majority of Europeans unrestrained competition can be very costly indeed. Even the wealthier European states may well have reached the stage when they can no longer rely on international trade to finance social security and other forms of public provision, especially in view of a growing surplus of labour, much of it old rather than young (and dependent rather than productive). France and Germany have recently joined the UK in undertaking a drastic reappraisal of the levels of state provision, especially for social insurance, education and public health.

These regressive effects of international trade on social redistribution add to the difficulties of European governments when trying to reconcile a commitment to democracy with one to freedom of trade. Increased competition outside the European market is unlikely, therefore, to be a preferred option for curing uncompetitiveness. Although an overt policy of protectionism is also unlikely, nevertheless, the majority of EU states, and the official EU doctrine itself, can be expected to continue to insist on multilateralism and gradualism as essential conditions of access to the internal market. The EU's current experiments in foreign policy might be interpreted as supporting just such a strategy, especially to preempt possible further efforts by the USA to impose global integration, under Western-dominated regulatory agencies. Europe's aspirations to a world role, therefore, may be explained – and justified internally as well as externally – as necessary in order to maintain a genuine and autonomous common commercial policy.

So far this 'regionalist' strategy is abetted by the former Third World. However, by fostering regionalism elsewhere the EU's member states might hope to secure not only useful allies against economic and political hegemony but also more efficient methods of influencing the commercial and industrial policies of their new competitors in trade, especially the NICs in Asia and Latin America. The practice of 'dialogue' with groups of trading 'partners' is a prudent way of forestalling possibly destructive conflicts and misunderstandings later on. If it should depict those partners' own policies to be less reasonable or even legitimate than they ought to be, such a practice also offers a useful defence of trade restrictions, or might justify other kinds of special pleading, in any future international legislative and police proceedings, for example in the WTO. Indeed, regionalism provides additional leverage for another discernible strategic shift in European policy, which is of somewhat earlier provenance: the attempt to link economic development with political and social issues.

EUROPE'S CIVILIZING MISSION

The TEU plainly states that the Union cooperates with developing countries for political, as well as economic, reasons. The new provisions on development cooperation require the Community to contribute in this area to the CFSP's general objective 'of developing and consolidating democracy and the rule of law, and to that of respecting human rights and fundamental freedoms'.[27] In fact, the Community's policy for overseas development began to be manifestly tinged with concern for the political and social conditions of economic development at least a decade ago. The tinge has now spread to a prominent colour.

Legal authority for 'conditionality' in the disposal of concessions in trade and aid was initially provided by a declaration of the Community's then 12 foreign ministers, meeting in Council on 21 July 1986, that the Community and its members administered overseas aid, and other external relationships, with a view to promoting 'fundamental rights'. A much stronger and more detailed legal basis was then provided by a resolution adopted by Council on 28 November 1991, just prior to the Maastricht agreement itself.[28] Agreements with states and regional organizations, as well as with the ACP, that include economically preferential treatment now specify *as a rule* any number of mutually desired political outcomes, namely: self-determination of peoples, respect for diversity and pluralism, good governance, administrative modernization, even the reduction of military expenditure. Whether these results should be achieved as a condition of preferential treatment is not always clear. Some measure of political and social reform on the part of the beneficiaries does seem to be expected, whether in order to maximize returns from European bene-volence, or as a more straightforward act of reciprocity. The general implication is clear enough: the EU believes itself to have a benign interest in fostering the cultivation of civilized values overseas and a special qualification and aptitude to pronounce on the political, as well as the economic, aspects of development.

Of course, these claims should, and will, be judged both by what Europeans do (and have done) to those on other continents, and by what they customarily do (and have done) to each other. Europe has gone a long way in the past 40 years to expiate a dubious past in both these respects. The gradual and painstaking process of European integration (a sense in which this precocious terminology for once duly applies) is a step towards atonement, reconstructing Europe as a civilian power, founded on a legal order bound to the respect of fundamental human and civic rights, a Union of nation-states, 'whose systems of government are founded on the princi-ples of democracy'.[29] Nevertheless, most Europeans are still only adapting to life under conditions of stable constitutional and democratic govern-ment.[30] The qualifications and aptitudes of Europeans, even in the west, to pronounce on civilized values are conditional on recent good conduct. Even this conduct begins to seem patchy enough, with growing evidence of the corruptibility and corruption of European liberal democracy in the second half of this century.

There are, indeed, various possible explanations for the increasing politicization of the EEC's external relations with less-developed coun-tries, and why this has now led to the formal assumption, endorsed by treaty, of a right to influence the domestic affairs of other sovereign states to moral ends. Even the EEC could never, in effect, entirely exclude political considerations from decisions to enter into formal international agreements with non-member states, singly or collectively, for commercial and other economic purposes. The most efficient internal cause of politicization has been the influence exercised by the Community's own member states, which have always been concerned, though some much more than others, to subordinate the actions taken legally by the Community's institutions to considerations of national interest, as embodied in the states' own foreign policies. The use of '*political dialogue*' to enhance the member states' collective influence outside the Community dates back to 1972 and the inauguration of the procedure of EPC on the eve of British accession.[31]

The use of EPC and of the European Council to intervene in external affairs for which the Community's own institutions were endowed with legal responsibility by treaty (and for primarily economic objectives) could be, and often was, confusing and vexing both for the Commission and for the foreign governments concerned, with which the Commission usually had a well-established diplomatic relationship of its own. The content of what the member governments declared or proposed was not always the main problem, since it mostly expressed opinions that individual governments had already voiced unilaterally or multilaterally in other international organizations, particularly the United Nations. However, it was often impossible to hide the facts, on the one hand, that one or more member states could and did interpret a 'common position' differently from others, and, on the other hand, that responsibility for implemention was assigned vaguely, if at all. The effect could be to contradict, or at least render equivocal, commitments already undertaken in the course of the Community's own diplomacy (even when this might be primarily economic in content).

The member states' collective attempts to influence the Community's use of its economic powers for political ends were often strongly influenced by considerations of security. Although, obviously enough, one major concern was to ensure that the Community's actions did not conflict with the obligations that most member states had assumed through their membership of NATO, there were, nevertheless, some famous disagreements with the USA (most notably, over the Middle East, South Africa and Central America).

However, EPC also provided an opportunity for individual member states to safeguard particular national economic interests against unfavourable trends in the Community's external policies. A leading example was the UK's reluctance during the 1980s to support economic sanctions against South Africa.[32] Generally, however, both member governments and the Commission have been concerned about the corrupt use, or sheer wastage, of development aid. One of the main shortcomings of the EDF, indeed, has been that the financial assistance that it makes available tends to be misspent or underspent. The Commission itself blames this defect partly on inadequate public administration in the recipient countries and has strengthened its own representation in the countries concerned as a means of rectifying it. These issues featured in the negotiations for the fourth Lomé Convention and, controversially, terms of 'conditionality' were written into the current ten-year agreement starting in 1990 and reinforced by the mid-term review in 1995. The terms of financial provision from the EDF now include assistance to various kinds of political and administrative reform, including the activities of 'non-governmental' organizations, while the Community's budget provides under various headings for financial and technical support for similar purposes outside ACP, and especially in Latin America.[33]

Another factor in politicization has been the growth of democracy within the Union. Members of the European Parliament, more especially since being directly elected, have not been deterred from voicing opinions on the political affairs of non-member states by their own institution's lack of competence to take more than declaratory actions, and even when the Community itself might have no moral or material sanction available. The expansion of financial means to promote political and social aspects of development overseas probably owes something to the Parliament's use of its budgetary powers. Parliament's influence became even more serious, after the Single European Act (SEA) of 1986 gave it means to bite, in the form of a right of 'assent' (*avis conforme*) to international agreements.

At the same time, the SEA confirmed and facilitated the *de facto* right of member states' governments to give collective political direction and ultimate approval to the use of powers legally transferred to the Community's own institutions. That right was, of course, further enhanced and enunciated by the TEU, which placed the CFSP and its execution beyond both accountability to Parliament and the jurisdiction of the Court of Justice.[34] Democratic pressures from within, therefore, cannot provide an adequate justification for the Community's, and later the Union's, assumption of a new civilizing mission on other, presumably darker, continents.

In effect, the Union can take, or desist from, action outside its own borders, including possible use of the Community's power to impose economic sanction, only when its member states' governments unanimously so determine, acting in conformity with their other various international obligations, including that, where applicable, to NATO. The overriding consideration in the constitutional arrangements for CFSP, as it was in the less formal procedures of EPC, is the defensive one of protecting each member government's nominal right to pursue national interest by diplomatic, economic or military means, whether on a unilateral or a multilateral basis. In theory, any state's government might be constrained by its own parliamentary, judicial or constitutional authorities from recommending, endorsing or specifically approving multilateral action under the TEU, just as it might be similarly constrained from undertaking unilateral action. No corresponding power is given to the Union's own Parliament and Court. Whenever they choose to make or execute foreign policy jointly, the state's governments are unaccountable; democracy and the rule of law apply to them, if at all, coincidentally. The TEU not only incurred in this regard a democratic deficit, but it also failed to realize a potential democratic surplus, in that collective parliamentary and judicial control (on behalf of European citizens as a whole) could have been, but was not, extended to the unilateral actions of member governments (to carry out nuclear tests, to sell arms to potential or actual belligerents, or to launch post-colonial adventures).

Indeed, the introduction, nominally and procedurally, of a common foreign and security policy significantly enhances neither the credibility nor the capability of external intervention by European states in support of political values in less-developed countries or elsewhere. There is still no way of binding a member state to act or refrain from acting, if it has not already given its approval in advance. Even if all member states do agree to be bound by some common position (and any joint action it may additionally entail) their self-appointed mission of promoting peace, democracy and justice, wherever these might be at risk, is circumscribed by the same conditions as it would be if they acted unilaterally or in any other way. Ultimately, and without unacceptable costs, there is no way from without of controlling the reactions of indigenous political or social forces, least of all in the turbulent conditions of late development. The hypothetical resort to armed intervention, even for 'peacekeeping' purposes, is inherently fraught with difficulty, while economic sanction must be of ever-diminishing potency, as an increasing number of developing states find the means to be economically competitive without changing their autocratic and inegalitarian ways.

In fact, there is significant variation, both between regions and between different states in the same region, not only in the practice of prescribed rules of good government, but also in the capacity for applying principles of democracy, equity and efficiency similar to those commonly identified with the mature civil society of Western Europe.[35] It is, of course, insensitive to set up general standards of political conduct, based on the expectations of advanced, industrialized countries, for much newer states, many of which have populations still massively poor, illiterate, unsettled and preoccupied with malnutrition, disease and dispossession. But more importantly, even where economic and political modernization have at least brought these primary deficiencies under some sort of control, or have occurred in spite of them, there is a risk of unduly prejudicing the local contest of political and social forces. This risk is especially dangerous to the extent that underdevelopment is rightly seen as a structural consequence of global economic integration.

Concepts like democracy, the rule of law, and above all 'good governance', are infamously ambivalent. The more they are applied as such, the more they are open to abuse, whether in spite of or on account of the technical guidance of political and other social scientists. On the one hand, internally, the invocation of Western values may provide externally educated and funded elites with an ideal rationalization of established state power. On the other hand, externally, Western moral benevolence may mask the seductive intent of economic and strategic interest. Often mere suspicion of these motives is enough to be destabilizing and to frustrate both the political and the economic purposes of development.

THE EUROPEAN MODEL OF REGIONAL INTEGRATION

To conclude: however desirable it might seem as a counterpoint to American power, the increasingly ambitious role projected for the European Union in overseas development so far lacks both legitimacy and efficiency. With respect to the economic aspects of development the Union's member states have been increasingly distracted by their own problem of 'competitiveness'. Paradoxically, these states seem unable to treat this problem (as might seem the logical thing to do) by accepting more external competition, without provoking a measure of social disparity for themselves that would be regarded as symptomatic of underdevelopment if it occurred elsewhere. Meanwhile, the Union not only wants efficient means to pursue political objectives of development on other continents but, more importantly, fails to realize those objectives itself. It is difficult to say in which respect the emperor's nudity most offends.

The question, therefore, is whether Europe's own experiment with regional integration could be transformed into something capable of leading the Third World by virtuous example. Less-developed communities in Africa, Asia and Latin America might find better means of self-reliant development in their own versions of multinational economic and political association, designed to transcend the artificial restrictions of political boundaries while accepting the diverse conditions in which development has to occur.[36] 'Regionalism' may offer the desired alternative to nationalism or internationalism, but it is still vague, while its inherently territorial denotation is unduly restrictive. 'Integration' is, moreover, a metapolitical conception, insufficiently existential as a guide to practice, even in a national context. The experience of European Union aptly illustrates the shortcomings of 'regional integration'.

First, with respect to security, the lesson seems to be that a wider global security, or at least balance of power, may be a condition of regional economic confederation, which thus on its own neither resolves problems of external dependency nor removes fundamental causes of insecurity among its own members, including their mutual confidence in each other. 'Regional integration', in other words, does not remove the need for states to defend themselves and to form military alliances between themselves and others, nor does it permanently and adequately guarantee peace, even on the borders of its own region.

Secondly, a regional common market may lessen economic disadvantages of both peripherality and scale, assisting the member states' management of domestic adjustment and enhancing their external bargaining power in conditions of increasingly global freedom of trade and capital mobility. On the other hand, a common market produces its own internal disparities, dividing the region itself between internal core and periphery. In any event, with increasingly global free trade there is a continuing temptation for both larger and smaller states who think they can afford it to play free-rider or simply cut and run. If the participating states' loss of fiscal and other means of redistribution and cyclical management could be substituted federally, or otherwise compensated for, the outcome might be more positive. 'Economic integration', therefore, seems to depend on the political conditions, and is unlikely to make a favourable contribution to welfare without suitable political decisions, which do not come about automatically.

Thirdly, indeed, left to itself 'regional integration' may not lead to a recognizable political entity, at least one capable of meeting demands for democracy and governance beyond the nation-state. Although the European Community owed much of its previous economic success to its quasi-federal institutions, too few members have been willing to insist on more federalism in the European Union, or to defend what there is, possibly fearing the effects of the likely withdrawal or exclusion of others. The outcome may, therefore, be disappointing for communities which, for whatever reason, expect new supranational authorities to provide a more liberal and stable regime than could be guaranteed by their existing awkwardly bounded, and perhaps ill-governed, states.

This relates to a fourth aspect of regionalism in which the experience of Europe so far is also disappointing. The EU's existing members have failed to agree on a common policy for treating foreigners who seek political or economic refuge within their borders and this is connected with the failure to provide for genuine European citizenship derived from human nature rather than nationality. A society that is so afraid of losing what it has that it cannot share its privileges with others can hardly be described as integrated.[37] Jurgen Habermas has cogently argued that the Europeans cannot reasonably detach citizenship from the restrictions of nationhood or nationality, unless they are at the same time capable of developing a new, *integral* conception of civic participation that is universally applicable, and thus capable also of admitting, on suitable conditions, those coming from outside the Union.[38] The problem for advocates of 'regional integration' is that, while the 'region' may be less than a nation-state writ large, it may nevertheless on the other hand be insufficiently integrated to apply a universal principle of civic participation. This issue has become critical for the EU's relations with its own neighbours and the further periphery overseas. It is also a crucial test of European integration itself, which thus emerges less as an issue of international relations than of political and moral theory.

Can the new Europe cultivate its own civil society sufficiently to qualify for the task of assisting the cultivation of others, indeed, of a global civil society, both by example and design? In fact, it has proved tragically difficult in Europe to transpose the 'constitutional patriotism' developed by the German Federal Republic since 1949 on to a larger scale. A European community founded on economic interest has remained bounded by it; most of the states most of the time have continued to feel too insecure about their immediate neighbours to permit a true community of shared civility to emerge. Regrettably, therefore, it seems that the altruistic project of a grand European republic has been, at best, postponed. The loss is not only Europe's; the dangers of Europe's indecision affect other continents too; the reasons for failure are of world-wide and millenial concern; the hope for speedy improvement must also be universal.

Notes

1. The author gratefully acknowledges the financial support of the *Generalidad Valenciana* in the form of a scholarship enabling him to work on this article at the European Peace University, Universitat Jaume I, Castellon, Spain, during 1996. It must nevertheless be stressed that the author assumes full personal responsibility for views and errors contained herein.

2. Hettne (1995) provides a valuable theoretical and historical introduction in the context of overseas development by a leading advocate of regionalism, who uses a much wider and more scholarly definition of 'Eurocentrism', namely: 'By Eurocentric development thinking I mean development theories and models rooted in Western economic history and consequently structured by that unique, although historically important, experience.' (p. 36). See also Melo and Panagariya (1993) and Robson (1993).

3. Commission of the European Communities, Secretariat-General, *European Council Meeting in Madrid on 15 and 16 December 1995: Conclusions of the Presidency*. SI (95) 1000. Brussels.

4. The task is being continued by the constituent inter-governmental conference that opened at Turin in March 1996, and may involve a new treaty between the Union's current 15 member states. The relevant *Provisions on a Common Foreign and Security Policy* make up *Title V* of the TEU (articles J–J11 inclusive). Other provisions of the same treaty relevant to external affairs form part of its *Title II: Provisions amending the Treaty establishing the European Economic Community with a view to establishing the European Community* (TEU article G). Reference to these other provisions will be made below by means of the abbreviated formula: EC, article... .

5. In Latin America the European Community had already developed special relationships with a group of six Central American states and with another six states belonging to the Andean Pact. The Madrid European Council made much of the recent signing (also in Madrid) on an *Inter-regional framework on trade and economic cooperation* between the EU and Mercosur (composed of Argentina, Brazil, Paraguay and Uruguay). With respect to South-east Asia an agreement between the EC and ASEAN (Brunei Darussalam, Indonesia, Malaysia, Philippines, Singapore, Thailand) has operated since 1983 (Vietnam became a member of ASEAN in 1995). The Madrid conference confirmed the proposed agenda for an Asia–Europe Meeting (ASEM), including ASEAN plus four other Asian states, which eventually took place in Bangkok in February 1996.

6. Commission of the European Communities, *Fourth ACP–EC Convention of Lomé as revised by the agreement signed in Mauritius on 4 November 1995*, The ACP–EC Courier, No. 155, January–February 1996. Lomé IV has 70 ACP participants, compared to 46 in Lomé I (which commenced in 1975). It provides for a budget, financed from the European Development Fund (EDF), of 12 million ECUs for the period 1990–4, multiplied nearly four times in money terms compared to Lomé I. The renegotiation of Lomé IV for its second five-year period was, however, extremely bitter, especially

over budgetary provision, which the British and Germans in particular sought to reduce.

7. This was adopted at Addis Ababa in June 1995. Military support from the EU may be supplied at the request of OAU, pursuant to a decision of the UN security council, and by means of the Western European Union (WEU). The EU has also contributed, in terms of coordinated diplomatic influence and technical assistance, to the transition to democracy in South Africa.

8. See, for example, Declaration of the Heads of State and Government participating in the meeting of the North Atlantic Council, Brussels, 10–11 January 1994, and for recent assessments of the prospects of independent European defence Chilton (1995), Taylor (1994).

9. See *European Council Meeting in Madrid, op. cit.*, annex 11.

10. Article 2 of the Treaty establishing the European Economic Community (EEC treaty). EC article 2 (as amended by the TEU) still describes those functions (or 'tasks') *inter alia* as '... to promote a harmonious and balanced development of economic activities' and now specifies also the promotion of 'a high level of employment and of social protection'. See note 2 above for an explanation of references.

11. EC article 3a.1. The principle is reiterated in the revised treaty, with specific reference to: economic policy (article 102a); monetary policy (article 105); and industrial policy (article 130, 'in accordance with a system of open and competitive markets').

12. EC article 110, unaltered since the original EEC treaty.

13. The treaty basis for these binding provisions is also extant in, respectively, EC articles 112, 131–6, and 234.

14. EC article 130u.1, which also enjoins the Community to foster 'the smooth and gradual integration of the developing countries into the world economy' and 'the campaign against poverty in the developing countries'. The Community's policy is described as 'complementary to the policies pursued by the Member States'.

15. For the effects of the Community's protectionism on less-developed countries generally, see McAleese (1993). The point about the internally benign effects is sustained by Hettne (1995).

16. See McAleese (1994).

17. The Lomé Conventions have provided, in addition, two schemes to insure ACP partners against the typical variability in earnings from the export of raw materials to the Community: STABEX, introduced in 1975, to cover a wide range of, mainly tropical, agricultural products; and SYSMIN, introduced in 1980, for a number of mineral products. Multilateral aid through Community instruments accounts for only a small proportion of total aid disbursed by its member states to less-developed countries (most of which is bilateral).

18. See, for example, Chikeka (1993), Grilli (1994), Lister (1988), Zartman (1993).

19. See Marin (1993).

20. The share of total imports from outside the Community attributed to trade with ACP fell from 7.3 per cent in 1980 to 4.3 per cent in 1989. Even

including the import of oil, the less-developed countries' share of total trade by EC member states in 1991 was 12.3 per cent of imports and 12.1 per cent of exports. See McAleese (1993, 1994).

21.   For a general critique of development theory, including analysis of the strengths and weaknesses of 'dependency' theory, see Hettne (1990) and Leys (1996). For the understanding of international trade and investment in terms of a theory of the world economy, see Wallerstein (1979). For statistical evidence of the trends in economic disparity in the world economy, see Hobsbawm (1994), pp. 344–72.

22.   In other words, in a neglected, but interesting sense, it is possible to question who is really dependent on whom. Earnings from the export of oil are inflated not only by cartelization but also by the seemingly inelastic demand for energy in the West (sustained by cultural rather than economic factors). Much acquisition of wealth in the periphery relies on Western addictions (to sugar and the three c's – caffeine, cocaine and cocoa); some of this trade is illicit and managed by another kind of cartel, not of governments but of international criminal organizations. On the wider significance of the capacity of transnational commerce, including crime, to evade political and legal control, see Strange (1994).

23.   Pelkmans (1993). On the political and social conditions of the NICs, see Leys (1996) pp. 19–25, 64–79. On the redundancy of 'Third World', see Hettne (1990).

24.   The Europeans have already begun to make wider use of more subtle instruments of protection for sensitive sectors in their own economies, such as 'voluntary export restraints' (VERs) and elaborated anti-dumping measures. See also note 21. For an optimistic view of the consequences of the EC's internal market on less-developed countries and others, see the contributions to Mayes (1993), and for a general defence of liberalism in international trade, see Keohane (1990). The crucial point, however, is that *this methodology itself, together with the liberal economic and legal discourse on which it is founded, are, in fact, redundant*; experience shows that governments as well as corporations (operating within or without the law) will inevitably and persistently undermine any given regulatory apparatus, not necessarily by breaking the rules, but by constantly finding new loopholes, valid exceptions or opportunities for avoidance.

25.   See McAleese (1993), Pelkmans (1993).

26.   The costs of allowing competition to promote competitiveness are, of course, far less for capital than for other interests, while in many respects the former will be actually better off. It is presumably of little moment to corporate investors whether they make an adequate return from Europe or Latin America or Asia.

27.   EC article 130u.2, see also TEU article J.1.2.

28.   The 1986 declaration, which was urged by the contemporary Dutch presidency, continued: 'so that individuals and peoples will enjoy to the full their economc, social and cultural rights and their civil and political rights'. (Cited in Nuttall 1992, p. 269). The 1991 resolution responded to an earlier communication from the Commission and confirmed that 'balanced and sustained development' required more than just the promotion of universal

human rights and should take account also of 'good governance' and military spending. Council set out detailed guidelines for the Community and its member states to adopt 'a consistent approach towards human rights, democracy and development in their cooperation with developing countries'.

29. TEU article F.

30. A substantial majority of those who currently enjoy citizenship of the Union must have recent forebears who, two generations ago, possibly only one, lived under (and may have directly served) some brutally tyrannical, militaristic, regime in which fundamental civil and human liberties were systematically undermined (and often worse).

31. The first 'dialogue' was initiated in 1992 with Turkey. On this and on the history of EPC in general, see Nuttall (1992), pp. 282–93 and passim.

32. The general ruling on conditionality actually made it easier to object to exceptional treatment of South Africa, since some of the Community's own ACP partners in Africa were also defective in democracy and human rights.

33. See Commission of the European Communities, *Report on the implementation of the resolution of the Council and of the Member States meeting in the Council on Human Rights, Democracy and Development, adopted on 28 November 1991.* SEC (92) 1915, Brussels, 21 October 1992. See also Babarinde (1995). These financial and technical measures compare with similar, though much more generously supported, ones adopted after 1990 for the formerly communist states of central and eastern Europe. Another explanation for the Community's growing confidence in seeking to influence political and social conditions in less-developed countries might be that it was encouraged by the experience of the Conference on Security and Cooperation in Europe (CSCE), which during the 1970s successfully extended the agenda of international diplomacy, even between the super-powers, to moral issues.

34. TEU articles J.8.1 and 2, and L. Parliament has the legal right (under TEU article J.7) only to be consulted by the presidency of Council, to be 'regularly informed' by the presidency and the Commission, to ask questions of Council and make recommendations to it, and hold an annual debate on CFSP.

35. See the various contributions on Latin America, Africa, Asia and the Middle East in Held (1993) pp. 312–406. On the current obstacles to democracy and 'good governance' in Africa, see Austin (1993). See also Bayart (1993), Leys (1996).

36. See Hettne (1995): 'There can be no fixed and final definition of development, only suggestions of what development should imply in particular contexts.' p. 15.

37. This problematic of the 'open society' that fears loss of the privileges that cause it to be 'open' in the first place, may correspond to that of the social limits to growth identified by Hirsch (1977) as endemic to the economic system founded on competitive markets.

38. See Habermas (1992). 'Only within the constitutional framework of a democratic legal system can different ways of life coexist equally. These

must, however, overlap within a common political culture, which again implies an impulse to open these ways of life to others. Only democratic citizenship can prepare the way for a condition of world citizenship which does not close itself off within particularistic biases, and which accepts a world-wide form of political communication.' (pp. 18–19).

References

Austin, Dennis (1993) 'Reflections on African politics: Prospero, Ariel and Caliban,' in *International Affairs* Vol. 69 No. 2, pp. 203–21.

Babarinde, Olufemi A. (1995) 'The Lomé Convention: An aging dinosaur in the European Union's foreign policy enterprise?', in Carolyn Rhodes and Sonia Mazey (eds.) *The State of the European Union* Vol. 3, (Boulder, CO: Lynne Reiner), pp. 469–96.

Bayart, Jean-François (1993) *The State in Africa: the Politics of the Belly* (London: Longman).

Chikeka, C.O. (1993) *Africa and the European Community 1957–1992* (London: Edwin Mellen Press).

Chilton, Patricia (1995) 'Common, Collective or Combined? Theories of Defense Integration in the European Union', in Rhodes and Mazey *op. cit.*, pp. 81–110.

Grilli, E. (1994) *The European Community and Developing Countries* (Cambridge: Cambridge University Press).

Habermas, Jurgen (1992) 'Citizenship and national identity: some reflections on the future of Europe', in *Praxis International* Vol. 12, No. 1, April 1992, pp. 2–19.

Held, David (ed.) (1993) *Prospects for Democracy* (Cambridge: Polity Press).

Hettne, Bjorn (1995) *Development Theory and the Three Worlds* 2nd edn, (Harlow: Longman).

Hirsch, Fred (1977) *Social Limits to Growth* (London: Routledge and Kegan Paul).

Hobsbawm, Eric (1994) *The Age of Extremes: the short twentieth century 1914–91.* (London: Michael Joseph).

Keohane, Robert O. (1990) 'International liberalism reconsidered', in Dunn, John, ed. (1990) *The Economic Limits to Modern Politics* (Cambridge: Cambridge University Press). pp. 165–94.

Leys, Colin (1996) *The Rise and Fall of Development Theory* (London: James Curry).

Lister, M. (1988) *The European Community and the Developing World: the role of the Lomé Convention* (Aldershot: Gower).

McAleese, Dermot (1993) 'The Community's external trade policy', in Mayes, David G. *The External Implications of European Integration* (Hemel Hempstead: Harvester Wheatsheaf), pp. 32–51.

McAleese, Dermot (1994) 'EC external trade policy, in El-Agraa', in Ali M., ed. *The Economics of the European Community*, 4th edn, (Hemel Hempstead: Harvester Wheatsheaf), pp. 450–70.

Marin, A. (1994) 'The Lomé Agreement, in El-Agraa', *op. cit.* pp. 472–89.

Mayes, David G. (1993) 'The Implications of Closer Integration in Europe for Third Countries', in Mayes *op. cit.* pp. 1–31.

Melo, J. De and Panagariya, A. (1993) *New Dimensions in Regional Integration* (Cambridge: Cambridge University Press).

Nuttall, Simon J. (1992) *European Political Cooperation* (Oxford: Clarendon Press).

Pelkmans, Jacques (1993) 'ASEAN and EC-1992', in Mayes, *op. cit.* pp. 123–45.

Robson, P. (1993) 'The New Regionalism and Developing Countries', in *Journal of Common Market Studies* Vol. 31 No. 3, September 1993.

Strange, Susan (1995) 'The Limits of Politics,' in *Government and Opposition* Vol. 30 No. 3, pp. 291–311.

Trevor Taylor (ed.) (1994) *Reshaping European Defence* (London: Royal Institute for International Affairs).

Wallerstein, Immanuel (1984) *The Politics of the World Economy* (Cambridge: Cambridge University Press).

Zartman, I.W. (ed.) (1993) *Europe and Africa: the new phase* (Boulder, CO: Lynne Reiner).

Appendix: Address to the European Parliament, Strasbourg, 8 March 1994

Václav Havel

Mr Chairman,
Members of Parliament,

I am most grateful to you for the honor of addressing the European Parliament, and I can scarcely think of a better way of using this opportunity than to try to answer three questions. First, why is the Czech Republic, which I represent here, requesting membership in the European Union? Secondly, why is it in the interest of all of Europe to expand the European Union? And thirdly, what, in my opinion, are the more general tasks confronting the European Union today?

Europe is a continent of extraordinary variety and diversity – geographically, ethnically, nationally, culturally, economically and politically. Yet at the same time all its parts are and always have been so deeply linked by their destiny that this continent can accurately be described as a single – albeit complex – political entity. Anything crucial in any area of human endeavor occurring anywhere in Europe always has had both direct and indirect consequences for our continent as a whole. The history of Europe is, in fact, the history of a constant searching and reshaping of its internal structures and the relationship of its parts. Today, if we talk about a single European civilization or about common European values, history, traditions, and destiny, what we are referring to is more the fruit of this tendency toward integration than its cause.

From time immemorial, Europe has had something that can be called an inner order, consisting of a specific system of political relations that circumscribed it and tried in one way or another to institutionalize its natural interconnectedness. This European order, however, usually was established by violence. The more powerful simply imposed it upon those less powerful. In this sense, the endless series of wars in Europe can be understood as an expression of the constant effort to alter the status quo and replace one order with another. From the ancient Roman Empire, through the Holy Roman Empire, and down to the power systems created by the Congress of Vienna, the Treaty of Versailles and finally by Yalta – all these were merely historical attempts to give European coexistence a certain set of game rules. A thousand times in its history Europe has been unified or divided in various ways; a thousand times one group has subjected another, forced its version of civilization on another and established self-serving political relations; a thousand times Europe's internal balance has been dramatically sought, found, transformed, and torn down. And a thousand times the French, the Swedes, the Germans or the Czechs have dealt with apparently internal matters, only to have their actions affect the rest of Europe.

I do not believe, therefore, that the idea of a European Union simply fell out of the sky, or was born in the laboratory of political theoreticians or on the drawing boards of political engineers. It grew quite naturally out of an understanding that European integrity was a fact of life, and from the efforts of many generations of Europeans to project the idea of unity into a specific 'supranational' European structure.

We may all be different, but we are all in the same boat. We can fight for our places and means of coexistence on this boat, but we also can agree on them peacefully. I understand European unity as a magnanimous attempt to choose the second of these possibilities, and to give Europe – for the first time in its history – the kind of order that would grow out of the free will of everyone, and be based on mutual agreement and a common longing for peace and cooperation. It would be a stable and solid order, one based not merely on military and political treaties, which anyone can break or ignore at will, but on such a close cooperation between European nations and citizens that it would limit, if not exclude, the possibility of new conflicts. This is not a mere dream. Soon half a century will separate us from the end of the Second World War. During that time all of Western Europe has successfully averted the threat of many potential conflicts, precisely by building, step by step, such an integrating system.

This alone is enough to demonstrate that this newest type of European order is not, or need not be, a mere utopia, but that it can work in real terms.

I do not perceive the European Union as a monstrous superstate in which the autonomy of all the various nations, states, ethnic groups, cultures, and regions of Europe would gradually be dissolved. On the contrary, I see it as the systematic creation of a space that allows the autonomous components of Europe to develop freely and in their own way in an environment of lasting security and mutually beneficial cooperation based on principles of democracy, respect for human rights, civil society, and an open market economy.

The Czech Lands lie at the very center of Europe and sometimes even think of themselves as its very heart. For this reason, they have always been a particularly exposed place, unavoidably involved in any European conflict. In fact, many European conflicts began or ended there. Like a number of other Central European countries, we have always been a dramatic crossroads of all kinds of European intellectual and spiritual currents and geopolitical interests. This makes us particularly sensitive to the fact that everything that happens in Europe intrinsically concerns us, and that everything that happens to us intrinsically concerns all of Europe. We are among the expert witnesses to the political reality of Europe's interconnectedness. That is why our sense of co-responsibility for what happens in Europe is especially strong, and also why we are intensely aware that the prospect of European integration presents an enormous historic opportunity to Europe as a whole, and to us.

I think I have essentially answered my first question – that is, why the Czech Republic wants to become a member of the European Union. Yes, we are able and happy to surrender a portion of our sovereignty in favor of the commonly administered sovereignty of the European Union, because we know it will repay us many times over, as it will all Europeans. The part of the world we live in can hope for a gradual transformation from an arena of eternally warring rulers, powers, nations, social classes and religious doctrines, competing for territories of influence or hegemony, into a forum of down-to-earth dialogue and effective cooperation between all its inhabitants in a commonly shared, commonly administered and commonly cultivated space dedicated to coexistence and solidarity.

I believe my thoughts about the interconnectedness of Europe have, to a considerable degree, answered the second question as well: why the European Union should gradually expand. Europe was divided artificially, by force, and for that very reason its division had to collapse sooner or later. History has thrown down a gauntlet we can, if we wish, pick up. If we do not do so, a great opportunity to create a continent of free and peaceful cooperation may be lost. Only a fool who has learned nothing from the millennia of European history can believe that tranquility, peace and prosperity can flourish forever in one part of Europe without regard for what is happening in the other. The era of the Cold War, when the enforced cohesion of the Soviet Bloc contributed to the cohesion of the West, is definitively over.

We must all accept that the world is radically different today than it was five years ago. The vision of Europe as a stabilizing factor in the contemporary international environment, one that does not export war to the rest of the world but rather radiates the idea of peaceful coexistence, cannot become reality if Europe as a whole is not transformed. The gauntlet simply must be taken up. What is going on in the former Yugoslavia should be a grave reminder to any of us who think that in Europe we can ignore with impunity what is going on next door. Unrest, chaos and violence are infectious and expansionary. We Central Europeans have directly felt the truth of this countless times, and I think it is our responsibility repeatedly to draw others' attention to this experience, especially those fortunate enough not to have undergone it as often as we have.

Western Europe has been moving toward its present degree of integration for nearly fifty years. It is clear that new members, particularly those attempting to shed the consequences of Communist rule, cannot be accepted overnight into the European Union without seriously threatening to tear the delicate threads from which it is woven. Nevertheless, the prospect of its expansion, and of the expansion of its influence and spirit, is in its intrinsic interest and in the intrinsic interest of Europe as a whole. There is simply no meaningful alternative to this trend. Anything else would be a return to the times when European order was not a work of consensus but of violence. And the evil demons are lying in wait. A vacuum, the decay of values, the fear of freedom, suffering and poverty, chaos – these are the environments in which they flourish. They must not be given that opportunity.

For if the future European order does not emerge from a broadening European Union, based on the best European values and willing to defend and transmit them, it could well happen that the organization of this future will fall into the hands of a cast of fools, fanatics, populists and demagogues waiting for their chance and determined to promote the worst European traditions. And there are, unfortunately, more than enough of those.

Members of Parliament, allow me now to turn to the third question I have posed. That is, the question of the tasks with which, in my opinion, the European Union is now confronted. There are certainly many of them, and all of them are difficult. One, however, appears to me especially important, and it is this I would like to talk about.

I confess that when I studied the Maastricht Treaty and the other documents on which the European Union is based, I had a somewhat ambiguous response. On the one hand, it is undoubtedly a respectable piece of work. It is scarcely possible to believe that a common framework could be given to such a complex and diverse legal and economic order, involving so many different European countries. It is amazing that common rules of the game have been created, that all the legislative, administrative and institutional mechanisms that enable the smooth running of this great body have been invented and that, in so colorful a political environment, agreement on an enormous number of concrete matters was reached and many different interests harmonized in a way that will benefit everyone. It is, I repeat, a remarkable labor of the human spirit and its rational capacities.

However, into my admiration, which initially verged on enthusiasm, there began to intrude a disturbing, less exuberant feeling. I felt I was looking into the inner workings of an absolutely perfect and immensely ingenious modern machine. To study such a machine must be a great joy to an admirer of technical inventions, but for me, whose interest in the world is not satisfied by admiration for well-oiled machines, something was seriously missing, something that could be called, in a rather simplified way, a spiritual or moral or emotional dimension. The treaty addressed my reason, but not my heart.

Naturally, I am not claiming that an affirmation of the European Union can be found in a reading of its documents and norms alone. They are only a formal framework to define the living realities that are its primary concern. And the positive aspects of those realities far outweigh whatever dry official texts can offer. Still, I cannot help feeling that my sensation of being confronted with nothing more than a perfect machine is somehow significant; that this feeling indicates something or challenges us in some way.

The large empires, complex supranational entities or confederations of states that we know from history, those which, in their time, contributed something of value to humanity, were remarkable not only because of how they were administered or organized, but also because they were always buoyed by a spirit, an idea, an ethos – I would even say by a charismatic quality – out of which their structure ultimately grew. For such entities to work and be vital, they always had to offer, and indeed did offer, some key to emotional identification, an ideal that would speak to people or inspire them, a set of generally understandable values that everyone could share. These values made it worthwhile for people to make sacrifices for the entity that embodies them, even, in extreme circumstances, the sacrifice of their very lives.

The European Union is based on a large set of values, with roots in antiquity and in Christianity, which over 2,000 years evolved into what we recognize today as the foundations of modern democracy, the rule of law and civil society. This set of values has its own clear moral foundation and its obvious metaphysical roots, whether modern man admits it or not. Thus it cannot be said that the European Union lacks a spirit from which all the concrete principles on which it is founded grow. It appears, though, that this spirit is rather difficult to see. It seems too hidden behind the mountains of systemic, technical, administrative, economic, monetary and other measures that contain it. And thus, in the end, many people might be left with the understandable impression that the European Union – to put it a bit crudely – is no more than endless arguments over how many carrots can be exported from somewhere, who sets the amount, who checks it and who will eventually punish delinquents who contravene the regulations.

That is why it seems to me that perhaps the most important task facing the European Union today is coming up with a new and genuinely clear reflection on what might be called European identity, a new and genuinely clear articulation of European responsibility, an intensified interest in the very meaning of European integration in all its wider implications for the contemporary world, and the re-creation of its ethos or, if you like, its charisma.

Reading the Maastricht Treaty, for all its historical importance, will hardly win enthusiastic supporters for the European Union. Nor will it win over patriots, people who will genuinely experience this complex organism as their native land or their home, or as one aspect of their home. If this great administrative work, which should obviously simplify life for all Europeans, is to hold together and stand the tests of time, then it must be visibly bonded by more than a set of rules and regulations. It must embody, far more clearly than it has so far, a particular relationship to the world, to human life and ultimately to the world order. Far more clearly than before, it must impress upon millions of European souls an idea, a historical mission and a momentum. It must clearly articulate the values upon which it is founded and which it intends to defend and cultivate. It also must take care to create emblems and symbols, visible bearers of its significance.

It should be perfectly clear to everyone that this is not just a conglomerate of states created for purely utilitarian reasons, but an entity that in an original way fulfills the longings of many generations of enlightened Europeans who knew that European universalism can – when projected into political reality – become the framework for a more responsible human existence on our continent. More than that, it is the way to achieve the genuine inclusion of our continent as a partner in the multicultural environment of contemporary global civilization.

Naturally, my intention is not to advise the European Union on what it should do. I can only say what I, as a European, would welcome.

I would welcome it, for instance, if the European Union were to establish a charter of its own that would clearly define the ideas on which it is founded, its meaning and the values it intends to embody. Clearly, the basis of such a charter could be nothing other than a definitive moral code for European citizens. All those hundreds of pages of agreements on which the European Union is founded would thus be brought under the umbrella of a single, crystal-clear and universally understandable political document that would make it obvious at once what the European Union really is. At the same time, it also would be to its advantage if it were made even more obvious who represents it and embodies and guarantees its values. If the citizens of Europe understand that this is not just an anonymous bureaucratic monster to limit or even deny their autonomy, but simply a new type of human community that actually broadens their freedom significantly, then the European Union need not fear for its future.

You will certainly understand that at this moment my concern is not so much any particular suggestion but something deeper: how to make the spirit of the European Union more vivid and compelling, more accessible to all. For it seems to me that this is a project of such historical importance that it would be an unforgivable sin were it to languish and ultimately disappoint the hopes invested in it only because its very meaning were drowned in disputes over technical details.

Ladies and gentlemen, I have come from a land that did not enjoy freedom and democracy for almost sixty years. You will perhaps believe me when I say that it is this historical experience that has allowed me to respond at the deepest level to the revolutionary meaning of European integration today. And perhaps you will believe me when I say that the very depth of that experience compels me to express concern for the proper outcome of this process and to consider ways to strengthen it and make it irreversible.

Allow me, in conclusion, to thank you for approving the Europe Agreement on the association of the Czech Republic with the European Union two weeks after it was signed. In doing so, you have shown that you are not indifferent to the fate of my country.

* Edited by Paul Wilson
Toward a Civil Society: Selected Speeches and Writings 1990–1994

ACKNOWLEDGEMENT

This paper is published with the kind permission of the Ministry of Foreign Affairs of the Czech Republic.

Index

Note: 'n.' after a page reference indicates the number of a note on that page.

accountability
  Common Foreign and Security Policy,
    235
  European integration, 76
  global security, 32, 35: cosmopolitan
    governance, 47
Acheson, Dean, 39
Adenauer, Konrad, 58, 107, 108
Aegean islands, 148
Afghanistan, 159, 160
Afro-Caribbean and Pacific (ACP) countries
  economic development, 228–9
  Europe's civilizing mission, 233
  regional integration, 224
aggression, 33
Alaska, 159
Albania, 162
Algeria, 226
altruism and ideals, 58–9, 62
Al Yamamah programme, 203
Anglo-Saxons, 20
Angola, 215n.18
Anti-Ballistic Missile (ABM) treaty, 156,
  170
anti-dumping measures, 242n.24
Aquinas, St Thomas, 16
Arabs, 41
Aristide, Jean-Bertrand, 45
armed neutrality, 207
Armenia, 152, 164
Arms Control and Disarmament Agency
  (ACDA), 196–7
arms trade, 187–8, 209–12
  change: post-Cold War opportunity for,
    195–200; proposals, 205–9
  control regimes, 194–5
  'new security order', need for, 200–5
  regulations, 38
  states and markets, 189–93
Asia, 223–4, 229–30
Aspin, Les, 217n.28
Association of South-East Asian Nations
  (ASEAN), 240n.5
Athens, 34
Australia Group of Suppliers, 194

Austria
  neutrality, 117, 185n.100: and arms trade,
    207, 209; parametric, 121, 123–4,
    125–8, 133–4
  Ottoman empire, 158, 161
authority and global security, 32
autonomy, 119
  Sweden, 129, 130
Azerbajzhan, 152, 164

balance of payments, and arms trade, 202
Baldwin, David A., 118
Barratt Brown, Michael, 213n.6
behaviourism, 106
Belgium, 89
belongingness, 64–5, 66
Belorussia, *see* Byelorussia
Bentham, Jeremy, 22
Bessarabia, 164
Bildt, Carl, 135
Biological Warfare Convention, 194
biological weapons, 194
Black Sea fleet, 167
Blackwill, Robert D., 185n.105, 186n.107
Bofors, 218n.36
Bolshevik Revolution, 37, 38
Bosnian war, *see* Yugoslavia, war in former
boundaries, nation-states, 65–7, 68
Braithwaite, Roger, 183n.78
Brandt Report, 6, 17
Brest-Litovsk Treaty, 159
Brezhnev, Leonid, 126
British Aerospace (BAe), 195, 199, 203
British American Security Information
  Council (BASIC), 217n.33
Brittan, Samuel, 203
Brown amendment, 178n.14, 185n.104
Bulgaria, 18, 158
Bull, Hedley, 23, 24, 43–4
bureaucracies, 71–2, 78
Burma, 45
Burundi, 36, 41
Bush, George, 39–40
Bush administration, 142
Buzan, Barry, 213n.5

Byelorussia
  nuclear-free buffer zone, 185n.101
  nuclear weapons, 153
  and Russia, relationship between, 167, 168
  secession and reincorporation, 164

Cameron, David, 109
Canada
  Conference on Security and Cooperation
    in Europe, 141
  Quebec, 18, 29
  and USA, analogy with Ukraine and
    Russia, 168
Canberra Commission on the Elimination of
  Nuclear Weapons, 155
Canetti, Elias, 86
carbon dioxide emissions, 22
Caribbean basin, 159
  see also Afro-Caribbean and Pacific
    (ACP) countries
Carr, E.H., 6
  global security, 42–3
  liberal internationalism, critique, 24
  relativist *Zeitgeist*, 26
  utopian approach, 23
Carter, Jimmy, 126, 139
Castro, Fidel, 17
centralization, 78
Chamberlain, Neville, 74
Chechnya, 29, 45
chemical weapons, 194
Chemical Weapons Convention, 194
Chemira, 218n.36
China
  Gulf War, 41
  human rights, 18, 22, 24
  and Russia: alliance with, 46, 176;
    border, 183n.84; expansionism, 157,
    159; nuclear weapons, 155; war,
    possibility of, 107
Chirac government, 109–10
Christian Democratic Party, Austria, 124
Church, Clive, 122–3
Churchill, Winston, 89, 161, 165
citizenship
  European, 69, 79–80, 82–3, 85–7, 239
  and nationality, 69, 82–3, 85
'clash' thesis, 46
Clemenceau, Georges, 37
Clinton, Bill, 140
Clinton administration
  enlargement doctrine, 46
  NATO expansion, 145, 146, 148, 149
Code of Conduct, arms trade, 207

Cohen, Hermann, 69
Cold War
  arms trade, 192, 194, 195
  global security, 39, 40
  International Relations, 6
  Peace Research, 2, 3–4
colonialism, 28, 33, 78
Combined/Joint Task Forces (CJTF), 145,
  146
commodification of values, 78
Common Agricultural Policy (CAP), 24,
  227, 228
  urbanization, 78
common commercial policy (CCP), 227
common external tariff (CET), 227, 228
Common Foreign and Security Policy
  (CFSP), 142
  Austrian role, 127
  constitutional arrangements, 235–6
  limitations, 224
  and neutrality, 132, 134, 135: arms trade,
    207
  objectives, 223, 225, 232
Common Security and Defence Policy, 75
Commonwealth of Independent States, 167
communitarianism, 26
competitiveness, European Union, 230–1,
  237
Comprehensive Test Ban (CTB) treaty, 155,
  156
Concert of Europe, 153
Conference on Security and Cooperation in
  Europe (CSCE; later Organization on
  Security and Cooperation in Europe,
  OSCE)
  Austria and Finland's role, 125, 126
  international diplomacy, agenda, 243n.33
  and NATO expansion, 140
  role, 141–3, 150
  Russian interest, 142, 169, 175–6
Confidence and Security Building Measures
  (CSBMs), 141
constitutional patriotism, 84, 239
constitutivism, 5
'constructive engagement', 45
constructivism, 5, 104
Conventional Forces in Europe (CFE)
  treaty, 150, 169, 199
Cooper, Richard N., 119
cooperative security, 175–7, 201
Coordinating Committee of Multilateral
  Export Controls (CoCom), 194
coordination reflex, 105, 110
copyright, intellectual, 24

cosmopolitan governance, 47
Costa Rica, 187
Council of Europe, 128
Cox, Robert, 6, 47
Crimea, 167
critical international theory, 5
Croatia, 152
Crusaders, 78
Cuba, 17, 159
cultural conditioning, global security, 42
Curzon Line, 161
cybernetic interconnectedness,
    disempowerment via exclusion
    from, 47
Cyprus, 148, 225
Czechoslovakia
    attitudes towards Soviet Union, 162
    Conference on Security and Cooperation
        in Europe, 143
    democracy, 147
    neutrality suggestion, 140
    Peace In Our Time approach, 59, 74
Czech Republic
    EC membership promised, 143
    Havel's speech to European Parliament,
        246, 247–8, 251
    NATO membership, 139

Dassault, 208
Dayton Peace Agreement, 33
Dean, Jonathon, 147n.18
defence spending, 38
defensive neutrality, 120–3, 133
demilitarization, 45
democracy
    community and state, 80, 81, 82
    European Union's civilizing mission,
        236–7
    growth in European Union, 235
democratic peace, 46–7
demographic issues, 226
demoi, European integration, 79–81, 82–5
demonic and ideals
    peace, 58, 59, 60
    prosperity, 62
    supranationalism, 69
Denmark, 57, 110
dependency theory, 17
depersonalization of the market, 78
Deutsch, Karl, 90
dignity and prosperity, 62
diplomatic sanctions, 17
disarmament
    League of Nations, role, 38

nuclear, 39, 45, 154–5
discrimination, European Union, 227
divine right of kings, 19
Dresden, bombing of, 16
dual nationality, 20, 86
dual-use goods, 194, 199, 207

E–3 Airborne Early Warning and Control
    System (AWACS) aircraft, 192
East Germany, 163–4
ecological crisis, 17–18
Economic and Monetary Union (EMU), 55,
    76, 109–10
economic development, Europe's
    contribution to, 226–32
economic liberalism, 214n.8
economics, 16–18
economic sanctions, 17, 234
economic warfare, 194
effective sovereignty, 119
Elster, Jon, 121, 128
employment, arms trade, 191, 201
enmeshment process, 103–4, 107, 110
environmental policy, 24
Erlander, Tage, 130
Estonia, 166, 167, 172
    cooperative security, 175
    population, 165
Ethiopia, 40
ethnic cleansing, 33, 45
ethnocentrism, 26
Eurocentrism, 26, 221
Eurofighter 2000, 203
Euro-Mediterranean partnership, 226
European Coal and Steel Community, 91,
    108, 149
European Commission, 77
    civilizing mission, 234–5
    enmeshment process, 104
    neofunctional analysis, 95, 97
European Council of Ministers, 81, 234
European Court of Justice (ECJ), 132
European Defence Community, 63
European Development Fund (EDF), 228,
    235
European Economic Area (EEA), 122, 123
European Free Trade Area (EFTA), 127
European Investment Bank (EIB), 228
European Parliament, 76, 235
    community and state, 81
    Havel's speech to, 246–51
European Political Community, 63
European Political Cooperation (EPC), 223,
    234, 236

European security, 139–40
  actors and institutions, 140–6
  cooperative, 175–7
  interests, balancing of, 173–5
  NATO expansion, 146–51
  nuclear weapons and materials, 153–6
  order, breakdown of, 151–3
  promotion, principles of, 171–2
  Russia's political and territorial
    aspirations, 156–9
  thinking about, 172–3
  threat to, 151, 169–71
European security and defence identity
  (ESDI), 142
European Union
  arms trade, 188, 196–8, 209–12: control,
    195; employment, 191; neorealism,
    190; new security order, 201–2,
    203–5; proposals for change, 205–9;
    technology, 192
  Austrian membership, 127, 131, 133–4
  community and state, 79–88
  fin-de-siècle crisis of meaning, 55–79
  Finnish membership, 128, 131, 133–4
  Havel's speech to European Parliament,
    246–51
  membership criteria, 148
  membership widening: costs, 225;
    debates, 25, 146; Havel's speech,
    246, 247–8, 251
  moral choice, 89–94, 105–11:
    intergovernmentalism and revision
    of neofunctionalism, 96–100;
    intergovernmentalism critique,
    100–3; neofunctionalist account of
    integration, 94–6; spillover and
    identity, 103–5
  and NATO expansion, 149
  neutrality, 117–18, 131–6: defensive, 133;
    parametric, 133–4; strategic, 134–6
  overseas development, 221–2: civilizing
    mission, 232–7; economic
    development, Europe's contribution
    to, 226–32; regional integration,
    237–9; world power, Europe as,
    222–6
  Swedish membership, 130–1, 134–6
  Swiss membership, 133
Euro-scepticism, 37
Exchange Rate Mechanism (ERM), 109
exclusionism, European Union, 227

Falklands War, 16
fallacy of origin, 26–7

fascism, 38, 39, 78
federalism, European integration, 67, 68,
  238–9
Federal Republic of Germany
  constitutional patriotism, 239
  European integration, 89
  and France, peace between, 57, 74
  NATO membership, 147
feminism, 21
Finland
  detachment from Sweden, 157
  neutrality, 117, 185n.101: and arms trade,
    207, 209; parametric, 121, 123–8,
    133–4
  and Russia, relationship between, 158,
    162, 166
Five Nation Contact Group, 153
foreign aid, 17, 22
foreign investments, 33
foreign policy
  arms trade, 191
  Austria, 127
  economic self-interest as motivating
    force, 100
  Finland, 125, 127
  moral terminology, 21
  Sweden, 117, 129–30
  Switzerland, 122, 123
Forland, Tor Egil, 194
formal sovereignty, 119
France
  arms trade, 192: advanced combat
    aircraft, 197; debts, 202; neorealism,
    190; second-hand market, 199;
    technology, 192
  communist parties, eviction, 147
  Conference on Security and Cooperation
    in Europe, 141
  cooperative security, 176
  defence expenditure, 185n.98
  European integration, 89: Exchange Rate
    Mechanism crisis, 109; identity,
    108–9, 110; impetus, 94; monetary
    controls, 109–10; Single European
    Act, 98
  European security and defence identity,
    142
  expansionism, 156
  fascism, rise of, 78
  film subsidies, 25
  and Germany: identity, 105, 106, 107;
    peace between, 57, 74, 75, 89;
    relationship between, 108–9,
    149

independent European military capacity, preference for, 224
military presence in Germany, 147
nuclear tests in the Pacific, 32, 48
Russian treaty commitments, 181n.56
state provision, 231
UN Security Council, 23
World Wars, 160
Franco, Francisco, 147
Frankfurt School, 71
free trade negotiations, 45–6
functional spillover, 94

Galtung, Johan, 3
Gasperi, Alcide de, 58
Gaulle, Charles de, 96, 108
GEC Underwater Systems, 209
Gehlen, General, 183n.81
General Agreement on Tariffs and Trade (GATT), 228, 230
general scheme of preferences (GSP), 228, 229
genocide, 45
Georgia, 152, 164, 183n.79
German Democratic Republic, 163–4
Germany
    aggression against neighbours, 40
    arms trade, 192, 208: advanced combat aircraft, 197; control, 195; employment, 201; neorealism, 190; second-hand market, 199
    Austrian neutrality, 124
    Central and Eastern Europe compared to, 147
    Conference on Security and Cooperation in Europe, 141
    Constitutional Court, 80, 85
    constitutional patriotism, 239
    cooperative security, 176
    defence expenditure, 185n.98
    demilitarization, 199
    European integration, 89: identity, 104, 107–8, 110; impetus, 94; interests, 107; self-containment, 108; Single European Act, 98
    European security and defence identity, 142
    expansionism, 156
    fascism, rise of, 38, 78
    Finnish neutrality, 124
    Forty Years War, 160–1
    and France: identity, 105, 106, 107; peace between, 57, 74, 75, 89; relationship between, 108–9, 149

Lomé IV, 241n.6
NATO: expansion, 143, 146, 149; joining, 147, 163
Nazism, 20, 160
nuclear weapons, 44
state provision, 231
Treaty of Brest-Litovsk, 159
Ukrainian support, 168
unification, 163–4
World War I, 38
Gilpin, Robert, 106, 213n.5
globalization, 189
global security, 31–48
Gorbachev, Mikhail
    Communism, collapse of, 163
    conciliatory policies, 155
    Conference on Security and Cooperation in Europe, 141
    criticisms, 169
    Eastern Europe military intervention ruled out, 163
    German unification, 163, 164
    new political thinking, 164, 172
    and Yeltsin, struggle between, 165–6
Gramsci, Antonio, 28
Great Britain
    arms trade, 190, 192, 199
    cooperative security, 176
    Cyprus invasion, 148
    defence expenditure, 185n.98
    European integration: enmeshment process, resistance to, 104; Exchange Rate Mechanism crisis, 109; identity, 91, 92, 107, 109; self-imposed exclusion, 108; Single European Act, 98
    expansionism, 159
    and Ireland, analogy with Russia and Ukraine, 168
    Lebanon and Jordan, military intervention, 159
    Lomé IV, 241n.6
    Napoleonic wars, 161
    Russian expansionism, concerns about, 156
    Russian treaty commitments, 181n.56
    Suez crisis, 179n.20
    UN Security Council, 23
    World War I, 160
    World War II, 160, 161
    see also United Kingdom
great powers, need for, 24
Greece
    Aegean islands, 148

Greece – *continued*
  arms trade, 199
  civil war, 148
  Cyprus invasion, 148
  independence, 158, 181n.59
  Macedonia, claims on, 152
  military junta's seizure of power, 148
  NATO membership, 146–7, 148
Greene, Grahame, 21, 29
Gripen JAS-39 fighter aircraft, 195
Grotius, Hugo, 17, 43
group rights, 18
Guam, 182n.64
Gulags, 78
Gulf War
  arms trade, 204
  economics, 17
  European security and defence identity,
    lack of, 142
  global security, 39–40
  great powers, need for, 24
  military research and development, 198
  NATO, role, 174

Haas, Ernst, on European integration, 93,
    94–5, 96, 97
  elite socialization and public opinion, 102
  identity formation, 103
Habermas, Jurgen, 35, 84, 239
Hafiz al-Asad, 29
Hague Conventions, 118, 121, 124
Haiti, 41, 45, 215n.18
Hakovirta, Harto, 123–4, 125, 126, 127
Hampshire, Stuart, 26
Happe, Nancy, 215n.21
Harkavy, Robert, 213n.4
Havel, Václav, 142, 246–51
Hawaii, 182n.64
Heidegger, Martin, 57, 88
Heine, Heinrich, 86
Held, David, 46–7
Hettne, Bjorn, 240n.2, 243n.36
Hiroshima, 16
Hirsch, Fred, 119
Hirst, Paul, 213n.7
historical conditioning, global security,
    36–41
Hitler, Adolf, 38, 59, 161
Hobbes, Thomas, 35, 43, 58
Hoffman, Stanley
  Melian dialogue, 34
  neofunctionalism critique, 96, 97–8, 101
Holbrooke, Richard, 179n.21, 179n.23
'home', and European integration, 84

Hong Kong, 229
Hospitalität, 20
Howard, Michael, 23
humanism, neoclassical, 88
humanitarian morality, 48
human nature and identity, 106
human rights, 18–19
  arms trade, 204
  failure to enforce, 22
  Soviet Union, 141
Hungarians, distribution, 152
Hungary
  EC membership promised, 143
  NATO membership, 139
  neutrality suggestion, 140
  and Russia, relationship between, 162
Huntington, Samuel P., 46
Hussein, Saddam, 17, 24

Iceland, 187
ideals, 56–62, 70–4
  idolatry, 77–9
  peace, 57–61, 74–5
  prosperity, 61–3, 75
  supranationalism, 63–70, 75–6
ideas, history of, 61
identities of states, 90–2
  European integration, 105–9, 110–11
  neofunctionalism, revision, 98
  and neutrality, 26
  Soviet Union, 165
  and spillover, 103–5
ideologies, 56
idolatry, 77–9
idyllic and ideals
  peace, 58, 59, 60
  prosperity, 62
  supranationalism, 68, 69
Ikle, Fred C., 179n.17
Indonesia, 204
instrumentalism, EC studies, 60
intellectual copyright, 24
intellectual history, 61
interests, national
  European integration, 105–6, 107
  intergovernmentalism, critique, 101,
    102
  and spillover, 103–5
Intergovernmental Conference (IGC), 55,
    74, 76, 77, 240n.4
  arms trade, 206
intergovernmentalism, 96–100
  critique, 100–3, 109, 110
International Monetary Fund (IMF), 122

'invisible hand', 73
Iran
  human rights, 24
  and Russia, relationship between, 176
  sovereign rights, constraints, 32
  and Soviet expansionism, 160
  war with Iraq, 202, 204
Iraq
  arms trade: embargo, 215n.18; Gulf War,
    204; Iran–Iraq war, 202, 204; UK
    sales, 203
  Gulf War: arms trade, 204; economics,
    17; global security, 40; great
    powers, need for, 24
  sovereign rights, constraints, 32
Ireland, Republic of
  economics, 17
  and Great Britain, analogy with Ukraine
    and Russia, 168
  neutrality, 126, 207
Irish School of Ecumenics, 1
Islamic fundamentalism, 226
Israel, 41
Italy
  arms trade, 192, 197
  Ethiopia, aggression against, 40
  European integration, 89
  fascism, rise of, 38, 78
  Forty Years War, 160–1
  US influence, 147

Japan
  arms trade, 204
  fascism, rise of, 38
  Forty Years War, 160–1
  Manchuria, aggression against, 40
  Sino–Russia alliance, 46
  trade with European Union, 229
  war with Russia, 157
Jewish nation, 64
Joenniemi, Perrti, 136
Jordan, 159
jus ad bellum, 16
jus in bello, 16

Kafka, Franz, 86
Kant, Immanuel, 19, 20, 46
Kantian morality, 35, 43
Karadzic, Radovan, 24, 29
Kazakhstan, 153, 166–7
Kekkonen, Urho, 125, 126
Kelleher, Catherine, 185–6n.105
Kennan, George, 39
Kennedy, John F., 125–6

Keohane, Robert O., 97–8, 101
Keynesianism, global, 17–18
Khrushchev, Nikita, 125–6, 167
Kissinger, Henry, 23, 140
knowledge, sociology of, 24
Kohnstamm, Max, 61
Kolko, Gabriel, 36
Korean War, 40–1, 176
Kosovo, 152
Krauss, Keith, 192, 198, 206, 214n.12
Kuwait, Gulf War
  arms trade, 204
  economics, 17
  global security, 40
  great powers, need for, 24

labour, 20
Latin America, 223–4, 229–30, 235
Latvia, 166, 167
Laurance, Edward, 213n.4
law
  global security, 22, 32–4
  Mosaic, 69
  neutrality, 124, 129
  supranationalism, 68
League of Nations
  cause of failure, 23
  limitations, 40
  responsibilities, 38
  Swiss membership, 122
Lebanon, 159
legitimacy, European integration, 72, 81
liberalism, 214n.8
Liberia, 215n.18
Libya, 182n.68, 215n.18
Lindberg, L.N., 94, 95
Lippmann, Walter, 39
Lithuania, 157, 166
Locke, John, 35
Lomé Conventions, 224, 227, 229, 235,
  241n.17
London Suppliers Group, 194
long-range missiles, 194
loyalty, 65, 86–7
Lugar, Richard G., 177n.2, 179n.28,
  184n.87
Luxembourg, 89
Luxembourg compromise, 131
Lysen, Goran, 207

Maastricht Treaty
  civilizing mission, 232, 235, 236
  Common Foreign and Security Policy,
    132, 223

Maastricht Treaty – *continued*
   community and state, 80, 85: citizenship,
      79, 82, 85
   defence policy, 142
   economic development, 227
   fin-de-siècle crisis of meaning, 55, 75–7,
      79
   Havel's speech to European Parliament,
      248–9, 250
   referenda, 110
Macedonia, 152
Machiavelli, Niccolò, 23, 28, 43
   ideals, rejection of, 61
   power, 118
MacIntyre, Alasdair, 26
Major, John, 75, 203
Malta, 225
Manchu empire, 157
Manchuria, 40
Marshall Plan, 17, 147
Marxist-Leninism, 156
Matlock, Jack F., 139, 184n.95
Mearsheimer, John, 44, 106
Melian dialogue, 34
Mercosur, 240n.5
Mexico, 159, 164
Middle East, 192, 226, 229–30
migration, 20–1, 24, 226
Milward, Alan, 90, 92, 100
Missile Technology Control Regime
   (MTCR), 194
Mitterand, François, 75
Mladic, Radko, 29
mobilization, European integration, 70
modernism, 78–9, 88
Moldavia, 164
Monnet, Jean, 58, 61, 108, 110
Moravcsik, Andrew, 98–100, 101, 102, 109,
   110
Morgenthau, Hans, 6
   human nature and identity, 106
   power, 118
   realism, 23, 39, 190
Mosaic law, 69

Nagasaki, 16
Nagorno-Karabakh, 152
Napoleonic wars, 161
nationalism, 19–21, 87, 88
nationality, 68–9, 82–3, 85
nation building, 66
nationhood, 63–5, 66
Nazi Germany, 20, 160
neoclassical humanism, 88

neofunctionalism, and European integration,
   92, 94–6, 100, 102, 110
   French monetary controls, 109
   interests, national, 103, 104–5
   revision, 96–100, 111
neo-imperialism, 228
neoliberalism, 189, 190
neo-realism
   arms trade, 190, 200–1
   European integration, 56
   global security, 45
Netherlands
   arms trade, 195, 199
   civilizing mission, 242n.28
   European integration, 57, 89
Neuhold, Hanspeter, 125
neutrality, 21
   and arms trade, 207–8, 209–12
   Central and Eastern Europe, 174–5
   defensive, 120–3, 133
   European Union membership
      compatibility with, 117–18, 131–6
   parametric, 121, 123–8, 133–4
   post-war, 118–31
   and special interest, 25
   strategic, 121, 128–31, 134–6
New Frankfurt school, 71
New International Economic Order, 17
newly industrialized countries (NICs), 229,
   230, 232
Nicaragua, 33
Nicoll, William, 132
Niebuhr, Reinhold, 23, 35
Nietzsche, Friedrich, 57
Nigeria, 204
Nitze, Paul H., 139
Nolan, Janne E., 185n.99
non-tariff barriers, 230
non-violence, militant, 36
Noricum, 218n.36
North Atlantic Cooperation Council
   (NACC), 144, 178n.12
North Atlantic Treaty Organization
   (NATO)
   arms trade, 199: expenditure, 198;
      new security order, 201, 204;
      second-hand market, 216n.25
   Combined/Joint Task Forces, 145
   Conference on Security and Cooperation
      in Europe, role, 141, 143
   European security: balancing interests,
      173–4; cooperative, 175, 177;
      promotion, 171–2
   European Union's obligations, 234, 235

Greek and Turkish accession, 146–7, 148
Gulf War, 174
membership expansion, 139–41, 143–4, 146–51, 176
military initiatives, 32
Partnership for Peace, 144–5
and Western European Union, 142
Yugoslavia, war in former, 41, 225
Northedge, Fred, 23
Northern Ireland, 18, 94, 104
North Korea, 32
nuclear first use policy, 155
Nuclear Non-Proliferation Treaty, 155, 194
nuclear weapons
control, 194
disarmament, 39, 45, 154–5
European security, 153–6, 170–1
French tests in the Pacific, 32, 48
Mearsheimer's views, 44
Peace Research, 2
World War II, 16, 39

Ohlson, Thomas, 202
Oppenheim, Felix, 118, 119
Organization for African Unity (OAU), 224
Organization for Security and Cooperation in Europe, *see* Conference on Security and Cooperation in Europe
origin, fallacy of, 26–7
originality, and nationhood, 64, 65
Ottoman empire, 157, 158
overseas development, European policy, 221–2
civilizing mission, 232–7
economic development, Europe's contribution to, 226–32
regional integration, 237–9
world power, Europe as a, 222–6

Paasikivi, J.K., 125
pacifism, 187, 213n.3
'Padania', 18
Paine, Thomas, 73
Palestine, 29
Palme, Olof, 131
Palme Report, 6
Palmerston, Viscount, 91
Panama, 159
parametric neutrality, 121, 123–8, 133–4
Partnership for Peace (PfP), 144–5, 148, 150, 175
patriotism
constitutional, 84, 239

global security, 37
peace
dividend, 197–8, 208
European integration: *fin-de-siècle* crisis of meaning, 57–8, 59, 73, 74–5; and prosperity, 61, 62
process, 93–4
Peace In Our Time approach, 59, 74
Peace Research (PR), 1–4, 5–6
Pedersen, Thomas, 133
Peloponnesian Wars, 34
Philippines, 182n.64
Plant, Raymond, 26
Poland
established as separate kingdom, 158
European Community membership promised, 143
and Germany, reconciliation between, 149
NATO membership, 139, 172
neutrality suggestion, 140
and Russia: expansionism, 157, 164; invasion, 167; relationship between, 162
World War II, 161
Polish minorities, 152
political spillover, 94–5
political union, European, 76
Popper, Karl, 117
population growth, 226
Portugal, 148
positivism, 3, 4, 5
postmodernism, 27, 79
post-positivism, 4–5
poverty, 17, 18, 62
power, 23, 118–19
privatization of defence industries, 189
prosperity, 61–3, 73, 75
protectionism, European Union, 227–8, 232
Puerto Rico, 159

Quebec, 18, 29

Reagan administration, 182n.65, 184n.88
realism, 22, 23–4, 29
arms trade, 190, 200, 205
criticisms, 37
European integration, 55, 56
global security, 34–5, 41–2, 44, 45, 48: national interests, 39; World War II, 39
refugees, 20, 45
regional integration, 221–2
economic development, 232

European model, 237–9
  world power, Europe as, 223–6
relativist *Zeitgeist*, 26–7
religion, 87
Roberts, Adam, 24
Romania, 158, 162
Romanians, distribution, 152
Rome Treaty, 61–2, 63, 195
Roosevelt, Franklin D., 40, 161, 165
Rotfield, Adam, 201
Russell, Bertrand, 119
Russia
  Alaska sold to USA, 159
  arms trade, 197, 201
  and China: alliance with, 46; war
    between, possibility of, 107
  Conference on Security and Cooperation
    in Europe, 141, 142
  European security: balancing interests,
    173–4; cooperative, 175–7;
    promotion, 171; thinking about,
    172–3; threat, 169–71
  and Germany, reconciliation between, 149
  NATO: expansion, 139, 144, 146, 150–1,
    155; special status, 150, 178n.12
  nuclear weapons, 153–4, 155–6, 170
  order, breakdown of, 153
  Partnership for Peace, 145, 150, 175
  political and territorial aspirations,
    156–61, 168–9: Eastern Europe,
    161–4; near abroad, 164–8
  political mobilization of nationalists, 144
  Revolution, 37, 38
  Western European Union, 142
  World War I, 37
Russian minorities, 152
Rwanda
  arms embargo, 215n.18
  humanitarian intervention, 36
  human rights, 18
  strategic interests, lack of, 41

Saab-Scania, 195
sacrifice, 58–9
Saferworld, 217n.33
Salisbury, Lord, 89
Salmon, Trevor C., 132
SALT, 125, 126
SALT II, 126, 156, 169
Sandholtz, Wayne, 97, 101
Sandinista government, 33
Sanhedrin, Talmud, 64
satellite telecommunications, 225
Saudi Arabia, 22, 203, 204

Schumacher, Fritz, 212
Schuman Plan, 57, 58, 109
Schuman, Robert, 58, 108, 110
security, global, 31–48
self-defence, 33
self-determination, nations' right to, 18, 29
self-interest, 90, 93, 100, 108
Serbia, 22, 29, 152
Sharp, Jane M.O., 149n.24
Shelley, Percy Bysshe, 42
Shevardnadze, Edvard, 155
Singapore, 229
Single European Act, 73–4
  European Parliament, 235
  intergovernmentalism, 100–1
  neofunctionalism, revision, 97–8
  neorealism, 100
Single European Defence Market (SEDM),
    206
slavery, 28
Slovakia, 143
Slovenia, 152
Smith, Ron, 202
social, and ideals, 60–1
social dimension of the market, 73
Socialist Party, Austria, 124
socialization, European integration, 71–2
sociology, 4, 24
Somalia, 41, 143, 215n.18
South Africa, 44, 234, 241n.7
South Korea, 229
sovereignty, 119, 136
  Sweden, 129, 130
Soviet Union, *see* Union of Soviet Socialist
    Republics
Spain
  arms trade, 199
  Euro-Mediterranean partnership, 226
  NATO membership, 147
  US expansionism, 159
spillover
  European integration, 110
  and identity, 103–5
  intergovernmentalism, critique, 102
  neofunctionalism, 94–5, 96, 102–3:
    revision, 97, 99
sport, 24
Sprout, Harold, 118
Sprout, Margaret, 118
STABEX, 241n.17
Stalin, Joseph, 161, 162
statehood, 63–4, 65–7
Stockholm International Peace Research
    Institute (SIPRI), 196–7, 214n.12

Strategic Arms Limitation Treaty, *see*
SALT; SALT II
Strategic Defence Initiative, 184n.88
strategic goods concept, 194
strategic neutrality, 121, 128–31, 134–6
structuralism, 3
Suez Crisis, 179n.20
supranationalism, 63–70, 73, 75–6, 87–8,
99
Sweden
arms trade: advanced combat aircraft,
197; controls, 195; and neutrality,
207–8, 209
Finland, detachment from, 157
foreign policy, 117, 129–30
identity, 110
neutrality, 185n.101: and arms trade,
207–8, 209; strategic, 121, 126,
128–31, 134–6
Russian expansionism, 157
Switzerland, 117, 121–3, 126, 133
SYSMIN, 241n.17

Taiwan, 229
Talbot, Strobe, 146
Taylor, Trevor, 199
technical spillover, 94
technology, military, 192, 198–9, 225
telecommunications, satellite, 225
territory and nationalism, 20
Theresa, Mother, 59
Third World countries
coalition, envisioned by Cox, 47
economic development, 229, 232
environmental policy, 24
equity demands, 43
foreign aid, 17
regional integration, 238
Thompson, Grahame, 213n.7
Thomson-CSF, 206, 208
Thucydides, 34
tolerance, 26
Tornado aircraft, 203
transcendent morality, 35
treaties, international, 82
Treaty of Rome, 61–2, 63, 195
Truman, Harry S., 162
Truman administration, 186n.110
Turkey
Aegean islands, 148
arms trade, 199
Cyprus invasion, 148
Macedonia, claims on, 152
NATO membership, 146–7, 148

political dialogue with EU, 243n.31
Turkish Straits, 158
war with Russia, 158

Ukraine
cooperative security, 175
Crimea, 167
nuclear-free buffer zone, 185n.101
nuclear weapons, 153
and Russia, relationship between, 151,
167–8, 172
secession and reincorporation, 164
US policy, Russian views of, 177n.2
Undén, Östen, 130
Union of Soviet Socialist Republics
arms trade, 191–2, 194
Austrian neutrality, 124, 127
break-up, 141, 152
Conference on Security and Cooperation
in Europe, 141
Finnish neutrality, 124–5, 127–8
Gulf War, 41
Korean War, 41
realist reasoning, 44
regionalism, 223
and USA, summits, 125–6
United Kingdom
arms trade: advanced combat aircraft,
197; balance of payments, 202;
Code of Conduct, 217n.33;
employment, 201; sales to Iraq,
203; technology, 192; Tornado
aircraft, 203
Conference on Security and Cooperation
in Europe, 141
Falklands War, 16
military presence in Germany, 147
post-positivism, 4
privatization of defence industry, 189
South African sanctions, reluctance to
support, 234
state provision, 231
Western European Union, 142
see also Great Britain; Northern Ireland
United Nations (UN)
arms trade, 205: embargoes, 215n.18;
Register of Conventional Arms, 208
Bull's views, 43
Charter, 40, 41
Cold War, 40
envisagement, 28, 40
humanitarian intervention, 36
human rights criticisms, 24
military initiatives, 32

United Nations – *continued*
  peacekeeping operations, 145
  role, 40
  Security Council, 23–4: force, 40;
    Gulf War, 40, 41; Korean War,
    40–1; membership broadening
    proposals, 25; military support to
    OAU, 241n.7; Stalin's hopes,
    182n.71; veto, 40, 130
  Swedish membership, 130
  Swiss non-membership, 122
  Universal Declaration of Human Rights,
    18–19
United States of America
  Aristide restored to power, 45
  arms trade, 191–2, 209: control regimes,
    194; economics, 203; new security
    order, 204; proposals for change,
    206; second-hand market, 199;
    technology, 192
  and British identity, 91
  and Canada, analogy with Russia and
    Ukraine, 168
  Conference on Security and Cooperation
    in Europe, 141, 143
  end of history, 55
  enlargement doctrine, 46
  European integration, 94
  European security: balancing interests,
    173, 174; cooperative, 175–6,
    185n.104
  and European Union: relationship
    between, 234; trade with, 229
  expansionism, 159, 164
  global integration, 232
  Gulf War, 39–40
  human rights criticisms, 24
  interwar years, 38–9
  League of Nations, refusal to join, 38
  Lebanon and Jordan, military
    intervention, 159
  as Lockean nation, 35
  military presence in Europe, 146, 147,
    149, 174
  NATO, expansion, 139, 141, 143–4:
    official rationale, 146, 147–8, 149–50
  'New Transatlantic Agenda', 224–5
  Nicaraguan intervention, 33–4
  nuclear weapons, 154, 155–6, 169, 170
  Partnership for Peace, 144–5
  post-positivism, 4
  regionalism, 223
  Republicanism, compared to European
    integration, 83–4

  role, 24
  Russian expansionism, 156
  and Soviet Union, summits, 125–6
  Ukrainian partisans supported by, 168
  United Nations Security Council, 23
  Western European Union, 142, 143
  World War I, 37
  World War II, 161
  Yugoslavia, war in former, 74
Universal Declaration of Human Rights
  (UDHR), 18–19
universalism, 15–29
urbanization, 78
utopian approach, 23, 43

Vetschera, Heinz, 217n.34
virtue and ideals, 59–60, 62
voluntary export restraints (VERs), 242n.24

Wake, 182n.64
Wakeham-Linn, John, 215n.21
Wallace, William, 119, 129
Waltz, Kenneth, 6, 106
Walzer, Michael, 26, 34
war, 16
  economic, 194
  economics and wealth, 17
  European integration, 90, 91, 105
  and law, 22
  normative horizons, 31–48
Wassenaar Agreement, 194
wealth, 16–18
Weil, Simone, 77
Welfare State, 83
Western European Union (WEU)
  arms trade, 201
  Combined/Joint Task Forces, 145
  and Conference on Security and
    Cooperation in Europe, 143
  defence policy, 142, 177–8n.5
  Forum of Consultation, 144
  German membership, 147
  membership criteria, 148
  military support to OAU, 241n.7
  and neutrality, 207
  role, 146
  structure and scope, 140
West Germany, *see* Federal Republic of
  Germany
Wight, Martin, 23, 43
William of Ockham, 57
Wilson, Woodrow, 34, 37–8, 39, 40, 42
  utopianism, 43
World Court, 33–4

World Development Movement, 217n.33
World Trade Organization (WTO), 46, 230, 232
World War I, 37–8
World War II
  and European integration, 57
  global security, 39
  Russian expansionism, 159, 161
  Swedish neutrality, 128–9

Yeltsin, Boris
  Chechnya, 29
  Commonwealth of Independent States, 167
  confrontation with Parliament, 144
  criticisms, 169
  and Gorbachev, struggle between, 165–6
  nuclear weapons, 154
Yugoslavia
  arms embargo, 215n.18

attitudes towards Soviet Union, 162
war in former: Conference on Security and Cooperation in Europe, 141–2; Dayton Peace Agreement, 33; great powers, need for, 24, 225; humanitarian intervention, 36; human rights, 18; lack of major intervention, 22; NATO, 41, 141, 225; order, breakdown of, 151–2, 153; peace, in European discourse, 74, 75; priorities, 28–9; Russia's role, 175; strategic interests, lack of, 41; US policy, 145, 155, 177n.2; US public opinion, 143; Western European Union, 142

Zeitgeist, relativist, 26–7
Zhdanov, Andrei, 162
Zysman, John, 97